Law, Religion and Homosexuality

Law, Religion and Homosexuality is the first book-length study of how religion has shaped, and continues to shape, legislation that regulates the lives of gay men and lesbians in the United Kingdom. Through a systematic examination of how religious discourse influences the making of law in the UK Parliament – in the form of official interventions made by faith communities and organisations, as well as by expressions of faith by individual legislators – the authors argue that religion continues to be central to both enabling and restricting the development of sexual orientation equality. Whilst some claim that faith has been marginalised in the legislative processes of contemporary Western societies, Johnson and Vanderbeck show the significant impact of religion in a number of substantive legal areas relating to sexual orientation, including: same-sex sexual relations, family life, civil partnership and same-sex marriage, equality in employment and the provision of goods and services, hate speech regulation, and education. *Law, Religion and Homosexuality* demonstrates the dynamic interplay between law and religion in respect of homosexuality and will be of considerable interest to a wide audience of academics, policy makers and stakeholders.

Paul Johnson is Anniversary Reader in Sociology at the University of York.

Robert M. Vanderbeck is Senior Lecturer in Human Geography at the University of Leeds.

Law, Religion and Homosexuality

Paul Johnson and
Robert M. Vanderbeck

LONDON AND NEW YORK
a GlassHouse book

First published 2014
by Routledge

Published 2014 by Routledge
2 Park Square, Milton Park, Abingdon, Oxfordshire OX14 4RN

and by Routledge
711 Third Avenue, New York, NY 10017

a GlassHouse Book

Routledge is an imprint of the Taylor and Francis Group, an informa business

First issued in paperback 2015

© 2014 Paul Johnson and Robert M. Vanderbeck

The right of Paul Johnson and Robert M. Vanderbeck to be identified as authors of this work has been asserted by them in accordance with sections 77 and 78 of the Copyright, Designs and Patents Act 1988.

All rights reserved. No part of this book may be reprinted or reproduced or utilised in any form or by any electronic, mechanical, or other means, now known or hereafter invented, including photocopying and recording, or in any information storage or retrieval system, without permission in writing from the publishers.

Trademark notice: Product or corporate names may be trademarks or registered trademarks, and are used only for identification and explanation without intent to infringe.

British Library Cataloguing in Publication Data
A catalogue record for this book is available from the British Library

Library of Congress Cataloging-in-Publication Data
Johnson, Paul (Paul James) author.
  Law, religion and homosexuality/Paul Johnson, Robert M. Vanderbeck.
  pages cm
  'A GlassHouse Book.'
  1. Gays – Legal status, laws, etc. – Great Britain. 2. Homosexuality – Law and legislation – Great Britain. 3. Homosexuality – Religious aspects – Christianity. 4. Law – Great Britain – Christian influences. 5. Religion and law – Great Britain. 6. Freedom of religion – Great Britain.
  I. Vanderbeck, Robert M., author. II. Title.
  KD4097.J64 2014
  342.4108'7 – dc23
  2013042620

ISBN 978-0-415-83268-7 (hbk)
ISBN 978-1-138-99885-8 (pbk)
ISBN 978-0-203-42750-7 (ebk)

Typeset in Galliard and Gill Sans
by Florence Production Ltd, Stoodleigh, Devon, UK

For Susan and Robert S. Vanderbeck

and in memory of Doreen Bogdányi

Contents

List of Abbreviations	xi
Introduction	1
A study of religion and lawmaking	2
Why study parliamentary discourse?	4
Secularisation and the changing religious landscape	6
Law, morality and religion	15
Transformations in religious discourse in Parliament	18
The formal role of religion in Parliament	22
Overview of the book	25

1 Religion and the legal regulation of homosexual sex   29

Law, religion and homosexuality in England: the formation of a relationship   29

From Roman canon law to statute law   30
The alignment between religion, statute law and (male) homosexual acts   36

Religion and the partial decriminalisation of male homosexual acts in England and Wales   40

Religion and homosexuality prior to the Wolfenden Report   40
The Wolfenden Report and the Church of England   44
Religion and the Sexual Offences Act 1967   47

The 'age of consent' debates   52

The assertion of Christian morality: the Sexual Offences (Amendment) Bill 1977   52
'Homophobia' and 'equality': the Criminal Justice and Public Order Act 1994   54

The triumph of equality over religion? The Sexual Offences (Amendment) Act 2000   60

The disappearance of religion? The decriminalisation of male homosexual acts   64

Conclusion   67

2 The boundaries of the family: religion and same-sex parenting   69

The Ashbourne–Ryder amendment   71

The contested moralities of same-sex parenting: the Adoption and Children Act 2002   72

Religion and child welfare   76
Religion and the 'evidence' of homosexual parenting   80
Religion and the symbolic politics of marriage   84

The marginalisation of religion? The Human Fertilisation and Embryology Act 2008   88

Religious opposition to the Human Fertilisation and Embryology Act 2008   90
The symbolism of fatherhood and the 'truth' of genetic heritage   93
Equalities and the morality of conception by assisted means   95

Conclusion   97

3 Religious exceptions from sexual orientation equality   99

Employment equality and religious exceptions   99

The Church of England and the sexual orientation exception   102
Parliamentary acceptance of the employment exception   105

Goods, services, facilities, premises and religious exceptions   107

Religious opposition to harassment protection for sexual minorities: the Equality Act (Sexual Orientation) Regulations (Northern Ireland) 2006   110
The threat to religious liberty: the Equality Act (Sexual Orientation) Regulations 2007   114

Resisting greater equality and defending exceptions: religious opposition to the Equality Act 2010   118

Retaining religious employment exceptions   119
Attempts to widen goods, services, facilities and premises exceptions   121

Further religious opposition to protection from harassment on the grounds of sexual orientation 122

Conclusion 123

4 The secular and the sacred: civil partnership and same-sex marriage 124

Avoiding a clash: civil partnerships as secular relationships 126
Appeasing religious opposition through secularism 129

The geography of separation: places of worship and religious freedom 132

Reaffirming separatism: same-sex marriage and religious rites 135

The 'quadruple lock' and the Church of England 136
Marriage 'locks' and the litigious homosexual 140
The Marriage (Same Sex Couples) Bill 2013 amendments 142

Distancing homophobia: a transformation in rhetoric 147
'Equality' not 'sameness' 148

Conclusion 151

5 Homophobic hate speech and freedom of religious expression 153

'Hatred on the grounds of sexual orientation' and the 'freedom of expression' saving provision 154
The logics of equalities 157
The special status of religious speech 161
Policing and the 'climate of fear' for people of faith 164
The persecution of people of faith? 169

The Pauline Howe case 170

Conclusion 172

6 Religion, homosexuality and state education 174

Religion and Section 28 175

The role of religion in the enactment of Section 28 176
Religion, sex education and the repeal of Section 28 181

Homosexuality and faith in the English school system 186

Maintained schools 186
Academies and free schools 187

Sexual orientation discrimination, victimisation and harassment in schools 189

Homosexuality as non-statutory knowledge … 190

Sequestering homosexuality from the National Curriculum 194
Sex education in academies and free schools 196

Religion and the teaching of same-sex marriage … 197

The 'Packer amendment' 199

Religion, curriculum and equalities … 201

Teaching homosexuality as sin 204

Conclusion … 205

Conclusion … **207**

Index … 210

List of Abbreviations

ACA 2002	Adoption and Children Act 2002
BA 1533	Buggery Act 1533
CDA 1998	Crime and Disorder Act 1998
CPA 2004	Civil Partnership Act 2004
CLAA 1885	Criminal Law Amendment Act 1885
CJIA 2008	Criminal Justice and Immigration Act 2008
CJPOA 1994	Criminal Justice and Public Order Act 1994
EA 2006	Equality Act 2006
EA 2010	Equality Act 2010
EASOR 2007	Equality Act (Sexual Orientation) Regulations 2007
EASORNI 2006	Equality Act (Sexual Orientation) Regulations (Northern Ireland) 2006
EESOR 2003	Employment Equality (Sexual Orientation) Regulations 2003
HFEA 1990	Human Fertilisation and Embryology Act 1990
HFEA 2008	Human Fertilisation and Embryology Act 2008
MA 1949	Marriage Act 1949
MSSCA 2013	Marriage (Same Sex Couples) Act 2013
OAPA 1861	Offences Against the Person Act 1861
POA 1986	Public Order Act 1986
SCA 1533	Submission of the Clergy Act 1533
SOA 1956	Sexual Offences Act 1956
SOA 1967	Sexual Offences Act 1967
SOA 2003	Sexual Offences Act 2003
SOAA 2000	Sexual Offences (Amendment) Act 2000

Introduction

> It is said that adultery and fornication are not criminal offences, so why should homosexuality be? The law answers that natural sin is different from unnatural vice. Natural sin is, of course, deplorable, but unnatural vice is worse; because, as the law says, it strikes at the integrity of the human race [...] The Bible calls it 'an abomination'; the Statute Book describes it as an 'abominable crime'; and the old lawyers, when they framed their indictments, thought it was a disgrace even to name it; and it was an offence not to be named amongst Christians [...] [T]he law should condemn this evil for the evil it is....
>
> Lord Denning, House of Lords, 1957[1]

> [M]any gay and lesbian people [...] want to enter not just into a civil partnership but a marriage: a lifelong commitment of love and fidelity, for better, for worse, for richer, for poorer, in sickness and in health [...] The point is that those who wish to enter into this most fundamental of human relationships should be able to do so legally [...] I believe in marriage. I believe, with the Jewish rabbi of old, that in the love of a couple there dwells the shekinah – the divine presence; or, to put it in Christian terms, that which reflects the mutual love of Christ and his church. I believe in the institution of marriage and I want it to be available to same-sex couples as well as to males and females.
>
> Lord Harries of Pentregarth, former Bishop of Oxford, House of Lords, 2013[2]

There has been a profound transformation since the mid-twentieth century in the relationship between law, religion and homosexuality in the United Kingdom. In this book we examine this relationship in the context of lawmaking, where religion and homosexuality have increasingly come into conflict. The once settled

---

1   HL Debate, 4 December 1957, cc.807–811.
2   HL Debate, 3 June 2013, c.969.

understanding of the relationship between law, religion and homosexuality amongst legislators that is exemplified in the speech by Lord Denning quoted above – where law is regarded as the vehicle to give direct expression to the religious (largely Christian) condemnation of (most usually male) same-sex sexual acts – no longer holds. The unravelling of this 'traditional' understanding of the relationship between law, religion and homosexuality is reflected in a now variegated religious discourse on homosexuality amongst legislators. Some, as demonstrated by the speech by Lord Harries of Pentregarth quoted above, openly support gay and lesbian legal equality and make their case for this on religious grounds. In contrast, others remain opposed to gay and lesbian law reform and increasingly vocalise the argument that their religious convictions have been marginalised. As Lord Mawhinney argued during debates about what became the Marriage (Same Sex Couples) Act (MSSCA) 2013, which made the solemnisation of same-sex marriage lawful in England and Wales:

> [A]s a practicing Christian, I have a problem with this legislation, because I do not believe that it respects faith and the sincerely held views of those in the faith community [. . .] For 40 years my life has been driven by Christian and Conservative convictions, and now I am led to believe that because I continue to hold those values and principles I am a swivel-eyed loon. I want to raise a flag for swivel-eyed loons, because at the very heart of our country and our party is a commitment to time-tested values and principles.[3]

The idea that conservative religion has become peripheral to lawmaking in the UK may be comforting to those concerned to safeguard and enhance equality based on sexual orientation, but it is profoundly misleading. Throughout this book we argue that religious disapprobation of homosexuality still maintains considerable influence upon lawmaking and continues to shape legislation in important ways. Although religious objections to homosexuality are no longer expressed using the language of Lord Denning, claims that law should give expression to a religious intolerance of homosexuality remain central to parliamentary discourse. As a consequence, contemporary law continues to bear the mark of a religious prejudice towards homosexuals.

A study of religion and lawmaking

Our aim in this book is to demonstrate how religion has shaped, and continues to shape, legislation that regulates the lives of gay men and lesbians. The focus of our study is on the role of religious discourse in the production of statute law. We investigate the influence of religious discourse on lawmaking in respect of six key thematic areas:

---

3 HL Debate, 3 June 2013, cc.1015–1016.

- same-sex sexual relations;
- family life, in respect of the adoption of children and access to assisted reproduction for same-sex couples;
- sexual orientation equality in employment and in the provision of goods and services;
- civil partnership and marriage for same-sex couples;
- protection for sexual minorities from homophobic hate speech; and
- education about homosexuality in schools.

By examining lawmaking in respect of each of these thematic areas we show how religion continues to influence the contemporary legal landscape inhabited by gay men and lesbians.

Our emphasis throughout the book is on the influence of religion on the making of statutory law by the UK Parliament. However, it is important to recognise that religion has an effect upon law at a number of other and sometimes competing legal sites. These sites include the domestic courts and the European Court of Human Rights, as well as the work of criminal justice practitioners such as police officers. Whilst we discuss the interaction between law and religion in the judicial interpretation and criminal justice enforcement of law when these elements are central to the shaping of law, our analysis remains fixed on lawmaking in the UK Parliament. Given the legislative complexities created by devolution in the UK, our focus on the UK Parliament means that our geographical coverage of law necessarily varies according to time period and issue. We give attention to Scotland and Northern Ireland when UK parliamentary debates relate to legislation applying to them, whereas in debates relating to devolved matters our emphasis is on English law.[4]

The primary data used throughout this study are debates in the UK Parliament about homosexuality from the mid-twentieth century to the present day. In examining the content of parliamentary debates we are concerned to show the influence of religious discourse about homosexuality on the formation of legislation. In the most general sense, we are interested in what parliamentarians say about religion and homosexuality, and how this serves to shape law in particular ways. Although we inevitably discuss specific parliamentary actors

---

4 For example, in Chapter 2 we focus specifically on English law when discussing UK parliamentary debates about the Adoption and Children Act 2002 given that the key issues are devolved matters, whereas, by contrast, the key issues that we discuss in respect of the Human Fertilisation and Embryology Act 2008 are reserved matters and therefore apply to England and Wales, Scotland and Northern Ireland. Similarly, our discussion of debates in the UK Parliament in respect of 'Section 28' of the Local Government Act 1988 relate to Great Britain, but our analysis of debates in respect of its repeal by the Local Government Act 2003 relates only to English law (reflecting the subsequent devolution of this aspect of local government legislation as it pertained to Scotland to the Scottish Parliament).

throughout the book, we are not principally concerned to provide an analysis of individual politicians or political parties. Our aim, following Michel Foucault, is not to explain or relate discourse about homosexuality 'to a thought, mind or subject which engendered it' but to consider the effects of discourse in 'the practical field in which it is deployed'.[5] In this sense, we approach Parliament as a discursive arena through which a wide range of individuals move over time but in which particular ways of talking about homosexuality endure, compete and are sometimes transformed. We are interested in the place of religion in this discursive environment, its significance within the broader context of debate about homosexuality, the mode of its deployment in the form of particular discursive strategies and tactics, the ambitions and objectives pursued through such strategies and tactics, and the effects of these upon the content of law.

Foucault's 'method' provides the principal framework for our study of parliamentary discourse and underpins five key questions that inform our analysis throughout the book. First, we ask what are the 'limits and forms of the *sayable*' about homosexuality in Parliament and how is religion implicated in this discursive delimitation?[6] Second, we ask what are the 'limits and forms of *conversation*' in Parliament in determining which religious claims and statements about homosexuality continue to circulate and have purchase, in contrast to those that decline and disappear?[7] Third, we ask what are the 'limits and forms of *memory*' in Parliament in influencing which religious discourses about homosexuality endure and are recognised as valid, as opposed to those that are abandoned and forgotten?[8] Fourth, we ask what are the 'limits and forms of *reactivation*' in Parliament in structuring the potential for particular religious discourses to be resuscitated from the past?[9] And, fifth, we ask what are the 'limits and forms of *appropriation*' in Parliament for individuals and groups seeking to deploy particular religious discourses about homosexuality?[10] These five questions are foundational to our overall objective of examining the significance of religious discourse in parliamentary debates about homosexuality.

Why study parliamentary discourse?

It is well recognised that legislative debates in Parliament have an importance that extends beyond the law that emerges from them. Parliamentary debates serve as

---

5 M. Foucault, 'Politics and the study of discourse', in G. Burchell, C. Gordon and P. Miller (eds), *The Foucault Effect: Studies in Governmentality: with Two Lectures by and an Interview with Michel Foucault*, Chicago, IL: Chicago University Press, 1991, p.61.
6 Ibid., p.59. Emphasis in original.
7 Ibid., p.60.
8 Ibid.
9 Ibid.
10 Ibid.

important platforms from which public opinion on key social issues is both shaped and reflected. Debate in Parliament acts as 'a powerful engine for recognitions and misrecognitions, for strengthening, marginalizing or disorganizing sexual/national identities and, in so doing, for conferring, limiting or withholding formal, as well as symbolic, citizenship'.[11] Particular narrative strategies and forms of storytelling feature strongly in Parliament, as legislators draw upon a range of devices – including correspondence from constituents, anecdotal accounts of interactions with 'ordinary' people, and media reports of particular events – to performatively reiterate ideas about 'society' and 'community'. The ontological effects of these discursive practices have been at different times to create, reinforce or challenge the symbolic and material exclusion of sexual minorities. For example, during the parliamentary passage of the MSSCA 2013, Prime Minister David Cameron expressed his optimism about the broader impact of parliamentary debate about same-sex marriage upon society:

> There will be girls and boys in school today who are worried about being bullied and concerned about what society thinks of them because they are gay or lesbian. By making this change they will be able to see that Parliament believes their love is the same as anyone else's love and that we believe in equality. I think this will enable them to stand that bit taller, be that bit more confident and I am proud of that.[12]

Although positivistic claims about a causal relationship between parliamentary debate and broader social change should be viewed with suspicion, it is incontrovertible that parliamentary discourse about sexual orientation is imbricated with the social and cultural construction of sexuality.

A study of Parliament as a discursive field cannot treat it as if it is hermetic. Parliament, as the theatre of the state,[13] is inevitably influenced by multiple and competing external discourses that emanate from various government departments, lobby groups, commercial interests and private citizens.[14] As some of the prominent debates that we examine show (including the progressive reform of the 'age of consent', the creation of civil partnership and the subsequent legalisation of same-sex marriage, and the adoption of children by same-sex couples), the substantial transformations in the social and cultural construction of homo-

---

11 D. Epstein, R. Johnson and D.L. Steinberg, 'Twice told tales: transformation, recuperation and emergence in the age of consent debates 1998', *Sexualities* 3, 2000, 5–30.
12 D. Cameron, contribution to *Pride in London, Love (and Marriage): Official Guide 2013*, London: Stream Publishing, 2013.
13 C.R. Kyle, *Theater of State: Parliament and Political Culture in Early Stuart England*, Redwood City, CA: Stanford University Press, 2012.
14 See: M. Rush (ed.), *Parliament and Pressure Politics*, Oxford: Oxford University Press, 1990.

sexuality have shaped parliamentary debate in important ways.[15] One principal impact has been upon the discursive strategies used by those parliamentarians who wish to oppose the extension of legal rights and protections to sexual minorities. There has been a significant move away from the dominant forms of parliamentary discourse that were evident during and after the passage of the Sexual Offences Act 1967, where legislators – even those supportive of the partial decriminalisation of male homosexual acts – often declared their personal disgust for homosexual practices. As we discuss below and throughout the book, the shift in public attitudes regarding homosexuality has meant a progressive decline in the most virulent anti-gay rhetoric in Parliament – in terms, for example, of stories of 'predatory' gay male sexuality, assertions that gay men have intrinsic paedophiliac tendencies, and claims about the mental and physical health risks of homosexual lifestyles – which have been replaced with an increasing concern by legislators to distance themselves from 'homophobia'.[16] Even those who oppose homosexual law reform now feel compelled to preface any parliamentary speech with claims such as 'I do not hold anti-homosexual views, nor do I advance them; in fact, I abhor homophobia. I fervently believe in a tolerant society but. . .'[17] Wider processes of social change are therefore influential in determining the limits and forms of discourse about homosexuality in parliamentary debates. In the next section, we consider this specifically in relation to the significant transformations in the religious landscape since the mid-twentieth century.

Secularisation and the changing religious landscape

Any understanding of the influence of religion on lawmaking must be situated in the broader context of religious change in Britain.[18] Perhaps the most significant aspect of this change involves what Callum Brown provocatively calls 'the death

---

15 For discussion of some aspects of the evolution of UK parliamentary discourse in relation to homosexuality but not specifically in relation to religion, see: J. Burridge, '"I am not homophobic *but* . . .": disclaiming in discourse resisting repeal of Section 28', *Sexualities* 7, 2004, 327–344; M. Durham, 'Abortion, gay rights, and politics in Britain and America: a comparison', *Parliamentary Affairs* 58, 2005, 89–103; D. Epstein, R. Johnson and D.L. Steinberg, op. cit.; S. Wise, '"New right" or "backlash"? Section 28, moral panic, and "promoting homosexuality"', *Sociological Research Online* 5, 2000.
16 For discussion, see: J. Burridge, op.cit.; D. Epstein, R. Johnson and D.L. Steinberg, op. cit.; J. Moran, 'Childhood sexuality and education: the case of Section 28', *Sexualities* 4, 2001, 73–89.
17 Lord Dear, HL Debate, 9 July 2009, c.800.
18 Patterns of religious change have differed in Northern Ireland, where powerful nationalist associations linked to religion have persisted. For an overview of differences in patterns of religious change between England and Wales, Scotland and Northern Ireland, see: M. Guest, E. Olson and J. Wolffe, 'Christianity: loss of monopoly', in L. Woodhead and R. Catto (eds), *Religion and Change in Modern Britain*, London: Routledge, 2012, pp.57–78.

of Christian Britain'.[19] Brown uses this term to signify not the disappearance of Christianity as such but rather the unravelling of a once hegemonic Christian culture and the interruption of the mechanisms through which that culture was reproduced – such as the intergenerational transmission of religious beliefs and practices. Whilst the principal causes of this religious transformation are disputed, there is little doubt that formal religious participation and affiliation have declined dramatically since the early 1960s and continue to do so. In addition to a substantial growth in the number of individuals who claim to have no religious belief, there have been increases in the number of adherents to non-Christian religions (something significantly influenced by patterns of immigration), shifts in the demographic composition of the population of self-identified Christians[20] and a turn by many away from organised religion towards forms of 'spirituality'.[21]

Although different data sources provide different estimates regarding the level of religiosity in Britain, the overall picture suggests a pattern of decline. In response to the question 'What is your religion?' in the 2001 and 2011 censuses in England and Wales, 71.8 per cent of respondents identified themselves as Christian in 2001, with this figure decreasing to 59.3 per cent by 2011.[22] These data provoke considerable consternation from secularist organisations that argue that the census question produces substantially inflated figures that reflect identification with a broader Christian heritage rather than any particular form of religious belief.[23] A poll conducted on behalf of the University of Lancaster in

---

19 C. Brown, *The Death of Christian Britain: Understanding Seculiarisation 1800–2000 (2nd edition)*, London: Routledge, 2009.
20 This population has aged substantially, giving it the oldest age profile of the major religions in Britain. There has also been a decline in the number of British Christians who identify as 'white', with this decline partially counterbalanced by growth in the population of Christians who have immigrated from Africa and other regions. See: Office for National Statistics, *Religion in England and Wales 2011*, 2012.
21 L. Woodhead, 'Introduction', in L. Woodhead and R. Catto (eds), op. cit., pp.1–33.
22 Office for National Statistics, *Religion in England and Wales 2011*, op. cit. The proportion of people in England and Wales declaring themselves to have no religion increased from 14.8 per cent to 25.1 per cent over the same period; 7.2 per cent of people did not answer the voluntary question on religion in the 2011 Census. Scotland's 2011 Census revealed that 54 per cent of people identified as belonging to a Christian denomination – a decrease of 11 per cent in a decade – while 37 per cent indicated that they had no religion. National Records of Scotland, *Statistical Bulletin: 2011 Census: Key Results on Population, Ethnicity, Identity, Language, Religion, Health, Housing and Accommodation in Scotland – Release 2A*, 26 September 2013.
23 Critics argue that the wording of the question and its placement immediately after a question about ethnicity produced responses much more related to family heritage and upbringing rather than religiosity. The British Humanist Association cites a subsequent YouGov poll in which respondents were asked 'What is your religion?' and 'Are you religious?'. While more than 53 per cent of respondents identified as Christian, only 29 per cent of respondents described themselves as religious. See: British Humanist Association, 'The Census campaign 2011'. Available online at https://humanism.org.uk/campaigns/old-campaigns/census-2011 (accessed on 4 December 2013).

2013 estimated that only 33 per cent of people in Britain would describe themselves as 'religious' or 'spiritual', and even fewer (15 per cent) reported engaging in any form of collective religious practice.[24] Data on the religious solemnisation of marriages – a common surrogate for the pervasiveness of Christian culture often employed by sociologists and historians – show evidence of steep decline. In England and Wales, for example, it is estimated that approximately 10 per cent of marriages were solemnised in civil ceremonies in 1872, with this figure rising to 20 per cent by 1908 and 30 per cent by 1963.[25] Since then, rates of religiously solemnised marriage have declined rapidly; by 2011 more than 70 per cent of marriages were solemnised in civil ceremonies (and of those marriages that continue to be religiously solemnised, many involve non-Christian faiths).

The precipitous decline in levels of religious observance and identification in Britain has typically been interpreted through the lens of 'secularisation'. However, theories of secularisation are highly contested and differ considerably in terms of defining secularity, determining its extent, and explaining its temporalities and spatialities. While in colloquial usage the word 'secular' tends simply to denote an absence of religion, secularisation theory in its diverse formulations has stressed the importance of three processes that may or may not occur in tandem:

1. a *decline* in religious belief and the influence of religious authority;
2. a *differentiation* of religion from other spheres of society (for example, government and the economy); and
3. a *privatisation* of religion whereby expressions of religious belief in the public sphere decline in significance and become restricted to 'private' times and spaces (such as the home or events involving co-religionists).[26]

In their early formulations, secularisation theories typically traced the origins of religious decline in Britain to the urbanisation and class transformations of the industrial revolution. However, while measures of formal religious participation

---

24 YouGov/University of Lancaster Survey Results. Available online at http://cdn.yougov.com/cumulus_uploads/document/mm7go89rhi/YouGov-University%20of%20Lancaster-Survey-Results-Faith-Matters-130130.pdf (accessed on 4 December 2013).
25 Office for National Statistics, *Trends in Religious and Civil Marriages, 1966–2011*, 26 June 2013. The drop in rates of religious marriage has been somewhat less precipitous in Scotland. Data from the Scottish Government show that 51 per cent of marriages in Scotland in 2010 were solemnised in civil ceremonies carried out by a registrar, compared with 31 per cent in 1971. See: General Register Office for Scotland, *Scotland's Population 2010: The Registrar General's Annual Review of Demographic Trends 156th Edition*, Edinburgh: Scottish Government, 2011.
26 J. Casanova and D. Yamane, 'Secularization on trial: in defence of a neosecularization paradigm', *Journal for the Scientific Study of Religion* 36, 1997, 109–122.

and membership seemingly declined during the period of industrial urbanisation,[27] scholars have subsequently argued that locating the origins of secularisation in this period underestimates the extent of religiosity amongst the urban working class and misidentifies its forms. Brown posits that – despite differences in denomination, class, region and other factors – one can identify 'a strong common Christian experience' in Britain that traversed the nineteenth century and extended to the 1950s.[28]

Far from there having been a steady decline in religious observance over the course of the twentieth century, it is now argued that the period between 1945 and 1960 represented a 'high point' for religious conformity in Britain, with evident increases in many indicators of Christian belief and practice.[29] Widespread religious decline in Britain was therefore a relatively sudden and rapid transformation originating in the early 1960s. Commentators in the 1960s and 1970s spoke of the rise of the so-called 'permissive society',[30] characterised by the weakening influence of traditional sources of religious authority and the loosening of moral codes that regulated, amongst other things, gender roles and sexual conduct. From the 1960s, Britain witnessed the rapid decline of what Brown calls *discursive Christianity*, or 'the people's subscription to protocols of personal identity which they derive from Christian expectations, or discourses, evident in their own time and place'.[31] New moral narratives – such as those associated with feminism, 'gay liberation', environmentalism and postcolonialism – proliferated, challenging the dominance and reproduction of Christian morality.[32] These narratives did not simply serve as mutually exclusive alternatives to once dominant religious morality. Rather, in some cases, new narratives developed alongside or were brought into conversation with religion – for example, in efforts by lesbian and gay Christians and their sympathisers to locate lifelong, monogamous relationships by same-sex couples within the boundaries of Christian morality.[33]

Whereas many theories of secularisation have given primacy to class-based processes for explaining religious decline, there have been recent moves to locate changing understandings of gender and sexuality at the core of secularisation. Transformations in gender and sexuality have not been epiphenomenal to religious

---

27 S. Bruce, *God is Dead: Secularization in the West*, Oxford: Blackwell, 2002.
28 C. Brown, op. cit., p.202.
29 C. Brown and G. Lynch, 'Cultural perspectives', in L. Woodhead and R. Catto (eds), op. cit., p.332.
30 G. Ganiel and P. Jones, 'Religion, politics and law', in L. Woodhead and R. Catto (eds), op. cit., pp.299–321.
31 C. Brown, op. cit., p.12.
32 Ibid., p.232.
33 R.M. Vanderbeck, J. Andersson, G. Valentine, J. Sadgrove and K. Ward, 'Sexuality, activism and witness in the Anglican Communion: the 2008 Lambeth Conference of Anglican Bishops', *Annals of the Association of American Geographers* 101, 2011, 670–689.

decline but, rather, are inextricably linked to it. The loosening of hegemonic religious codes regulating gender roles and sexual behaviour have been interpreted as central elements of a larger cultural shift whereby, as Linda Woodhead argues, 'an increasing number of men and women in affluent democracies have come to rely on inner convictions, emotions, and intuitions as the authentic source of wisdom in the living of life'.[34] For this reason, the relationship between changes in the social construction of sexuality and religion are important in understanding secularisation. Such changes contributed to a reconsideration of the broader relationship between religion and sexual morals, with a growing number of people – both inside and outside the churches – questioning the extent to which legal regulation was an appropriate means to enforce religiously based (Christian) sexual morality (an issue we explore in greater detail below, and in Chapter 1).[35]

Against this broader social transformation since the 1960s, Brown asserts that 'the churches have become increasingly irrelevant in the new cultural and ethical landscape' that most people inhabit.[36] However, despite the loss of the hegemony of 'normative Christian culture',[37] Christianity maintains a privileged cultural and political status in relation to other faiths in Britain, and continues to exert an influence greater than one might infer simply through an analysis of trends in church attendance, rates of baptism or other measures. While it is now commonplace to hear assertions that Britain is a 'secular' society, a number of scholars have disputed some of the assumptions about secularism and the unidirectional trajectory of secularisation. Some have questioned whether reliance on various statistical indicators results in overstated claims for the disappearance of religion. For example, Grace Davie suggested that Britain, at the time she wrote in the 1990s, was characterised by 'believing without belonging'[38] (although, since then, polls suggest that a belief in God or a higher spiritual power has also waned rapidly).[39]

---

34 L. Woodhead, 'Sex and secularization', in G. Loughlin (ed.), *Queer Theology: Rethinking the Western Body*, Oxford: Blackwell, p.239.

35 Hugh McLeod's account of the 1960s, for example, stresses the importance of changes within the churches in enabling the process of homosexual law reform that led to the partial decriminalisation of male homosexual acts in England and Wales. See: H. McLeod, *The Religious Crisis of the 1960s*, Oxford: Oxford University Press, 2007. Callum Brown stresses, however, the importance of remembering that 'the existence of Christian proponents of these reforms cannot detract from the fact that their opponents were Christians in their own churches'. See C. Brown, op. cit., p.218. We explore the role of the Church of England in this aspect of homosexual law reform in detail in Chapter 1.

36 C. Brown, op. cit., p.229.

37 C. Brown and G. Lynch, 'Cultural perspectives', in L. Woodhead and R. Catto (eds), op. cit., p.333.

38 G. Davie, *Religion in Britain since 1945: Believing without Belonging*, Oxford: Blackwell, 1994.

39 Other evidence suggests that decline in belief in 'God' is especially pronounced amongst young people. A recent poll of British youth (ages 18–24) by YouGov suggests that 25 per cent express belief in God, 19 per cent believe in a 'spiritual greater power' that is not God, and 38 per cent believe in neither God nor a greater spiritual power. See:

Assumptions about the privatisation of religion have also been challenged by the resurgence of religious voices in public debates since the 1990s, leading some commentators to argue that Britain is witnessing a 'deprivatisation'[40] of religion and entering a period of 'desecularisation'[41] or 'postsecularity'.[42] The idea of the 'postsecular society' has gained increasing attention over the past decade with a seeming resurgence in religious discourse in the public sphere.[43] Various explanations have been provided for this, which include the increased vocality of conservative religious organisations and pressure groups who, in the face of what they perceive as hostile cultural and political transformations, seek to influence law and policy.[44]

Claims that Britain is a secular society also arguably underestimate the extent to which religion is embedded in public institutions associated with government, the school system and other aspects of contemporary British society. As Jim Beckford argues, despite the assumptions of secularisation theory about the increased differentiation of religion from other spheres, it is necessary to recognise that:

> the British state is not secular at any level – national, regional, or local. There is no principled or legal separation of the state from religions. On the contrary, there is a long and complex intertwining of the monarchy, the Church of England, the Church of Scotland, Parliament, and the major institutions of the state such as the armed forces, health services, emergency services, and prisons. Other Christian denominations and leading representatives of Hindu, Jewish, Muslim, and Sikh faith communities have also gained admission in various ways to this pragmatic 'settlement' – often through the channels of interfaith cooption and cooperation.[45]

Moreover, within the context of an increasingly multicultural society, religious groups and leaders are often included as part of strategies of consultation aimed at facilitating the inclusion of minority interests. As a consequence, Kim Knott

---

W. Dahlgreen, 'British youth reject religion', YouGov, 24 June 2013. Available online at http://yougov.co.uk/news/2013/06/24/british-youth-reject-religion (accessed on 4 December 2013).

40 L. Woodhead, 'Introduction', in L. Woodhead and R. Catto (eds), op. cit., p.32; J. Casanova, *Public Religions in the Modern World*, Chicago, IL: University of Chicago Press, 1994.

41 P. Berger (ed.), *The Desecularization of the World: Resurgent Religion and World Politics*, Grand Rapids, MI: Wm. B. Eerdmans Publishing, 1999.

42 J.A. Beckford, 'Public religions and the postsecular: critical reflections', *Journal for the Scientific Study of Religion* 51, 2012, 11–19.

43 For example: J. Habermas, 'Notes on post-secular society', *New Perspectives Quarterly* 25, 2008, 17–29.

44 However, a perception of religious resurgence in Britain should not be confused with increased levels of overall religiosity. See C. Brown, op. cit.; J. Beckford, op. cit.

45 J. Beckford, op. cit., 13.

suggests that representatives of many religions have relatively recently gained 'a place at the table of government, are consulted regularly on policy issues, and are treated with a degree of seriousness quite unimaginable in the late 1970s'.[46]

Although religion therefore remains embedded in public life in multiple (sometimes under-recognised) ways, there has nevertheless emerged a growing rhetoric in Britain about the marginalisation of religion within the public sphere.[47] This rhetoric has been promulgated by leaders of organised religions, including the Church of England, as well as by evangelical and fundamentalist organisations and pressure groups. The process of social secularisation since the 1960s, through which religion has changed from being a 'majority' to a 'minority' affair,[48] has encouraged a 'consolidation of conservative religious sub-cultures'[49] that, over time, have become more politically active. The issue of homosexuality has served as a major locus for the lobbying efforts of these groups. Organisations such as the Evangelical Alliance, the Christian Institute, Christian Action Research and Education (CARE) and Focus on the Family actively seek to influence political debate and shape the law relating to sexual orientation. These pressure groups have become skilled at presenting arguments that support their religious positions but avoid the explicit use of religious discourse.[50] We demonstrate this in Chapter 1 in respect of recent changes in conservative religious discourse about homosexual sex. And in Chapter 2 we show how evangelical pressure groups widely distributed 'scientific research' on the effects of gay parenting during parliamentary debates over adoption by same-sex couples (which was influential in both Houses).

In recent years, conservative religious groups have also increasingly appropriated the discourse of equality. It has become common to hear the claim that religious individuals are positioned at the bottom of an equalities hierarchy in which sexual orientation is privileged. This is not simply a rhetoric that circulates in Britain but one that is deployed in many Western countries where religion is

---

46 K. Knott, 'Becoming a "faith community"': British Hindus, identity, and the politics of representation', *Journal of Religion in Europe* 2, 2009, 88.
47 For discussion see: D. Cooper and D. Herman, 'Up against the property logic of equality law: conservative Christian accommodation claims and gay rights', *Feminist Legal Studies* 21, 2013, 61–80; S. Hunt, 'Saints and sinners: the role of conservative Christian pressure groups in the Christian gay debate in the UK', *Sociological Research Online* 8, 2003; C.F. Stychin, 'Faith in the future: sexuality, religion and the public sphere', *Oxford Journal of Legal Studies* 29, 2009, 729–755; C.F. Stychin, 'Closet cases: "conscientious objection" to lesbian and gay legal equality', *Griffith Law Review* 18, 2009, 17–38; G. Valentine and L. Waite, 'Negotiating difference through everyday encounters: the case of sexual orientation and religion and belief', *Antipode* 44, 2011, 474–492.
48 L. Woodhead, 'Introduction', in L. Woodhead and R. Catto (eds), op. cit., p.26.
49 C. Brown and G. Lynch, 'Cultural perspectives', in L. Woodhead and R. Catto (eds), op. cit., p.341.
50 D.R. Walhof, 'Habermas, same-sex marriage and the problem of religion in public life', *Philosophy & Social Criticism* 39, 2013, 232.

argued to have become disadvantaged *vis-à-vis* sexual orientation. For example, commenting on a case of alleged religious discrimination in Canada, Bruce Ryder contends that religion is now 'the new gay':

> [J]ust as the display of minority sexual orientations in the public sphere invited persecution in Canada in the past, now religious and public servants [. . .] are being asked to choose between keeping their jobs and acting in accordance with their religious beliefs.[51]

This is one aspect of a more general trend, prevalent in Britain, of 'traditional' Christians and other religious believers claiming that they are alienated minorities in fear of persecution from the state. For example, former Archbishop of Canterbury George Carey articulated this view during debates over the MSSCA 2013, suggesting that Prime Minister David Cameron, in his support for same-sex marriage, had 'done more than any other recent political leader to feed these anxieties':

> The danger I believe that the Government is courting with its approach both to marriage and religious freedom, is the alienation of a large minority of people who only a few years ago would have been considered pillars of society [. . .] The Government risks entrenching a very damaging division in British society by driving law-abiding Christians into the ranks of the malcontents and alienated – of whom there are already far too many.[52]

In recent years, claims about the 'persecution' of Christians in Britain have reached such a pitch that there have been calls for a moderation of this rhetoric even from sources often otherwise sympathetic to conservative moral agendas. For example, a recent inquiry conducted by Christians in Parliament, with support from the Evangelical Alliance, concluded that:

> Christians in the UK are not persecuted. To suggest that they are is to minimise the suffering of Christians in many parts of the world who face repression, imprisonment and death if they worship, preach or convert [. . .] Some of the legal activity, associated campaigning and media coverage has been unwise and possibly counter-productive to the positive role that Christians play in society.[53]

---

51 B. Ryder, 'The Canadian conception of equal religious citizenship', in R. Moon (ed.), *Law and Religious Pluralism in Canada*, Vancouver, BC: UBC Press, 2008, p.100.
52 G. Carey, 'The PM's done more than any leader to make Christians feel they're persecuted', *Daily Mail*, 29 March 2013.
53 Christians in Parliament, *Clearing the Ground Inquiry: Preliminary Report into the Freedom of Christians in the UK*, February 2012.

Nevertheless, it is frequently posited that there is a 'clash'[54] between religion and sexual orientation that is created by competition over access to legal recognition and rights. We demonstrate the pervasiveness of this discourse in recent parliamentary debates and show its influence on fashioning legislation. However, it is important to note that this polarised framing of contemporary social relations often risks both obscuring the diversity of religious positions in relation to homosexuality and reproducing an oversimplified view that homosexual law reforms are themselves secular (as opposed to, for some people, religious) victories. Substantial divisions exist in many Christian traditions over homosexuality, not least within the Church of England, for which issues of sexual orientation have taken on a global resonance (given the position of the Archbishop of Canterbury as not only the most senior figure in the Church of England but also the 'focus of unity' for an international Anglican Communion that is experiencing schism between its provinces as a result of conflicts over homosexuality).[55] While groups such as Anglican Mainstream seek to preserve 'the traditional biblical teaching on marriage, the family and human sexuality',[56] other groups have put forward a 'liberal' Christian perspective on these issues.[57]

A number of organisations have emerged that exist specifically to serve and represent the interests of non-heterosexuals in particular faith groups.[58] As well as functioning as sources of mutual support, these groups have contributed to the circulation of discourses challenging the view that homosexuality is intrinsically incompatible with religious faith. These groups differ in the extent to which they align themselves with the realm of 'secular' politics. Some groups actively collaborate with non-religious groups that campaign for legal equality; others, however, are more cautious about adopting discourses of rights and equality given the tendency for anti-gay religious groups to claim that the promotion of 'gay rights' is an essentially secular agenda being forced upon sacred institutions. Many people of faith who favour widened gay inclusion have sought to rework dominant notions of sexual morality, suggesting, for example, that a faith's ethic of care not only permits but demands a more liberal approach to human sexuality. These pro-gay religious discourses now pervade and inform parliamentary debates about homosexuality and, in some cases, are deployed to combat and neutralise the voices of conservative religious groups.

---

54 For a discussion, see: R. Wintemute, 'Religion vs. sexual orientation: a clash of human rights', *Journal of Law & Equality* 1, 2002, 125.
55 R.M. Vanderbeck, J. Andersson, G. Valentine, J. Sadgrove and K. Ward, op. cit.
56 Anglican Mainstream, www.anglican-mainstream.net.
57 For example: J. Clatworthy, *Liberal Faith in a Divided Church*, Hampshire, UK: O Books, 2008; A.K.T. Yip, 'Attacking the attacker: gay Christians talk back', *British Journal of Sociology* 48, 1997, 113–127.
58 The most well-known of these is the Lesbian and Gay Christian Movement (an inter-denominational group). Others include Changing Attitude (a specifically Anglican group), Accepting Evangelicals, Imaan (a Muslim group) and Sarbat (Sikh).

Law, morality and religion

Within the context of the religious transformations described above, one of our key concerns in this book is to consider the extent to which religious morality continues to exercise authority in lawmaking. In focusing predominantly on law reforms relating to homosexuality from the mid-twentieth century, we inevitably only consider a short historical period of the relationship between law, religion and morality that is long established in the UK. Scholars have sought to explicate the nature of this relationship since at least the time that Thomas Aquinas attempted to determine the connection between eternal, divine, natural and human law.[59] In the sixteenth century, Coke provided a summation of the belief – dominant in that era – that 'the law of nature' is 'part of the law of England' and that the 'immutable' law of nature, which existed 'before any judicial or municipal law' was written, is 'that which God at the time of creation of the nature of man infused into his heart, for his preservation and direction'.[60] The endurance of this idea in the nineteenth century is evident in Stephen's comparison of law and religion with 'surgery and medicine' to demonstrate the impossibility of separating the 'temporal and spiritual' aspects of law.[61] The fortunes of Judeo-Christian natural theories of law, in which secular law is imagined as derived from or to be entwined with fundamental moral principles originating from God, have fluctuated in light of various theories that have contended with them. But even after sustained attacks over two centuries encouraged by legal positivists – chief amongst them Bentham[62] and Hart,[63] who were instrumental in separating the concept of law from (religious) morals – a concern with religious morality has remained present in lawmaking in the UK.

Although the contemporary relationship between religious morality and law has been determined by a range of issues – such as abortion, blasphemy, cloning, euthanasia and suicide – homosexuality has been and remains a touchstone concern. Religious morality, as we demonstrate in Chapter 1, underpinned the long history of legal regulation of homosexual conduct in England that originated in the Middle Ages. The partial decriminalisation of male homosexual acts in England and Wales in 1967 was achieved not in spite of religious morality about homosexuality but, as we demonstrate, significantly encouraged by it. The conception of homosexuality that dominated at that time, amongst both those supporting and opposing law reform, was inextricably linked to Christian morality. When Anthony Grey, a leading figure in the Homosexual Law Reform Society,

---

59 T. Aquinas, *Summa Theologica (Part 2.1, 'Treatise on law' QQ 90–108)*, Milton Keynes: Authentic Media, [1265–1274] 2012.
60 *Calvin's Case* [1608] 7 Coke Report 1a at 12b; 77 ER 377 at 391–392.
61 J.F. Stephen, *Liberty, Equality, Fraternity (2nd edition)*, London: H. Elder and Co., 1874, p.xlii.
62 J. Bentham, *A Fragment on Government*, London: T. Payne *et al.*, 1776.
63 H.L.A. Hart, *The Concept of Law*, Oxford: Oxford University Press, 1961.

wrote in 1954 that 'homosexual relationships can never be "moral" in the sense that marriage is the only truly moral sexual relationship',[64] he reiterated the established Christian view of homosexual sex as, to paraphrase the current formulation of the Church of England, falling short of the ideal.[65] Homosexual law reform in the 1960s did not challenge the hegemony of a Christian moral condemnation of homosexuality but, as exemplified by the 'Wolfenden Report', sought only to create 'a realm of private morality and immorality which is, in brief and crude terms, not the law's business'.[66] Because homosexuality was agreed to be antithetical to social (Christian) morality, no attempt was made during the twentieth century to repeal the suite of laws regulating buggery, gross indecency and solicitation by men.[67]

For those concerned to retain criminal sanctions against male homosexual acts in order to enforce a religious moral code, their progressive decriminalisation has been a cause of disappointment. For example, when the European Court of Human Rights upheld a complaint about the criminalisation of consensual homosexual acts between adult males in Northern Ireland,[68] which resulted in a defeat of the 'Save Ulster from Sodomy Campaign' led by the Reverend Ian Paisley MP, Paisley was dismayed that 'an outside body who is not committed to the moral values [of] the people of Northern Ireland [. . .] is prepared to say "you will legislate perversion and immorality"'.[69] Similar complaints about a separation between religious morality and law have accompanied every aspect of legal change relating to sexual orientation since that time. For example, the Archbishop of York, John Sentamu, in response to the legislative reforms that we discuss in Chapter 2 in respect of legal recognition for same-sex parents of children conceived through the use of reproductive technologies, protested against the 'severance of law from morality and religion':

> Religion, morality and law were once intermingled, which helped to shape both the common law and the statutes of this land, and greatly influenced the way in which judges interpreted them. However, the law is now regarded

---

64 A. Grey, *Quest for Justice: Towards Homosexual Emancipation*, London: Sinclair-Stevenson, 1992, p.281.
65 On 11 November 1987 the General Synod of the Church of England passed by 403-8 the motion that 'sexual intercourse is an act of total commitment which belongs properly within a permanent married relationship' and that 'homosexual genital acts also fall short of this ideal'. The subsequent lawfulness of same-sex marriage under English statute law does not trouble this view since Church of England Canon law continues to maintain that marriage is exclusively heterosexual.
66 Home Office, *Report of the Committee on Homosexual Offences and Prostitution* (Cmnd. 247), London: Home Office, 1957, § 24.
67 S.12–13 and S.32 Sexual Offences Act 1956.
68 *Dudgeon v the United Kingdom*, no. 7525/76, 22 October 1981, Series A no. 45.
69 For a fuller discussion, see: M.D. Goldhaber, *A People's History of the European Court of Human Rights*, New Brunswick, NJ: Rutgers University Press, 2009.

purely as an instrument for regulating our personal affairs and as being completely severed from morality and religion.[70]

A similar complaint was made by the then Archbishop of Canterbury, Rowan Williams, on behalf of non-Anglican religions when he argued that, at a time dominated by a 'secular legal monopoly', there is 'a great deal of uncertainty about what degree of accommodation the law of the land can and should give to minority communities with their own strongly entrenched legal and moral codes'.[71] Williams' comment was prompted by the introduction of the Equality Act (Sexual Orientation) Regulations 2007, which we discuss in Chapter 3.

In many ways, Sentamu and Williams are correct. The progressive acceptance of a conceptual distinction between religious morals and secular law amongst legislators – itself influenced by the processes of religious change described above – has been foundational to many of the law reforms relating to homosexuality since the 1990s. In turn, such law reforms have themselves influenced the social and cultural construction and deployment of homosexuality, and given rise to arguments promoting further separation between religious morality and law. The result has been a gradual diminishment of the conception of homosexuality as 'sin' that was once the dominant paradigm in UK parliamentary debates. At the point that same-sex marriage was made lawful in England and Wales in 2013, opposition on the grounds that it was contrary to 'the biblical definition of marriage [that] God gave [...] to us in his precious word'[72] was no longer sufficient to halt this fundamental legal change. After more than half a century of homosexual law reform, the influence of explicit faith-based moral condemnations of homosexuality on lawmaking is near redundant.[73]

However, contrary to claims that law is increasingly being severed from religious morality, we demonstrate throughout this book that such morality remains central to the process of lawmaking in respect of homosexuality. Whilst

---

70 HL Debate, 19 November 2007, cc.704–705.
71 R. Williams, 'Civil and religious law in England: a religious perspective', lecture to the Temple Foundation at the Royal Courts of Justice, 7 February 2008.
72 W. McCrea, HC Debate, 21 May 2013, c.1168.
73 Laws J provided a trenchant critique of the influence of religious morality upon lawmaking in *McFarlane v Relate Avon Ltd* which is illustrative of a shift in judicial understanding: 'The Judaeo-Christian tradition, stretching over many centuries, has no doubt exerted a profound influence upon the judgment of lawmakers as to the objective merits of this or that social policy [...] But the conferment of any legal protection or preference upon a particular substantive moral position on the ground only that it is espoused by the adherents of a particular faith, however long its tradition, however rich its culture, is deeply unprincipled. It imposes compulsory law, not to advance the general good on objective grounds, but to give effect to the force of subjective opinion' ([2010] EWCA Civ 880, § 21). However, by contrast, see our discussion in Chapter 3 of the decision by Weatherup J in *An Application for Judicial Review by The Christian Institute and Others* [2007] NIQB 66.

the relationship between lawmaking and religious morality has undoubtedly changed in recent history, our analysis shows that religious morality continues to exert considerable influence upon the legislative process. Whereas religious morality no longer provides a basis for coercive law designed to regulate private and consensual sexual conduct, it continues to mould law in particular ways that limit the rights and protections afforded to gay men and lesbians. For example, as we demonstrate in Chapter 4, religious morality provided the basis for a suite of provisions in the MSSCA 2013 that enforce a default exclusion of same-sex couples from solemnising marriage on religious premises and according to religious rites (which includes nearly 16,000 churches of the Church of England[74]) unless religious organisations decide otherwise. Similarly, as we show in Chapter 3, the assertion of religious morality (specifically to prevent 'the gay lobby [. . .] seeking to impose its morality on [. . .] religious communities'[75]) was foundational in ensuring religious exceptions from sexual orientation equality legislation. In sum, we argue throughout the book that Lord Denning's well-known argument that '[w]ithout religion there can be no morality: and without morality there can be no law'[76] is still relevant to lawmaking in the UK.

Transformations in religious discourse in Parliament

Although religion remains significant in shaping law relating to sexual orientation, its influence upon the legislative process has changed over time. Most importantly, as we noted above, there has been a fundamental decline in the authority of explicitly anti-gay religious rhetoric in Parliament. Throughout this book we chart that decline, showing the progressive demise of the once commonplace and unquestioned religious condemnations of homosexuality that dominated parliamentary debates. The consequence of the displacement of 'traditional' religious discourse by the discourse of equality and human rights is that those with faith-based objections to homosexuality must now compete in a 'symbolic economy'[77] that is predominantly hostile to them. The recent growth in religious discourse supportive of sexual orientation equality has further peripheralised explicitly hostile faith-based condemnations of homosexuality. The result of this has been a marked suppression of anti-gay religious rhetoric, and in its place religious opponents have developed new discursive strategies designed to resist legal

---

74 *Church Statistics 2010/11: Parochial Attendance, Membership and Finance Statistics Together with Statistics of Licensed Ministers for the Church of England January to December*, London: Archbishops' Council, 2012.
75 Viscount Bledisloe, HL Debate, 21 March 2007, c.1316.
76 Lord Denning, quoted in E. Davies, 'Lord Denning: Christian activist and judge', *The Denning Law Journal* 1, 1986, 42.
77 P. Bourdieu, *Language and Symbolic Power*, Cambridge: Polity Press, 1991.

change. For instance, no longer easily able to directly condemn homosexuals, religious opponents of legal change increasingly claim that the extension of equal rights and protections to gay men and lesbians is being used to 'trample over people's deeply held beliefs'.[78]

We do not want to suggest that the transformation in religious discourse about homosexuality in Parliament follows a straightforward or chronological trajectory. However, it is possible to discern broad temporal patterns of change in respect of religious discourse in Parliament since the middle of the twentieth century. We identify four periods that are distinguishable by the dominance of particular religious discourses. The following schema outlines periodic changes in religious discourses in Parliament, indicates the dominant content of each period, and locates this in the context of homosexual law reform.

- *1954–1967 Decriminalising male homosexual acts as a pastoral solution to sexual deviancy*
  From the time that the body that became the 'Wolfenden Committee' was announced in 1954 until the partial decriminalisation of male homosexual acts in England and Wales in 1967, parliamentary debate about the appropriate regulation of male homosexual sexual conduct by the criminal law was dominated by a near-universal acceptance of a Christian condemnation of homosexuality. The partial decriminalisation of male homosexual acts in England and Wales was significantly encouraged by the argument that the separation of 'crime' and 'sin' would more effectively enable society (and particularly churches) to address the problem of homosexuality. Claims that partial decriminalisation would maximise the enforcement of Christian morality and suppress homosexual conduct gained considerable authority. These arguments – and the Christian morality that underpinned them – provided the basis for the creation of a legal framework in England and Wales designed to maintain a strict control of male homosexuality in the public sphere.

- *1968–1993 Discouraging homosexuality through the legal enforcement of religious morality*
  A parliamentary debate about the 'age of consent' for male homosexual acts in 1977 – the first debate about homosexual law reform since the partial decriminalisation of male homosexual acts in England and Wales – marked the beginning of a period of continuous and forceful assertion of religious morality to prevent any further legislative reform. Although the partial decriminalisation of male homosexual acts was extended to Scotland in 1980, this was encouraged by a religious discourse about 'pastoral care' similar to that found in earlier parliamentary debates concerning England and Wales. The absence of broad support for this view amongst representatives

78 E. Leigh, HC Debate, 29 January 2013, c.801.

for Northern Ireland meant that the partial decriminalisation of male homosexual acts there was not achieved by consensus in the UK Parliament but was compelled by the European Court of Human Rights.[79] However, the European Court of Human Rights was clear that its judgment did not challenge religious morality nor make 'any value-judgment as to the morality of homosexual relations'.[80] During this period, religious discourse provided a vital support for resistance in Parliament to legislative reform of the higher minimum age set for male homosexual acts. Religious discourse was also conspicuous in the enactment of the anti-gay 'Section 28' which stated that no local authority shall 'intentionally promote homosexuality'. Throughout this period, religious discourse was frequently deployed to oppose any legislative change that would constitute the 'thin end of the wedge' in the development of gay and lesbian legal equality.

- *1994–2000 Challenging 'equality'*
  Between 1994 and 2000, the deployment of religious discourse was fundamental in resisting a range of legislative reforms driven by an ascendant discourse of sexual orientation equality. Discourses of gay and lesbian equality, while not without antecedents, began to circulate widely in Parliament during this period. Those utilising religious discourse to oppose sexual orientation equality increasingly began to encounter – and explicitly attempted to resist – the charge of 'homophobia' (although accusations of homophobia remained more commonly levied outside than inside Parliament).[81] The discourse of 'rights' provided a further competitor to religious opposition to homosexuality with a notable rise in reference to 'gay rights' in Parliament during this period. Religious discourse was foundational to resisting reform of the 'age of consent' for male homosexual acts in a protracted series of parliamentary debates that spanned this period. The

---

79 *Dudgeon v the United Kingdom*, op.cit.
80 Ibid., § 54. For a discussion, see: P. Johnson, *Homosexuality and the European Court of Human Rights*, Abingdon: Routledge, 2013.
81 Our analysis of Hansard suggests that the first use of 'homophobia' in a parliamentary debate was by Ken Livingstone MP, who used the term in a debate regarding the publication of materials for children about homosexuality (HC Debate, 15 December 1987, c.1012). A year earlier, the Earl of Halsbury, when advocating a provision that would prove to be an important precursor to Section 28 (see Chapter 6), stated that he would be accused of being a 'homophone' (it is unclear whether this is a transcription error for 'homophobe' or an error on his part) (HL Debate, 18 December 1986, c.310). Usage of the terms 'homophobia' and 'homophobe' seems to have remained uncommon until approximately 1995–6 when their use by parliamentarians accelerated rapidly. Use of the terms 'heterosexist' and 'heterosexism' appear to predate the use of 'homophobia' in Parliament. These terms were used by Baroness Cox in 1986 in her derisive discussion of advice being given on sex education by local education authorities which encouraged the challenging of 'heterosexism' (HL Debate, 30 October 1986, c.803).

equalisation of the age of consent by Parliament in 2000 marked a significant displacement of anti-gay religious discourse.

- *2001–2013 Protecting religious human rights*
  Since 2001, the progressive mainstreaming of a discourse of gay and lesbian equality and human rights has further displaced anti-gay religious discourse in Parliament. Religious opposition has failed to halt a range of legislative reforms relating to sexual offences, partnership and family rights, equality in employment and in the provision of goods and services, and hate speech. In addition, faith-based support for legal equality in respect of sexual orientation has increased in parliamentary debates during this period. As a consequence, religious opponents of homosexuality have modified their discourse in particular ways, routinely distancing themselves from homophobia (and in some cases attributing same-sex relationships with a degree of moral worth – but not *equal* worth). A nodal point for religious discourse has been 'religious conscience', around which have circulated a number of claims that faith-based 'conscientious objection' to homosexuality has no equivalence with 'discrimination'. A major discursive shift has involved the now commonplace appropriation by religious opponents of rights-based discourses previously deployed by gay and lesbian groups. Religious discourse has become increasingly orientated towards claiming that religious groups and individuals require greater protection from litigious homosexuals. Operating in a defensive mode orientated towards preserving particular religious boundaries, religious opposition to law reform has been effective in shaping law to either limit its scope or exempt religious organisations from its provisions.

Since the beginning of the twenty-first century, then, explicit religious condemnations of homosexuality have become infrequent in parliamentary debates, and religious opponents have increasingly deployed a new discursive arsenal orientated towards defending religious rights and freedoms. It is now common for parliamentarians who wish to advance faith-based arguments against legislative reform to profess personal opposition to homophobia while, at the same time, arguing that measures either go 'too far' (such as the frequent claim that the 'gay community' seek special rights rather than equal rights)[82] or conflict with the rights of other groups (particularly religious groups) and the interests of the 'wider public'. An example of this can be seen in the argument made by Baroness Paisley during the Equality Act 2010 debates about whether to permit civil partnership ceremonies on religious premises:

> [A]ny partnership between two people of the same sex is not a marriage and cannot be called a marriage because God's word does not allow that. It is in

---

82 C. Brickell, '"Whose "special treatment"? Heterosexism and the problems with liberalism', *Sexualities* 4, 2001, 211–235; J. Burridge, op. cit.

total contravention of the marriage which God ordained when he made mankind and put mankind into the world. It is totally wrong and I do not believe that any Christian church which is founded on the word of God can possibly be forced to carry out such partnerships in its places of worship. Although we are told that they will not be forced to, I fear that pressure will be put on churches to do so against their consciences, otherwise there will be a cry of discrimination. I do not believe in discrimination because of a person's orientation, whether sexual, religious or anything else, but it is wrong and dangerous to overthrow certain limits.[83]

The primary limit to which Baroness Paisley refers is the provision in the Civil Partnership Act 2004, originally enacted in response to similar objections grounded in religious morality and theology, which prohibited same-sex couples from registering a civil partnership on religious premises. That prohibition has since been repealed and we discuss this, and the relevance of arguments like those made by Baroness Paisley to the reshaping of law, in Chapter 4. The point we make here is that Paisley's discursive 'style' is typical of how religious objections to law reform are now formulated and deployed. The key aspects of such opposition are: an eschewal of any explicit condemnation of homosexuality; the denial that religious opposition constitutes the expression of homophobia; and the claim that religious conscience is made victim by zealous homosexuals. Such a discursive strategy 'works' insofar as, to use the words of the Bishop of Oxford, John Pritchard, those who deploy it are often not 'accused of being homophobes' but are characterised as being concerned with 'safeguarding religious liberty' and upholding the 'traditional ethical teaching on sexual morality of the Christian churches and many other faiths'.[84] Religious opposition to legislative reform, whilst not always successful, remains the most effective counter-discourse to gay and lesbian legal equality because it often avoids 'the accusations of being homophobic, toxic, [or] odious'.[85] This form of religious discourse resists being labelled as homophobic because, as Bourdieu argues, it utilises linguistic devices such as 'traditional ethical teaching' to appeal to notions of commonly shared and long-established beliefs.[86] This accounts, in part, for why religious (Christian) discourse continues to have significant authority in Parliament.

The formal role of religion in Parliament

Religious discourse also remains prominent in UK lawmaking as a result of the status of the Church of England in the UK Parliament. The formal and

---

83 HL Debate, 23 March 2010, c.870.
84 HL Debate, 15 December 2011, c.1420.
85 Baroness O'Cathain, HL Debate, 15 December 2011, c.1446.
86 P. Bourdieu, op. cit.

institutionalised relationship between Parliament and the Church of England is a direct result of the religious settlement that emerged during the sixteenth-century English Reformation. Following the Acts of Supremacy 1534 and 1558, the latter of which definitively determined that all 'Jurisdictions Privileges Superiorities and Preheminences Spirituall and Ecclesiasticall [. . .] shall for ever [. . .] be united and annexed to the Imperiall Crowne of this Realme',[87] the British monarch has simultaneously been both Head of State and Defender of the Faith and Supreme Governor of the Church of England. As Supreme Governor of the Church of England, the monarch, on the advice of the prime minister (informed by the Crown Nominations Commission), appoints the Church of England's archbishops, bishops and other senior clergy. Although there has always been ecclesiastical representation in Parliament[88] (save for during the Commonwealth of England[89]), the current settlement permits 26 Lords Spiritual to sit and vote in the House of Lords.[90] These comprise the Archbishops of Canterbury and York, the Bishops of London, Durham and Winchester, and the longest-serving of the other qualifying diocesan bishops.

The influence on parliamentary business by the Lords Spiritual is minor in relation to the overall legislative work of the House of Lords. The Lords Spiritual make up only 3 per cent of the membership of the House of Lords, and in recent years at least one bishop has been in attendance at approximately 17 per cent of sittings.[91] However, as previous studies have shown, the Lords Spiritual are more likely to attend the House of Lords and make contributions from their benches on issues of 'obvious moral or ethical concern'.[92] As we demonstrate throughout this book, the Lords Spiritual are a consistent presence in debates relating to homosexuality. Although no positivistic claims can be made about the influence of the Lords Spiritual upon the outcome of divisions in the House of Lords in

---

87   S.8 'An Acte restoring to the Crowne thauncyent Jurisdiction over the State Ecclesiasticall and Spirituall, and abolyshing all Forreine Power repugnaunt to the same' 1558 (1 Eliz. 1 c.1).

88   For a discussion of the pre- and post-Reformation arrangements of Parliament, see: G. Drewry and J. Brock, 'Prelates in Parliament', *Parliamentary Affairs* 24, 1971, 222–250.

89   'An Act for disinabling all persons in Holy Orders to exercise any temporall Jurisdiccion or authoritie' 1640 (16 Cha. 1 c.27) stated that no 'Archbishop or Bishop or other person that now is or hereafter shall be in Holy Orders shall [. . .] have any Seat or place suffrage or Voice or use or execute any power or authority in the Parliaments of this Realm'. This was repealed by 'An Act for Repeal of an Act of Parliament Entituled An Act for disinabling all persons in Holy Orders to exercise any Temporall Jurisdiccion or Authority' 1661 (13 Cha. 2 St.1 c.2).

90   The current number of Lords Spiritual permitted to sit in the House of Lords was set by the Bishopric of Manchester Act 1847.

91   Data for parliamentary sessions 2005/2006 to 2010/2011. M. Purvis, 'House of Lords: religious representation', *House of Lords Library Note*, LLN 2011/036, 2011.

92   D. Shell, *The House of Lords*, Manchester: Manchester University Press, 2007, p.54.

respect of legislation relating to homosexuality – although, where divisions have been decided by relatively small majorities, we pay attention to the voting records of the Lords Spiritual – we examine their significant contribution to shaping the limit and form of parliamentary discourse on homosexuality. As each chapter demonstrates, the Lords Spiritual have participated in all of the major legislative reforms relating to homosexuality and this has given the Church of England direct influence upon this aspect of lawmaking.

In the House of Commons, the Church of England has a presence in the form of the Second Church Estates Commissioner who is an elected Member of Parliament appointed by the Crown. The Second Church Estates Commissioner provides a link between the House of Commons and the Church Commissioners, responding to questions about a wide range of issues including those related to sexual orientation. For example, the current Second Church Estates Commissioner took an active role in the recent House of Commons debates during the passage of the MSSCA 2013, arguing against it on the grounds that it would 'alter the intrinsic nature of marriage as the union of a man and a woman as enshrined in human institutions throughout history'.[93] The Second Church Estates Commissioner is a member of the Ecclesiastical Committee, made up of membership from both Houses, which considers draft Measures presented to it by the Legislative Committee of the General Synod of the Church of England. A Church of England Measure is primary legislation relating to 'any matter concerning the Church of England, and may extend to the amendment or repeal in whole or in part of any Act of Parliament'.[94] The Ecclesiastical Committee decides whether a Measure is expedient and, if so, submits it to both Houses of Parliament where it is voted on. This arrangement, which enables the Church of England to independently legislate on the understanding that Parliament does 'not legislate over and above, or directly at, the Church of England',[95] provides it with considerable legislative authority. However, although unconventional in practice, Parliament retains the capacity to legislate directly in matters relating to the Church of England and an example of this can be seen in the Civil Partnership Act 2004 which provided that '[a] Minister of the Crown may by order make such amendments, repeals or revocations in any [. . .] Church legislation relating to pensions, allowances or gratuities'.[96] There has been debate about the extent to which this provision challenges the legislative autonomy of the Church of England.[97]

---

93 T. Baldry, HC Debate, 5 February 2013, c.145.
94 S.3(6) Church of England Assembly (Powers) Act 1919. Parliament has no role in Church of England Canon law, which is promulged by the General Synod under Royal Assent and Licence.
95 Lord Cormack, HL Debate, 15 December 2011, c.1437.
96 S.255(1) Civil Partnership Act 2004.
97 See: S. Slack, 'Church autonomy and the Civil Partnership Act: a rejoinder', *Ecclesiastical Law Journal* 9, 2007, 206–207.

There is no constitutional arrangement for representation in Parliament of organised religions or faith groups other than the Church of England. The Church in Wales and the Church of Ireland, by virtue of their disestablishment, have no representation in the UK Parliament.[98] The Church of Scotland, although an established church, has no representation in the UK Parliament and has never participated in the House of Lords.[99] For these churches, as well as all other religious groups, representation in Parliament is therefore determined by indirect means. The religious affiliation of individual Members of Parliament or Lords Temporal (life Peers, as well as the remaining hereditary Peers) may provide links between faith groups and Parliament. In the debates that we examine throughout the book we show that individual Peers in the House of Lords have, for example, frequently given expression to the concerns of the wider faith groups to which they belong. However, life Peers are not appointed to the House of Lords on the basis of their religious affiliations nor to represent particular religious groups. Similarly, many parliamentarians belong to All-Party Parliamentary Groups – such as Christians in Parliament, Christian and Jewish Relations, Faith in Society – but these have no legislative function. In light of the lack of direct representation, many faith groups have become increasingly more organised in establishing lobbying mechanisms – for example, by providing evidence to parliamentary committees or circulating materials to parliamentarians (some of which, as we show, are cited directly in parliamentary debate). The loss of Christianity's cultural 'monopoly'[100] has encouraged parliamentarians seeking to oppose aspects of sexual orientation law reform to invoke the views of non-Christian faiths to complement and substantiate the viewpoint of 'traditional' Christians.

Overview of the book

As we stated above, the organisation of this book is thematic rather than chronological. Each chapter focuses on a particular substantive area of law relating to homosexuality and considers the role of religion in relation to it. We adopt this thematic approach for two main reasons: first, focusing on the influence of religion on discrete areas of law affords greater analytic depth and coherence; second, and relatedly, this approach allows an exploration of the temporal complexities and discontinuities that characterise the relationship between law, religion and homosexuality. Although gay and lesbian law reform is often understood to be a progressive and causational history, whereby each legislative change is an incremental step towards achieving full legal equality, we demonstrate that

---

98 Irish Church Act 1869; Welsh Church Act 1914.
99 J. Lewis-Jones, *Reforming the Lords: The Role of the Bishops*, London: UCL Constitution Unit, 1999.
100 M. Guest, E. Olsson and J. Wolffe, 'Christianity: loss of monopoly', in L. Woodhead and R. Catto (eds), op. cit.

lawmaking does not always conform to this linear narrative. Whilst, in some cases, changes in one legal area relating to homosexuality have undoubtedly encouraged reform in others – in either progressive or regressive ways – it is also the case that some legal reforms are the result of indirect and extraneous influences. For instance, it is possible to approach the history of gay and lesbian law reform in the UK as a loosely connected series of legislative changes influenced by a number of broader social, political and legal shifts including, for example, the development of left-wing and socialist politics in the post-war period[101] or the progressive ascendency of human rights.[102] Our focus on substantive legal areas in each chapter avoids a totalising historical account of legislative change, as well as affording a more nuanced account of the influence (and interest) of religion in respect of a number of different issues.

In Chapter 1 we consider the relationship between the criminal law and religion in respect of the regulation of homosexual sex. Although the focus of this chapter is on law reform in the second half of the twentieth century, we begin by providing an historical account of the relationship between law, religion and homosexual sex in England from the thirteenth century. This longer history is important to understanding the role of religion during the twentieth century in respect of the progressive decriminalisation of male homosexual acts and the associated changes in the minimum legal ages for these acts. We demonstrate that the long-established role of religion in this sphere of lawmaking has remained highly influential since the middle of the twentieth century in fashioning the legislative landscape in which male homosexual acts have been – and remain – subject to specific social control.

In Chapter 2 we examine the role of religion in debates over two pieces of legislation that bear directly on the ability of same-sex couples to engage in legally recognised practices of parenting: the Adoption and Children Act 2002 and the Human Fertilisation and Embryology Act 2008. The reforms benefiting same-sex couples made by these statutes were subject to concerted religious opposition based not only on the practical implications of these legal changes (which enabled and offered legal recognition to lesbian and gay practices of parenting) but also on the symbolic significance of the changes in undermining the privileged social and legal position of heterosexual marriage and mother–father models of parenting. As we show, moral and religious arguments about the unfitness of gay men and lesbians to serve as parents had lost considerable authority, and attempts by religious opponents to deploy scientific 'evidence' in support of their position also proved insufficiently persuasive. Indeed, as we demonstrate, many supporters of reform successfully characterised religious opposition to the reforms as the

---

101 L. Robinson, *Gay Men and the Left in Post-war Britain: How the Personal Got Political*, Manchester: Manchester University Press, 2007.
102 R. Wintemute, *Sexual Orientation and Human Rights: The United States Constitution, the European Convention, and the Canadian Charter*, Oxford: Clarendon Press, 1995.

'immoral' position. We argue that the debates over the Human Fertilisation and Embryology Act 2008 exemplify the increasing tendency for opponents of legal reform to seek recourse to claims of religious discrimination and marginalisation in the face of the declining authority of religious discourses on homosexuality.

In Chapter 3 we consider the influence of religion on legislation designed to protect sexual minorities from discrimination in employment, in the provision of goods and services, and in access to facilities and premises. Our analysis in this chapter focuses on the ways in which religious groups and individuals have attempted to halt the introduction, or significantly curtail the scope, of this legislation. We show the ways in which these groups and individuals have drawn upon a range of discursive strategies to secure significant exceptions in equality law. As we demonstrate, organised religions have secured a unique exception from law prohibiting sexual orientation discrimination in employment. Furthermore, religious organisations are afforded considerable scope to restrict the provision of goods and services and the use of facilities and premises on the grounds of sexual orientation. In addition, we show how religious opposition resulted in the exclusion of sexual orientation from provisions in equalities legislation prohibiting harassment outside of employment.

In Chapter 4 we examine the evolution of legislation that has enabled same-sex couples to register civil partnerships and solemnise marriages. Our analysis of this sphere of lawmaking demonstrates the considerable impact that religious opposition has had upon shaping and limiting successive legislation. In charting the development of this we consider the discursive strategies that have been adopted by religious opponents in their attempt to fashion law in particular ways. Whilst these strategies have been heterogeneous, we show that their fundamental aim has been to maintain distinctions in law between same-sex and opposite-sex partnerships. As we demonstrate, such strategies have been successful in shaping legislation to reflect and maintain the hostility of mainstream organised religions to the legal equivalence of same-sex and opposite-sex partnerships.

In Chapter 5 we provide a critical analysis of the role of religion in the creation of a new criminal law regulating 'hatred on the grounds of sexual orientation' in England and Wales. The scope of this law, which is popularly understood to criminalise forms of anti-gay 'hate speech', was strongly determined by religious opposition. We show how opponents of the law deployed particular representations of 'traditional' Christians and other religious believers as minorities in need of protection from gay and lesbian individuals and groups. By invoking a particular equalities hierarchy, where religion and sexual orientation were imagined to be in competition, opponents were successful in significantly limiting the scope of the law. As a result of this, a higher threshold has been set for speech and behaviour intended to stir up hatred on the grounds of sexual orientation than that set in respect of race.

In Chapter 6 we examine the influence of religion on the legal frameworks that govern the inclusion and exclusion of knowledge about homosexuality within the curricula of English schools. We begin the chapter by examining the role of religion in relation to the passage and later repeal of Section 28, which left a significant legacy for the legal framework governing sex education in Britain. We then explore how religious discourse has been significant in sequestering the discussion of homosexuality outside the requirements of the National Curriculum. We also consider how the recent legalisation of same-sex marriage in England and Wales has instigated debates that remain unresolved about the legal obligation of schools to teach about the importance of marriage. Throughout the chapter, we argue that although religious arguments for severely circumscribing the discussion of homosexuality in schools have lost considerable persuasiveness, religious interests and considerations have contributed to shaping the law in ways that permit religiously inflected understandings of homosexuality to remain dominant in schools with a legally designated religious character.

Chapter 1

Religion and the legal regulation of homosexual sex

In this chapter we consider the relationship between law and religion in respect of the regulation of homosexual sex. We begin with an historical account that traces the development of the relationship between English law, religion and homosexual sex from the thirteenth to the mid-twentieth century. We provide this account of the long and complex relationship between law and religion in order to contextualise and situate our analysis of the role of religion in homosexual law reform from the mid-twentieth century onwards. The subsequent parts of this chapter are devoted to an analysis of UK parliamentary debates during three key moments of legislative reform: first, the partial decriminalisation of male homosexual acts in England and Wales by the Sexual Offences Act 1967; second, changes to the minimum age for male homosexual acts that culminated in the Sexual Offences (Amendment) Act 2000; and, finally, the repeal of male homosexual offences by the Sexual Offences Act 2003. Although the twentieth-century history of homosexual law reform in the UK has been well documented, there has been insufficient analysis of the role of religion in shaping it. Our analysis shows a dynamic historical interplay between law and religion, and demonstrates the significant role of religion throughout this period in fashioning the legislative landscape in which male homosexual acts have been – and remain – subject to specific social control.

Law, religion and homosexuality in England: the formation of a relationship

It is often asserted that laws that criminalise homosexual acts are expressions of a perpetual Judeo-Christian concern to regulate homosexuality.[1] However, an

---

1 For example, the Christian Institute has argued against all stages of reform of the criminal law in the UK in respect of male homosexual acts on the grounds that the 'historic Christian faith has *always* affirmed Biblical teaching that homosexual acts are *always* wrong'. The Christian Institute, *Age of Consent: The Case Against Change*, Newcastle upon Tyne: The Christian Institute, 1999. Our emphasis.

examination of English history repudiates any claim for a stable alignment between law, religion and homosexuality. Rather, the historical evidence demonstrates the fluidity of the relationship between forms of law (especially canon and statute), religion (particularly pre- and post-Reformation Christianity) and cultural conceptions of human erotic behaviour (specifically in respect of the social construction of homosexuality). In this section we provide a short account of the changing formations between law, religion and homosexuality since the thirteenth century. An understanding of this history is important, because claims about it have often been central to the arguments used by legislators since the mid-twentieth century who have sought to either defend or challenge particular approaches to enforcing religious morality through law.

From Roman canon law to statute law

The legal regulation of same-sex sexual acts in England originated, as it did in other European states, in ecclesiastical forms of control. The earliest records of English law relating to acts that would now be classified as homosexual are in thirteenth-century treatises that described penalties for 'sodomites'.[2] Medieval ecclesiastical courts independent of the royal courts dealt with the offence of sodomy and, whilst there is dispute amongst scholars about the extent of their regulation of it,[3] the ecclesiastical authorities would almost certainly have been influenced by Roman canon law relating to sexual conduct.[4] However, although

---

2   *Fleta* (circa 1290) states: '*Contrahentes vero cum Judæis vel Judæabus pecorantes & Sodomitæ in terra vivi confodiantur, dum tamen man' oper' capti per testimonium legale vel publice convicti*'. *Fleta, seu Commentarius Juris Anglicani*, London: H. Twyford, T. Bassett, J. Place, & S. Keble, 1685, p.54. Bailey translates this as: 'Those who have dealings with Jews and Jewesses, those who commit bestiality, and sodomists, are to be buried alive, after legal proof that they were taken in the act, and public conviction.' D.S. Bailey, *Homosexuality and the Western Christian Tradition*, London: Longmans, 1955, p.145. However, the word 'Sodomitæ' is now more commonly translated as 'sodomite'. *Britton* (circa 1290) states that 'sodomites' who are 'publicly convicted' 'shall be burnt'. F.M. Nichols, *Britton: An English Translation and Notes*, Washington, DC: John Byrne & Co., 1901, p.35. There is no mention of sodomy in earlier accounts of English law, such as *Glanvill* (circa 1187). G.D.G. Hall (ed.), *The Treatise on the Laws and Customs of the Realm of England Commonly Called Glanvill*, Oxford: Clarendon Press, 1965. For an historical discussion of sodomy in Scottish law, see: D. Hume, *Commentaries on the Law of Scotland, Respecting the Description and Punishment of Crimes*, Edinburgh: Bell & Bradfute, 1797; J.H.A. MacDonald, *Practical Treatise on the Criminal Law of Scotland*, Edinburgh: William Peterson, 1867.
3   J. Boswell, *Christianity, Social Tolerance, and Homosexuality*, Chicago, IL: University of Chicago Press, 1980.
4   For a discussion of the influence of Roman canon law on the ecclesiastical courts of medieval England, see: F.W. Maitland, *Roman Canon Law in the Church of England: Six Essays*, London: Methuen and Co., 1898; R.H. Helmholz, *Roman Canon Law in Reformation England*, Cambridge: Cambridge University Press, 1990. Pollock and

in contemporary societies several biblical sources – most commonly Leviticus[5] – are frequently cited as evidence of a constant Christian concern to single out and regulate sodomy between males, the history of canon law suggests otherwise. In his survey of the development of canon law up until the twelfth century, Bailey argues that although same-sex sexual acts were 'often denounced (though not actually specified) in many general enactments against the sins of the flesh, and especially those regarded as contrary to nature', there is no 'convincing proof of an implacable ecclesiastical animus against the sodomist'.[6] Whilst early canon law regulated acts of 'defilement' and 'unseemliness' between males, it was only later, from the eleventh century onwards, that it defined sodomy as in violation of the natural function of sex as proscribed by God.[7] The control of sodomy by the ecclesiastical courts in late-medieval England was therefore shaped by the application of the conceptual apparatus of sodomy invented by theologians as a 'category for classifying – for uniting and explaining – desires, dispositions, and acts that had been earlier classified differently and separately'.[8]

References to sodomy in canon law, whilst undoubtedly relating to same-sex sexual acts between males, were not limited to them. Some scholars have argued, for example, that the medieval Christian preoccupation with sodomy was not

    Maitland note that the medieval punishment of sodomy in England 'may betray a trace of Roman law'. F. Pollock and F.W. Maitland, *The History of English Law Before the Time of Edward I (Volume 2) (second edition)*, Cambridge: Cambridge University Press, 1898, p.556. Pollock and Maitland provide a discussion of the relationship between Roman law and Roman canon law in medieval English jurisprudence.

5 In early English translations, Leviticus (20:13) states: 'If a man sleepeth with a man, by lechery of a woman, ever either hath wrought unleaveful thing, die they by death; their blood be on them' (Wycliffe Bible, circa 1382). Some twentieth-century English translations make explicit reference to homosexuality: 'If a man practices homosexuality, having sex with another man as with a woman, both men have committed a detestable act. They must both be put to death, for they are guilty of a capital offense' (New Living Translation, 2007).

6 D.S. Bailey, op. cit., pp.98–99.

7 Jordan argues that the Christian concept of and concern with sodomy (*sodomia*) as particularly sexual sin emerged in eleventh-century theology and became progressively incorporated into Roman canon law. He distinguishes the eleventh-century turn in comprehending 'sodomitical vice' – exemplified by Peter Damian's (circa 1051) *Liber Gomorrhianus* – as a significant departure from earlier and different conceptions of 'Sodom' that did not relate exclusively to sex. M.D. Jordan, *The Invention of Sodomy in Christian Theology*, Chicago, IL: University of Chicago Press, 1997. There is now a large literature that discusses the etymology of sodomy in medieval Christian theology, the particular sexual acts that it describes, and its relation to same-sex sexual practices. See, for example: W. Burgwinkle, *Sodomy, Masculinity, and Law in Medieval Literature: France and England, 1050–1230*, Cambridge: Cambridge University Press, 2004.

8 M.D. Jordan, op. cit., p.1. See also: M. Goodich, 'Sodomy in ecclesiastical law and theory', *Journal of Homosexuality* 1, 1976, 427–434.

explicitly focused on homoerotic sex but encompassed a range of sexual acts that were prohibited because they involved either unmarried partners or were not directed towards procreation.[9] When sodomy eventually began to be tried as a statutory crime in England, the requirement that 'emission of seed' be proven rather than simply penetration reflected an established Christian concern with erotic practices not related to reproduction.[10] A large literature now exists in which there is general agreement between scholars that medieval canon law on sodomy principally existed as one aspect of a more general framework designed to assert a distinction between 'natural' (that is, procreative) and 'unnatural' acts which, consequently, brought same-sex acts within its ambit.[11] The 'utterly confused category'[12] of sodomy enabled the Roman Church to enforce a moral order in respect of both clergy and laity through a system that comprised canon law as well as penitentials and other theological writings. There is dispute over whether ecclesiastical institutions drove an increasing intolerance of sodomy from the eleventh century onwards or whether it reflected a more widespread social hostility.[13] However, the regulation of sodomy by the medieval ecclesiastical courts of England can be seen as enforcing a moral intolerance rooted in Christianity.

When sodomy (or buggery[14]) first became regulated by English statute – as a result of the 'Buggery Act' (BA) 1533 passed by the Parliament of England which made 'the detestable and abominable Vice of Buggery committed with mankind or beast' a felony punishable by death[15] – the statute law continued to express

---

9   See, for example: K. Borris (ed.), *Same-Sex Desire in the English Renaissance: A Sourcebook of Texts, 1470–1650*, London: Routledge, 2003.
10 Until the early nineteenth century, proof of 'spermatic injection' was required to secure a conviction for buggery. S.18 Offences Against the Person Act 1828 made 'penetration only', rather than 'actual emission of seed', the means by which 'carnal knowledge' was proven. This signified less a change in Christian ideas about the importance of 'seed' and more a response to addressing the difficulty of securing convictions created by courts requiring proof of both 'penetration' and 'emission' (as the 1828 Act stated: 'Offenders frequently escape by reason of the Difficulty of the Proof which has been required'). For a discussion, see: H. Montgomery Hyde, *The Other Love: An Historical and Contemporary Survey of Homosexuality in Britain*, London: Heinemann, 1970.
11 See: D. Moon, 'Religious views on homosexuality', in D. Richardson and S. Seidman (eds), *Handbook of Lesbian and Gay Studies*, London: Sage, 2002, pp.313–328; A. Clark, *Desire: A History of European Sexuality*, Abingdon: Routledge, 2008, pp.73–74.
12 M. Foucault, *The History of Sexuality Volume 1: An Introduction*, London: Penguin Books, 1979, p.101.
13 J. Boswell, op. cit.
14 Coke attributes the existence of buggery ('bugeria') in England to the Lombards who 'brought [it] into the realm' in the Middle Ages and reports complaints about this in the Parliament of Edward III. E. Coke, *The Third Part of the Institutes of the Laws of England (the Fourth Edition)*, London: Printed for A. Crooke et al., 1669, p.58.
15 'An Acte for the punyssheement of the vice of Buggerie' 1533 (25 Hen. 8 c.6). The English buggery statute was originally enacted on a temporary basis and subsequently continued in 1536 (28 Hen. 8 c.6) and 1539 (31 Hen. 8 c.7) until it was made perpetual in 1540

the religious morality that had hitherto been enforced by the ecclesiastical courts. However, by incorporating buggery into statute law the BA 1533 ended the near exclusive jurisdiction of the ecclesiastical courts that had previously possessed the capacity to try and sentence a person convicted of buggery to death[16] (a power commonly found in other European nations[17]) and relinquish them to the state for execution.[18] There is general agreement that the enactment of the BA 1533 was not motivated solely by theological ambitions but, rather, represented a secular expression of political power by Henry VIII. As Hyde argues, '[i]ts primary object was part of Henry's policy in general towards the Church [which] included the progressive reduction of the jurisdiction of the ecclesiastical courts'.[19] Understood this way, the BA 1533 was essentially one element of a broader set of legislative changes designed to diminish the legal authority of the ecclesiastical courts.[20] Appearing at a critical point of the English Reformation – it was enacted in the same year as the Submission of the Clergy Act 1533[21] and one year before the Act of Supremacy 1534[22] – the BA 1533 can be seen to reflect a strongly anti-papist sentiment.[23] It was the assertion of a correlation between male same-sex sodomy and Catholicism that underpinned the design of the statute to allow the

(32 Hen. 8 c.3). For an extensive account of the observance of English statute in Wales, and the piecemeal statutory changes to ensure this, in the sixteenth century, see: J. Reeves, *History of the English Law from the Time of the Saxons to the End of the Reign of Philip and Mary: Volume 4 (Third Edition)*, London: Reed and Hunter, 1814. Buggery was incorporated into statute law in Ireland by 'An Act for the punishment of the vice of Buggery' 1634 (10 Cha.1 Sess.2 c.20). Sodomy was not incorporated into statute in Scotland but was a capital offence at the common law. Unlike in England and Wales and Ireland, the offence of sodomy in Scotland related exclusively to acts between males. See: G. Mackenzie, *The Laws and Customs of Scotland in Matters Criminal*, Edinburgh: Thomas Brown, 1678.

16 According to *Britton*, although the 'Holy Church shall make their inquests of [...] sodomites [...] if the king by inquest find any persons guilty of such horrible sin, he may put them to death, as a good marshall of Christendom'. This suggests that although the ecclesiastical courts commonly tried the offence of sodomy, the royal courts could also exercise independent authority. F.M. Nichols, op. cit., pp.35–36.
17 J.A. Brundage, *Law, Sex, and Christian Society in Medieval Europe*, Chicago, IL: University of Chicago Press, 1987.
18 There appears to be no recorded history of any case of execution by the state following a conviction for buggery in an ecclesiastical court in England. See, for example: K. Borris, op. cit.
19 H. Montgomery Hyde, op. cit., p.39.
20 For a general overview of the decline of the ecclesiastical courts in England, see: R. Outhwaite, *The Rise and Fall of the English Ecclesiastical Courts 1500–1860*, Cambridge: Cambridge University Press, 2006.
21 'An Acte for the submission of the Clergie to the Kynges Majestie' 1533 (25 Hen. 8 c.19).
22 'An Acte concernynge the Kynges Highnes to be supreme heed of the Churche of Englande & to have auctoryte to refourme & redresse all errours heresyes & abuses yn the same' 1534 (26 Hen. 8 c.1).
23 A. Bray, *Homosexuality in Renaissance England*, London: Gay Men's Press, 1982.

state to seize the 'goods chattels debts lands tenements and hereditaments' of any convicted clergy.[24] However, although its primary motivation may have been secular and its principal target may have been acts between males, the BA 1533 criminalised buggery as an 'abominable' behaviour whether committed between two men or a man and a woman, and, in so doing, reflected contemporary Christian attitudes about 'unnatural' sexual acts.[25] As Coke later described it, buggery was a 'detestable, and abominable sin, among Christians'.[26]

The various repeals and re-enactments of the buggery statute between 1533 and 1563 demonstrate its strategic political *and* spiritual role. For example, the Henrician statute was repealed in 1547 in the first Parliament of Edward VI[27] and a new statute was enacted in 1548 that included reformed rules in respect of heredity and possessions. The 1548 Act omitted the term 'abominable' (but retained 'detestable') and introduced a statute of limitations of six months, prohibited witnesses giving testimony if they would profit from a conviction, and repealed provisions relating to attainder and 'corruption of blood'.[28] The 1548 Act was wholly repealed under the reign of Mary I from the point of her succession in 1553[29] as one of a number of measures 'intended to restore the former jurisdiction of the ecclesiastical courts'.[30] The Henrician statute was re-enacted in perpetuity under Elizabeth I in 1563 and, although it was usually only enforced throughout the sixteenth and seventieth centuries 'when public figures were involved and political motives were present',[31] it expressed the sentiment that the 'horrible and detestable Vice of Buggery' was a 'high displeasure of Almighty God'.[32] Whereas the category of sodomy in canon law had previously

---

24 Makeover describes the Buggery Act 1533 as one of several 'less important laws' by which the 'benefit of clergy was likewise taken away'. F. Makeover, *Constitutional History and Constitution of the Church of England*, Whitefish: Kessinger Publishing, [1895] 2003, p.447.
25 Although it is not possible to say for certain whether the buggery statute when first enacted in 1533 was intended to include heterosexual acts within its ambit, the English courts came to interpret it that way. See: *R. v Wiseman* (1718) Fortes Rep 91.
26 E. Coke, op. cit., p.58.
27 'An Acte for the repeale of certaine Statutes concerninge treasons felonyes &c.' 1547 (1 Ed. 6 c.12).
28 'An Acte againste Buggorie' 1548 (2–3 Ed. 6 c.29).
29 'An Acte repealing certayne Treasons Felonies and Premunire' 1553 (1 Mary Sess.1 c.1).
30 H. Montgomery Hyde, op. cit., p.40.
31 B.R. Burg, 'Ho hum, another work of the devil. Buggery and sodomy in early Stuart England', *Journal of Homosexuality* 6, 1980/81, 69–78.
32 'An Act for the punishment of the Vyce of Sodomye' 1562 (5 Eliz. 1 c.17). It is interesting to note that whilst the word 'sodomye' appears in the title of this Act as recorded on the Rolls of Parliament in Chancery, the word 'buggorye' appears in the title of the Act preserved in the Parliament Office (see: *Statutes of The Realm: from Original Records and Authentic Manuscripts (Volume 4)*, 1819). This suggests that these terms were used interchangeably by legislators.

been inclusive of a wide range of 'unnatural' acts, the English buggery statute was progressively interpreted to regulate the specific acts of penile penetration of the anus of a man or a woman, and anal or vaginal penetration involving a man or woman and an animal.[33]

The emergence of the statutory regulation of buggery, therefore, was not premised on any straightforward relationship between Christianity and 'homosexuality'. Prior to the sixteenth century, 'sodomites' were discursively constructed as deviants equivalent to arsonists, sorcerers, renegades and heretics.[34] Furthermore, whilst statute from the sixteenth century onwards framed buggery as a 'sin' – for instance, in the Navy Act 1661 which explicitly stated that it was an 'unnatural and detestable sin'[35] – it was linked to other sinful practices such as pride, excess of diet, idleness, and contempt of the poor.[36] Although from the beginning of the eighteenth century Christian-inspired buggery law began to be increasingly enforced to regulate sexual acts between a wide range of men,[37] it continued to do so without making any delimitation of offenders on the basis of sexual identity or orientation. In the trials of male sodomites that became progressively common in Georgian England, men were, for example, prosecuted for 'Wicked Crimes of Un-natural Leudness with their own Sex, contrary to the order of Humane Nature' and were said to have done this because they lacked 'the Fear of God before their Eyes'.[38] Foucault's well-known argument that the sodomite was a 'temporary aberration' before the homosexual became a 'species'[39] is therefore applicable to this period of English legal history because of the now generally accepted fact that, prior to the late nineteenth century, neither the concept of homosexuality nor 'the homosexual' existed.[40] The regulation of

---

33 The English courts would not accept, for instance, that fellatio between males constituted an offence of buggery. See *R. v Jacobs* (1817) Russ & Ry 331. This interpretation of buggery contrasts with other jurisdictions which maintained more inclusive definitions of buggery or sodomy that covered a wider range of genital acts. For a discussion, see: W. Naphy, *Sex Crimes from Renaissance to Enlightenment*, Stroud: Tempus, 2002.

34 *Britton* states: 'Let inquiry also be made of those who feloniously in time of peace have burnt others' corn or houses, and those who are attainted thereof shall be burnt, so that they may be punished in like manner as they have offended. The same sentence shall be passed upon sorcerers, sorceresses, renegades, sodomites, and heretics publicly convicted.' F.M. Nichols, op. cit., p.35.

35 'An Act for the Establishing Articles and Orders for the regulateing and better Government of His Majesties Navies Ships of Warr & Forces by Sea' 1661 (13 Cha. 2 St. 1. c.9).

36 E. Coke, op. cit., p.59. For discussion see: I. McCormick (ed.), *Secret Sexualities: A Sourcebook of 17th and 18th Century Writing*, London: Routledge, 1997.

37 R. Norton, *Mother Clap's Molly House: The Gay Subculture in England 1700–1830 (Second Edition)*, Romford: Chalford Press, 2006.

38 'Trial of Sodomites, 1707' in R. Norton (ed.), *Homosexuality in Eighteenth-Century England: A Sourcebook.* Available online at www.rictornorton.co.uk/eighteen/tryal07.htm (accessed on 4 December 2013).

39 M. Foucault, op. cit., p.43.

buggery by statute law prior to the 'invention' of homosexuality was therefore not concerned with the conduct of discrete or identifiable (homo)sexual *persons*[41] but, like the canon law that preceded it, focused on the delimitation of unnatural and ungodly *acts*. As Blackstone described it, buggery was an 'infamous crime against nature', something 'dark in nature', a 'disgrace to human nature', a 'crime not fit to be named', an act against the 'express law of God' and '*peccatum illud horribile, inter christianos non nominandum* [that horrible crime not to be named among Christians]'.[42]

The alignment between religion, statute law and (male) homosexual acts

The process by which buggery became synonymous with homosexuality in English statute law involved a progressive funnelling of the long-standing Christian concern with unnatural acts into an explicit focus on male same-sex genital activity. When the Offences Against the Person Act (OAPA) 1861 closely associated the 'abominable crime' of buggery with the offence of 'any indecent assault upon any male person', it gave statutory coherence to an established concern to regulate 'immoral' practices between men.[43] The OAPA 1861 therefore represents a significant moment in the progressive evolution of Christian-inspired statute law to focus on same-sex sexual acts. The Criminal Law Amendment Act

---

40 The word 'homosexual' first appeared in English in the 1892 translation of: R. von Krafft-Ebing, *Psychopathia Sexualis*, London: The F.A. Davis Co. Publishers, 1892.

41 For a discussion of the relationship between sodomy and sexual identities, see: S. Salih, 'Sexual identities: a medieval perspective', in T. Betteridge (ed.), *Sodomy in Early Modern Europe*, Manchester: Manchester University Press, 2002, pp.112–130.

42 W. Blackstone, *Commentaries on the Laws of England 1765–69 (4th Book)*, Chicago, IL: University of Chicago Press, 1979, pp.215–216.

43 S.61 ('Unnatural Offences') Offences Against the Person Act 1861 regulated 'the abominable Crime of Buggery, committed either with Mankind or with any Animal'. It repealed the capital penalty as specified in S.15 Offences Against the Person Act 1828 and S.18 Offences Against the Person (Ireland) Act 1829, and consolidated the law on buggery in England and Wales and Ireland. S.62 Offences Against the Person Act 1861 made provision in respect of the 'attempt to commit the said abominable Crime', 'any Assault with Intent to commit the same', and 'any indecent Assault upon any Male Person'. This gave a statutory focus to sexual acts between 'male persons' that had previously been expressed in gender-neutral terms. For example, when in 1825 statute was expanded to include amongst the 'infamous crimes' 'every Attempt or Endeavour' to commit the 'abominable Crimes of Sodomy or Buggery' or 'every Solicitation, Persuasion, Promise, Threat, or Menace, offered or made to any Person, whereby to move or induce such Person to commit or to permit the said abominable Crimes' ('An Act for the Amendment of the Law as to the Offence of sending threatening Letters' 1825, 6 Geo. 4 c.19; subsequently consolidated by 'An Act for consolidating and amending the Laws in England relative to Larceny and other Offences connected therewith' 1827, 7 & 8 Geo. 4 c.29), no reference was made to the male acts that were the implicit focus of regulation.

(CLAA) 1885 represents a further stage in this evolution because of its expansion of law to regulate '[a]ny male person who, in public or private, commits, or is a party to the commission of, or procures or attempts to procure the commission by any male person of, any act of gross indecency with another male person'.[44] The criminalisation of 'gross indecency' provided an encompassing statutory framework to regulate what contemporary commentators on the CLAA 1885 termed 'men [who] have been guilty of filthy practices together, which have not been sufficiently public to have constituted indecent exposure, or which have not had sufficiently direct connection with a more abominable crime to allow of an indictment'.[45] The CLAA 1885 gave clear expression to a pervasive moral attitude towards male same-sex sexual acts and, categorising them as 'outrages on decency', enabled the state to more effectively encroach into the private sphere and enforce public morality.[46] As Weeks argues, the 'general moral framework' that the state sought to inject into private life through the CLAA 1885 'was unquestionably that of the Christian tradition'.[47]

However, whilst the CLAA 1885 gave expression to Christian morality, the enactment of the gross indecency provision did not result from any concerted religious campaign to regulate male same-sex sexual practices through the expansion of statute law. The gross indecency section of the CLAA 1885, the result of an amendment introduced by Henry Labouchere MP,[48] produced

---

44 S.11 Criminal Law Amendment Act 1885. This extended to Ireland and Scotland. There is disagreement over the extent to which S.11 Criminal Law Amendment Act 1885 widened the scope of statute law in respect of private sexual acts committed between men. Cocks, for example, argues that it 'did not enlarge the scope of the law any further' (H.G. Cocks, *Nameless Offences: Homosexual Desire in the 19th Century*, London: I.B. Taurus, 2003, p.30). This is correct insofar as S.62 Offences Against the Person Act 1861 already criminalised 'any indecent Assault upon any Male Person' and therefore enabled the regulation of sexual acts other than buggery committed in private between men. However, the 1885 Act can be seen as an expansion in the scope of statute law because it provided a framework for regulating all sexual acts deemed to constitute 'gross indecency' when committed in private between men regardless of consent. This meant that unlike in cases of sexual acts between men tried as 'assault' – where it had been established that '[i]f anything is done by one being upon the person of another to make the act a criminal assault, it must be done without the consent and against the will of the person upon whom it is done' (*R v Wollaston* (1872) 26 LT 403 at 404) – consent could no longer provide a defence. The 1885 Act also provided, for the first time, a unitary statutory framework for regulating sexual practices (other than buggery) between men in private across the whole of the United Kingdom.
45 F. Mead and A.H. Bodkin, *The Criminal Law Amendment Act 1885 with Introduction, Notes, and Index*, London: Shaw and Sons, 1885.
46 For a discussion of the social, cultural and political aspects of 'gross indecency', see: M. Cook, *London and the Culture of Homosexuality 1885–1914*, Cambridge: Cambridge University Press, 2003.
47 J. Weeks, *Sex, Politics and Society: The Regulation of Sexuality since 1800*, London: Longman, 1981, p.82

no debate in the House of Commons and, when reaching the Lords, its inclusion in a Bill generally designed to regulate the sexual exploitation of girls was accepted by stealth rather than because of any religious fervour for it.[49] Even those Peers, such as Earl Fortescue, who spoke passionately about the problems of a 'population destitute of religious principles or moral convictions' and in need of 'religious, moral, and educational' instruction made no reference to the gross indecency provision.[50] In their commentary on the CLAA 1885, Mead and Bodkin expressed puzzlement about the inclusion of a section that focused on sexual acts committed between men[51] which suggests that, at a time when law increasingly sought to compel decent and respectable behaviours in line with Christian morality, a discrete concern with male homosexual acts was not readily acknowledged, even by lawyers. This is because in late-nineteenth-century England 'the existence or extent of sex between men was, with rare exceptions, denied or ignored by the legislature, the national newspapers and the medical profession'.[52]

Religion was instrumental in maintaining a culture of denial and silence about same-sex sexual relationships in Victorian England and this had a significant impact upon the shape of law. This is demonstrated by the failure of a proposed amendment to the Criminal Law Amendment Bill 1921 that sought to criminalise 'gross indecency between female persons' in the same way that the CLAA 1885 regulated men. The idea of criminalising gross indecency between women originated in a suggestion by a Metropolitan Police Magistrate who appeared as an expert witness before the Joint Select Committee considering the Bill,[53] where it was quickly decided that the 'subject did not require serious attention'.[54] Nevertheless, a subsequent amendment tabled in the Commons by Frederick Macquisten MP, which proposed to criminalise acts of indecency between women,

---

48 HC Debate, 6 August 1885, c.1397.
49 For example, Earl Beauchamp stated that because 'there was little chance of their Lordships being able to alter the decisions which had been arrived at by the House of Commons' in respect of the gross indecency provisions, they should not 'imperil [the] object [of the Bill] by rejecting any of the Amendments the Commons had made'. HL Debate, 10 August 1885, cc.1550–1551.
50 HL Debate, 10 August 1885, c.1552.
51 'It is difficult to understand why the section is limited to conjoint acts by two or more persons and to male persons.' F. Mead and A.H. Bodkin, op. cit., p.69.
52 S. Brady, *Masculinity and Male Homosexuality in Britain, 1861–1913*, Basingstoke: Palgrave-Macmillan, 2005, p.1.
53 Report by the Joint Select Committee of the House of Lords and the House of Commons on the Criminal Law Amendment Bill [HL], Criminal Law Amendment (No.2) Bill [HL], and the Sexual Offences Bill [HL], 30 November 1920, p.74. For a discussion of the Joint Select Committee proceedings, see: L.L. Doan, *Fashioning Sapphism: The Origins of a Modern English Lesbian Culture*, New York, NY: Columbia University Press, 2001.
54 Earl of Malmesbury, HL Debate, 15 August 1921, c.568.

was adopted.[55] Whilst the Lords concurred that gross indecency between females was 'a most disgusting and polluting subject',[56] they rejected its criminalisation on the basis that the law would dangerously publicise and potentially promote practices of which the vast majority 'have never even heard a whisper'.[57] The Earl of Malmesbury stated that 'these cases are best left to their own determination' – whereby 'these unfortunate specimens of humanity exterminate themselves by the usual process' – because '[t]he more you advertise vice by prohibiting it the more you will increase it'.[58] Significantly, the Archbishop of Canterbury, Randall Davidson, explicitly stated he did not support the amendment.[59] Similarly, the Bishop of Norwich, Bertram Pollock, argued that the criminalisation of female acts of gross indecency was 'utterly irrelevant and undesirable'.[60]

By the middle of the twentieth century, statute law had therefore evolved piecemeal to enforce Christian morality through the regulation of 'unnatural' and 'indecent' practices between men. The Sexual Offences Act (SOA) 1956, reflecting the widespread growth of scientific discourse about the problem of sex in Western European societies,[61] codified the offences of buggery and gross indecency as unnatural and specifically 'sexual' offences.[62] In a subsequent amendment to the SOA 1956 by the Sexual Offences Act (SOA) 1967, these sexual acts between men were described in statute law as 'homosexual' for the first time.[63] More than 400 years after the enactment of the BA 1533 and more than 80 years after the enactment of the CLAA 1885, the SOA 1967 named buggery and gross indecency between men as 'homosexual acts'.[64] It was, therefore, in 1967 that English statute law gave expression to a concern to regulate distinctly 'homosexual' practices. In the remainder of this chapter, we consider the influence of religion in shaping law from the point that the homosexual first

---

55 The amendment was adopted 148-53. HC Debate, 4 August 1921, Division No.328. For a discussion of the Commons debate, see: F. Tamagne, *A History of Homosexuality in Europe: Berlin, London, Paris 1919–1939: Volume I and II*, New York, NY: Algora Publishing, 2004.
56 Earl of Malmesbury, HL Debate, 15 August 1921, c.568.
57 Viscount Birkenhead, HL Debate, 15 August 1921, c.574. For a discussion of how in the nineteenth century the legal regulation of homosexuality became regarded as problematic because it encouraged knowledge and interest in homosexual acts, see: H.G. Cocks, op. cit.
58 HL Debate, 15 August 1921, c.570. The Earl of Malmesbury expressed the contemporary idea that female homosexual 'vice has been increasing partly owing to the nervous conditions following on the [First World] war'.
59 Ibid., c.576.
60 Ibid., c.577.
61 These concerns were largely the result of the dissemination of ideas associated with a number of sexologists. See: L. Bland and L. Doan, *Sexology Uncensored: The Documents of Sexual Science*, Chicago, IL: University of Chicago Press, 1999.
62 S.12–13 Sexual Offences Act 1956.
63 For a discussion, see: L.J. Moran, *The Homosexual(ity) of Law*, London: Routledge, 1996.
64 S.1(7) Sexual Offences Act 1967.

appeared in English criminal law in 1967 to his departure in 2003.

Religion and the partial decriminalisation of male homosexual acts in England and Wales

In this section we consider the relationship between religion and law in the period of reform that culminated in the partial decriminalisation of male homosexual acts in England and Wales in 1967. This reform, driven by changes in attitudes about the role of the criminal law in regulating male homosexual acts committed by consenting adults in private, is now often characterised as the result of both the liberalisation and secularisation of British society. However, whilst questions of personal liberty and private morality were key features of the *Report of the Committee on Homosexual Offences and Prostitution* ('Wolfenden Report') that underpinned law reform,[65] of the broader social debate that was exemplified in the exchange between Devlin[66] and Hart,[67] and of the political activism of those seeking law reform,[68] these were not the defining characteristics of parliamentary debates about homosexuality during this period. Although legislators increasingly began to concede that adult males should not be criminalised for engaging in consensual homosexual acts in private, this was not articulated as a commitment to either liberalism or secularism. Rather, as we demonstrate below, a Christian-inspired commitment amongst legislators to the regulation of 'unnatural' sexual acts between men was central to law reform in this period.

Religion and homosexuality prior to the Wolfenden Report

Between the announcement in 1954 by the UK Government of an 'investigation by a well-qualified body' of the 'scope and nature of [the] difficult and controversial problems' that are raised by homosexuality in society[69] and the partial decriminalisation of male homosexual acts in private by the SOA 1967, there had been a considerable shift in attitudes amongst legislators about male homosexual sex. A central element of this change was a decline in the willingness to accept that the criminalisation of private homosexual acts was both necessary and justified. This change did not represent a wholesale acceptance by legislators of a liberal approach to individual sexual liberty,[70] nor was it propelled by an obvious

---

65 Home Office, *Report of the Committee on Homosexual Offences and Prostitution* (Cmnd. 247), London: Home Office, 1957.
66 P. Devlin, *The Enforcement of Morals*, Oxford: Oxford University Press, 1965.
67 H.L.A. Hart, *Law, Liberty and Morality*, Oxford: Oxford University Press, 1963.
68 For example, in the work of the Homosexual Law Reform Society and the Albany Trust. See: A. Grey, *Quest for Justice: Towards Homosexual Emancipation*, London: Sinclair-Stevenson, 1992.
69 H. Lucas-Tooth, HC Debate, 28 April 1954, c.1756.

decline in the Christian condemnation of homosexual acts. When Desmond Donnelly MP first called for a Royal Commission to investigate 'the law relating to and the medical treatment of homosexuality', his expressed motivations were neither to promote the sexual liberty of homosexual men nor to attribute them with any moral value.[71] Rather, legislative reform during this period was orientated towards addressing the efficacy of law in respect of the policing, treatment and moral rehabilitation of male homosexuals.[72]

Although 'homosexuals' were rarely discussed in Parliament prior to the 1950s, a Lords debate in 1937 shows the roots of the discourse about homosexuality that later gained prominence. Lord Dawson of Penn approached the issue of 'homo-sexuality' – which appears to be the first usage of the term in a parliamentary debate[73] – during debates about the Marriage Bill 1937 in an unsuccessful attempt to make 'the practice of homo-sexuality' an explicit ground for divorce.[74] Dawson used the then novel term to avoid using the word 'sodomy' which, he argued, denoted 'a rather vulgar crime which is only open to the male' whereas homosexuality 'refers to both sexes'.[75] Dawson's specific legislative aim was to promote 'equality of treatment between men and women' in divorce law, to 'protect the man against the Lesbian just as you protect a woman against a male homo-sexualist'.[76] However, Dawson also made the more general argument that the 'progress of knowledge has altered our conception' and that, 'although it is true that the law must take cognisance of homosexuality and punish it in order to act as a preventive to potential offenders, the more reasonable view is gradually being adopted that it at any rate has one foot in the realm of disease and it is not wholly in the realm of crime'.[77] This view of homosexuality, which Dawson acknowledged was within 'the region of prophecy',[78] interested the Archbishop of Canterbury, Cosmo Gordon Lang, who asked Dawson 'whether it is not the case in his experience, as it certainly is in mine, that even these unfortunate

---

70   B. Mitchell, *Law, Morality and Religion in a Secular Society*, Oxford: Oxford University Press, 1967.
71   HC Debate, 28 April 1954, c.1745.
72   Existing practices of policing were increasingly understood to employ 'methods of great dubiety' that only 'intensify the squalor by which [homosexuality] is surrounded, and widen the areas in which the underground flourishes' (R. Boothby, HC Debate, 28 April 1954, c.1749), the imprisonment of homosexual men was also increasingly recognised as ineffective in rehabilitating them to a 'normal' sexual orientation, and developments in psychology were considered favourably in respect of the treatment of adult males.
73   HL Debate, 28 June 1937, c.829. Lord Dawson of Penn subsequently stated the issue was 'a matter which is almost foreign' to parliamentary debate. HL Committee, 7 July 1937, c.144.
74   HL Committee, 7 July 1937, c.140.
75   Ibid., c.141.
76   Ibid., c.145.
77   Ibid., c.141.
78   Ibid.

tendencies can be cured, and whether this is not a case of a disease, if it can be called a disease, which is incapable of cure?'[79] However, Lord Atkin, a judge who had 'come across this subject' and who had had 'the privilege for seven years of being President of the Medico-Legal Society in which this kind of subject was discussed', robustly rejected the idea that homosexuality was 'the result of something in the nature of disease'.[80] Rather, he argued that homosexuality was 'the result of wicked impulses which, like other wicked impulses, are capable of being controlled'.[81] Atkin, in opposing Dawson's proposal, concluded that 'this is a subject which requires very careful scientific examination' and, '[i]f some time or other a Select Committee or a Departmental Committee considered this subject in all its branches, the result might be a very valuable Report upon which the criminal law and the civil law might very well be amended'.[82]

When it was proposed that a Departmental Committee consider the subject of homosexuality in the 1950s – which led to the formation of the Departmental Committee on Homosexual Offences and Prostitution ('Wolfenden Committee') – Lord Dawson of Penn's 'prophecy' that homosexuality should not wholly be in the realm of crime had become central to parliamentary debate. As Desmond Donnelly MP argued:

> I think it is quite unusual for the law to interfere in what is essentially a moral issue. The Church of England Moral Welfare Society makes this clear in a wise, sane and sober pamphlet [which] states 'In no other department of life does the State hold itself competent to interfere with the private actions of consenting adults'. It goes on to say 'A man and woman may commit the grave sin of fornication with legal impunity, but a corresponding act between man and man is liable to life imprisonment, and not infrequently is punished by very long sentences, five, 10 or even more years'.[83]

The pamphlet to which Donnelly referred, *The Problem of Homosexuality: An Interim Report* published by the Church of England Moral Welfare Council, expressed a developing argument in the Church in favour of a conceptual distinction between 'crime' and 'sin' in respect of homosexuality.[84] Similar policy formulations were advanced by bodies in the Catholic, Methodist and Unitarian

---

79 Ibid., c.142.
80 Ibid., c.145.
81 Ibid.
82 Ibid.
83 HC Debate, 28 April 1954, c.1748.
84 It was followed by: D.S. Bailey (ed.), *Sexual Offenders and Social Punishment: Being the Evidence Submitted on Behalf of the Church of England Moral Welfare Council to the Departmental Committee on Homosexual Offences and Prostitution, with Other Material Relating Thereto*, Westminster: Published for the Church of England Moral Welfare

churches, as well as by the Religious Society of Friends, and these were highly influential in shaping parliamentary debate during this period.[85] Robert Boothby MP exemplified the view of these faith groups that an examination of the relationship between religious morality, law and homosexuality was necessary when he stated that '[w]hat consenting adults do in privacy may be a moral issue between them and their Maker, but in my submission it is not a legal issue between them and the State'.[86]

A new enthusiasm to loosen the legal regulation of the 'filthy, disgusting, unnatural vice of homosexuality'[87] was not representative of a decline amongst parliamentarians in the commitment to a Christian condemnation of homosexual acts. Rather, as the Bishop of Southwell, Russell Barry, argued, the desire for reform was based on a wish to reconfigure the relationship between law and homosexuality in order to more effectively achieve the Christian regulation of homosexual acts in a society regarded as increasingly sexually permissive:

> [Homosexuality] is a moral and religious problem, and the long-term solution can be sought only in those terms. I wholly [deplore] the levity with which this and similar forms of sexual irregularity are at the present moment condoned and almost taken for granted. It is time that some strong stand was taken against it. The whole subject is intensely repugnant, and raises intense moral indignation in many minds, and perhaps some kind of primitive subconscious racial horror. Society – our society, at any rate – reacts very violently against it, because it feels, and rightly feels, that such practices are injecting poison into the bloodstream [...] Heaven forbid that I should in any way seem to minimise the gravity of the problem before us! But further medical and psychological knowledge may lead us to a more enlightened or, at any rate, to a different approach to the whole question, and to yield to a clamour for vindictive action or for even harsher punitive measures may easily defeat our ends.[88]

At the point that the Wolfenden Committee was formed, therefore, there was growing support amongst legislators for the idea that the criminal law was not necessarily the most effective way to enforce Christian sexual morality. However,

---

Council by the Church Information Board, 1956. For a historical discussion of Church of England policy, see: M. Grimley, 'Law, morality and secularisation: the Church of England and the Wolfenden Report', *Journal of Ecclesiastical History* 60, 2009, 725–741.
85 For a discussion of the history of the Church of England Moral Welfare Council and the policy of other religious organisations in this period, see: G. Willett, 'The Church of England and the origins of homosexual law reform', *Journal of Religious History* 33, 2009, 418–434.
86 R. Boothby, HC Debate, 28 April 1954, cc.1750–1751.
87 Earl Winterton, HL Debate, 19 May 1954, c.739.
88 HL Debate, 19 May 1954, cc.751–752.

there was no question amongst legislators that homosexuality was antithetical to Christian morality and in need of regulation. A study produced by a key figure in the Church of England Moral Welfare Council, Derrick Bailey, clearly showed that 'liberal' members of the Church of England encouraged reform only insofar as it addressed 'homosexual perversion' as 'a corrosion which has already left its mark upon marriage and family life and, if left unchecked, may ultimately undermine the whole social order'.[89] In contemporary accounts it has become common to misunderstand and misrepresent the Church of England during this period – for example, by suggesting that it 'acknowledged that the rights of homosexual men were being violated and in the name of justice and humanity [. . .] called for a change in law'[90] – which obscures the expressed reasoning underpinning its commitment to law reform.

The Wolfenden Report and the Church of England

The publication of the Wolfenden Report in 1957 established a new conceptual apparatus for considering the relationship between law, religion and homosexuality. The Wolfenden Report premised its key recommendation, that consensual adult homosexual acts in private be decriminalised, on a distinction between public (Christian) morality and the private behaviours of individuals. The Wolfenden Report recognised that '[c]ertain forms of sexual behaviour are regarded by many as sinful, morally wrong, or objectionable for reasons of conscience, or of religious or cultural tradition'[91] but stated that 'moral conviction or instinctual feeling, however strong, is not a valid basis for overriding the individual's privacy'.[92] On this basis, the Wolfenden Report recommended the partial decriminalisation of private homosexual acts involving two consenting adults over the ages of 21 years. The recommendation to reform the law on the basis of a distinction between public (Christian) and private morality produced fierce opposition. Devlin, for example, argued that the Wolfenden Report confused 'private morality' with 'private behaviour in matters of morals'[93] and rejected the Millian-inspired[94] claim that homosexual acts committed in private have no impact on the 'moral structure' of a Christian society.[95]

The Wolfenden Report's recommendation regarding the partial decriminalisa-

---

89 D.S. Bailey, op. cit., p.166.
90 J. Cooper, 'Perpetuating persecution: when will the Church of England condemn the criminalization of LGBTI identity?', *Huffington Post*, 29 July 2013. Available online at www.huffingtonpost.co.uk/jonathan-cooper/church-of-england-lgbti_b_3632337.html (accessed on 4 December 2013).
91 Home Office, op. cit., § 14.
92 Ibid., § 54.
93 P. Devlin, op. cit., p.9.
94 The Wolfenden Report implicitly reiterates J.S. Mill's understanding of liberty and harm outlined in *On Liberty* (1859) – specifically, 'that the sole end for which mankind are

tion of male homosexual acts was premised on a conceptual separation of 'crime' and 'sin'. It proposed to relinquish legal control of certain behaviours commonly regarded as sinful, providing that these were done in private so as not to offend collective Christian morality. Whilst there was parliamentary support for this approach, it was not founded on any significant commitment to sexual liberalism. Rather, as Devlin caricatured it, the proposals found favour in 'the deeply religious person who feels that the criminal law is sometimes more of a hindrance than a help in the sphere of morality, and that the reform of the sinner – at any rate when he injures only himself – should be a spiritual rather than a temporal work'.[96] This was certainly the view of Lord Pakenham who introduced the first debate on the Wolfenden Report in the Lords by stating that although 'Christians of all denominations' regarded homosexuality as a 'grievous sin', there was a need to reconsider 'our duty to protect society and our duty also to induce the sinner to abandon his evil ways'.[97] Homosexuals, Pakenham argued, 'might be prepared to seek medical or spiritual assistance, if the criminal taint were withdrawn'.[98]

This was certainly the view of the Archbishop of Canterbury, Geoffrey Fisher, who, reiterating the will of the Church Assembly, gave his support for the Wolfenden recommendations.[99] Although Fisher stated that he was not speaking from 'any particular Christian grounds' but from those of 'every reasonable and responsible citizen', he argued for the need 'to think about and compare the sphere of crime and the sphere of sin'[100] in order to more effectively enforce Christian morality in respect of homosexuality. Fisher regarded the criminalisation of homosexual acts to encourage undesirable forms of social organisation amongst homosexuals – 'freemasonry from which it is not at all easy to escape' – that was

---

warranted, individually or collectively, in interfering with the liberty of action of any of their number, is self-protection' – in order to sustain the argument that private homosexual acts are not socially harmful. See: J.S. Mill, *On Liberty (2nd edition)*, Boston, MA: Thickner and Field, 1863, p.23.

95 Devlin argued that 'when all who are involved in the deed of [homosexual acts] are consenting parties and the injury is done to morals, the public interest in the moral order can be balanced against the claims of privacy'. P. Devlin, op. cit., p.18.

96 Ibid., p.4.

97 HL Debate, 4 December 1957, c.735.

98 Ibid., c.744.

99 The Church Assembly voted 155-138 in favour of the Wolfenden recommendations in November 1957. Wolfenden wrote to the Archbishop of Canterbury on 19 November 1957: 'The incredible thing about the Assembly's vote was not that it was, as the *Times* said, "by a majority of only 17". The staggering thing is that the Church Assembly should vote by any majority at all in that direction. If you or I had said five years ago that in November 1957 the Church Assembly would decide by a majority that adult consenting homosexual acts should be taken out of the criminal law, we should have been removed to a lunatic asylum.' M. Barber, S. Taylor and G. Sewell (eds), *From the Reformation to the Permissive Society: A Miscellany in Celebration of the 400th Anniversary of Lambeth Palace Library (Church of England Record Society 18)*, Woodbridge: Boydell Press, 2010.

100 HL Debate, 4 December 1957, c.753.

strengthened by 'the glamour and romance of chosen and select rebels against the conventions of society and the forces of the law'.[101] He argued that partial decriminalisation was a vital means to combat homosexuality through the restoration of Christian morality:

> At once, I am quite certain, the fresh air of normal morality will begin to circulate amongst [homosexuals] far more easily. Those who are involved in it will be set free to talk to others outside without giving anybody away to the law. They will seek advice openly – indeed, they will be free, if they like, to seek protection by the police from molestation by their former companions without bringing in the question of prosecution for illegal offences. It will be all the more easy, I think, to convince them of the restraints of common sense and Christian morality when they are delivered from the fears, the glamour and even the crusading spirit of the rebel against law and convention who can claim to be made a martyr by persecution.[102]

Although Fisher recommended that the 'extreme offence' of sodomy should remain a criminal offence in private – a view that he argued 'can be upheld on moral grounds'[103] – he supported the partial decriminalisation of other genital acts between men in private.[104] Some commentators have characterised this support for law reform as evidence of the 'dechristianisation' of British society and English law.[105] Yet, far from providing straightforward evidence of declining religious opposition to homosexuality, Fisher's commitment demonstrates a desire to reformulate law in order to better enforce Christian morality in society. It was this commitment that underpinned a letter published in *The Times*, signed by 33 people, including the Bishops of Birmingham (Leonard Wilson) and Exeter (Robert Mortimer), which stated that '[t]he present law is clearly no longer representative of either Christian or liberal opinion in this country'.[106]

There was general agreement between 'Christian' and 'liberal' supporters of law reform in Parliament that homosexuality was immoral but that the existing legal framework failed to sufficiently regulate it. Whilst some parliamentarians strongly opposed reform on religious grounds,[107] an emerging consensus in favour of reform was perceptible during initial considerations of the Wolfenden

---

101   Ibid., c.756.
102   Ibid., cc.756–757.
103   Ibid., c.757.
104   The recommendation effectively meant that the Archbishop of Canterbury supported partial decriminalisation of the offence of gross indecency, first introduced by the Criminal Law Amendment Act 1885, but not of buggery.
105   See, for discussion: C.G. Brown, *Religion and Society in Twentieth-Century Britain*, Harlow: Pearson-Longman, 2006.
106   Letter published in *The Times*, 7 March 1958.
107   'Statements have been made this afternoon about the attitude of the churches on this matter [. . .] It has been stated, for instance, by the Homosexual Law Reform Society that

Report. As Rev. Llywelyn Williams MP, a self-described 'normal person [...] whose physical and sexual life is happily integrated in a satisfactory marital relationship', stated:

> [W]hile society could never give moral approval to [homosexual] behaviour, nevertheless, since it takes place in the privacy of a household, it should not rank as a criminal offence any more than heterosexual behaviour between consenting adults in private, such as adultery and fornication, to which again society could never give moral approval, should rank as a criminal offence.[108]

The debate about the appropriate relationship between 'crime' and 'sin' continued throughout the various parliamentary debates regarding homosexuality that preceded the enactment of the SOA 1967. The frequent defeat of efforts to implement the Wolfenden recommendations was partly the result, as one MP argued at the time of the first unsuccessful attempt,[109] of 'the difficulty for all of us who call ourselves Christians [in knowing] how far the State can legislate in order to make men and women into moral creatures'.[110]

Religion and the Sexual Offences Act 1967

When the first of several Bills to implement the Wolfenden recommendations was introduced in the Lords in 1965,[111] it was given public support by the Bishops of Birmingham (Leonard Wilson), Bristol (Oliver Tomkins), Exeter (Robert Mortimer), London (Robert Stopford) and St Albans (Edward Jones).[112] The Archbishop of Canterbury, Michael Ramsey, who was unequivocal in his view that

> the utterances of the churches have been overwhelmingly in favour of the implementation of the recommendation. I do not believe that that is an accurate statement of the opinion of the churches at all. It is a fact that the Church of Scotland, the Church of Ireland and the Salvation Army have all expressed themselves against this recommendation. My own church, the Baptist Church, is certainly not in favour of it, and when we come to the other churches which have given more or less qualified support it is interesting to look at what the voting figures have been.' C. Black, HC Debate, 26 November 1958, cc.461–462.

108 HC Debate, 26 November 1958, c.488.
109 Kenneth Robinson MP moved the motion 'That this House calls upon Her Majesty's Government to take early action upon the recommendations contained in Part Two of the Report of the Wolfenden Committee' on 29 June 1960 in the House of Commons and was defeated 213-99 (Division No.126).
110 A. Greenwood, HC Debate, 29 June 1960, c.1500.
111 Sexual Offences Bill 1965, HL Debate, 13 May 1965, c.268.
112 These bishops signed a letter to *The Times* on 11 May 1965 which stated: 'Seven years ago a distinguished list of signatories wrote to your columns that the existing law clearly no longer represented either Christian or liberal opinion in this country, and that its continued enforcement would do more harm than good to the community as a whole. We hope that [...] Her Majesty's Government will now recognize the necessity for this reform and will introduce legislation.'

'homosexual acts are always wrong in the sense that they use in a wrong way human organs for which the right use is intercourse between men and women within marriage', also gave his support.[113] This support has since become somewhat mythologised. In 2013, a subsequent Archbishop of Canterbury, Justin Welby, praised Ramsey during debates over same-sex marriage for 'vigorously' supporting decriminalisation and being one of the few 'notable exceptions' in the Church, which overall had 'not served the LGBT communities in the way it should'.[114] However, Welby's account of Ramsey's commitment to partial decriminalisation misrepresents the stated aims of those in the Church of England who were not concerned with service to the homosexual community. Ramsey was explicit that his commitment to partial decriminalisation was in no way an expression of tolerance or acceptance of homosexuality:

> There will be no question of [. . .] declaring homosexual practices to be a right use of sex. Rather will there be a greater possibility for some to find their way from wrong uses of sex and to be helped towards better uses of their energies. In the moral state of our country we need all the forces available to combat evils, of which homosexual practices are one. The proposed reforms would, I believe, help greatly by enabling a greater balance between the forces of law, morality, remedial science and the cure of souls, by promoting what is good and right.[115]

Ramsey argued that the criminalisation of homosexual acts 'helps morality no more than would a law which made fornication a crime' and 'hinders the deliverance of those who are caught in these practices'.[116] A similar view was expressed by the most 'liberal' religious organisation of the period, the Religious Society of Friends, who although promulgating a unique religious toleration for some discrete and monogamous homosexual relationships also regarded law reform as necessary to address 'promiscuous and degraded' homosexuals.[117] The commitment to legal reform as a means to better achieve the 'deliverance' of homosexual men from sin characterised much of the parliamentary debate about the Wolfenden recommendations. The Bishop of Worcester, Lewis Charles-Edwards, gave expression to a consensus amongst parliamentarians on the relationship between law reform and Christian morality:

---

113 HL Debate, 12 May 1965, c.80.
114 HL Debate, 3 June 2013, c.953.
115 HL Debate, 12 May 1965, c.84.
116 Ibid., c.82.
117 'Only if Society is prepared to [. . .] accept even degraded homosexuals as human beings, can they be helped to face the moral implications of their selfish relationships.' Religious Society of Friends, *Towards a Quaker View of Sex: An Essay by a Group of Friends (revised edition)*, London: Friends Home Service Committee, 1964, p.42.

[D]uring a ministry of nearly 40 years it has been my privilege to give what help I can to a number of homosexuals [. . .] and a homosexual is often a man desperately in need of help. He lives his life in constant fear of discovery and the publicity of a trial and prison sentence. He is, as many of your Lordships have said, faced by possible blackmail. He feels an outcast from society, which tends to classify him as different from other men. He knows that his sexual impulses, which to him are normal impulses, are considered by others to be abnormal. Why he is and what made him so, he does not know. Often he is a man of great genius, endowed with many gifts, yet his life is dogged by a sense of guilt which drives him more and more into himself. So it is that very often such a man may come under the care of a doctor or a parson, desperately hoping that in some way they can help him to become an integrated personality [. . .] My very small experience has taught me to believe that ethical considerations and religious observances enable some, perhaps many, to lead chaste lives, but that the present severe penalties for homosexuality between consenting adults make their often heroic and self-denying efforts still more difficult [. . .] I have felt over and over again, in trying to help such cases, that these men need desperately the help of a psychotherapist who is familiar with their problem and skilled in treating such conditions. Yet over and over again one finds that a man is afraid to seek this help because, if he goes to a clinic, it may be discovered that he is a homosexual, and that might lead to a prison sentence [. . .] My Lords, frankly, to me, this is primarily a pastoral problem.[118]

Charles-Edwards epitomised the Church of England's approach to law reform in which the commitment to partial decriminalisation was founded not on a desire to protect the sexual liberty of homosexual men but on a concern to create more favourable social conditions in which to achieve their moral reorientation. Although some commentators have correctly observed that 'there were divisions within the Church about the issue' of homosexuality and that 'it was the liberals who had gained the upper hand',[119] it is misleading to suggest that the 'liberal' bishops in Parliament were any more committed to relativism in the sphere of sexual morals than their 'orthodox' colleagues. Nor is it correct to understand the bishops' support for reform as representative of secularisation in which 'the churches themselves became agents of permissiveness in 1960s Britain'.[120] The commitment of the bishops to partial decriminalisation was expressly motivated by neither liberalism nor secularism but rather, as the Bishop of Southwark, Mervyn Stockwood, argued, by a desire to ensure the legislative reform necessary

118 HL Debate, 12 May 1965, cc.133–135.
119 G. Willett, op. cit., 428.
120 S. Brooke, *Sexual Politics: Sexuality, Family Planning, and the British Left from the 1880s to the Present Day*, Oxford: Oxford University Press, 2011, p.177.
121 HL Debate, 12 May 1965, cc.153–154.

for Christianity to most effectively help those 'who have lost their way' and exist in a legal and social 'atmosphere [. . .] vitiated by a sense of fear'.[121] This echoed the view of the Homosexual Law Reform Society which argued that fear of prosecution hampered contact between 'maladjusted homosexuals' and 'medical men' and limited advances in understanding of 'causes', 'treatment' and 'cure'.[122]

Evidence that the bishops were not engaging in pragmatic parliamentary rhetoric but held genuinely strongly intolerant views on homosexuality is shown by the arguments made by those who supported the partial decriminalisation of private homosexual acts between consenting adults but also made strong faith-based arguments in favour of the increased legal regulation of other homosexual acts. For instance, the Bishop of Chichester, Roger Wilson, argued for an increase in the maximum penalties for homosexual acts involving males aged over 21 years with those aged between 16 and 21 years[123] to ensure the 'preservation of moral standards in society, and for retaining a strong public opinion on this matter'.[124] The Archbishop of Canterbury, Michael Ramsey, expressed the concern of several bishops that those moral standards must be enforced particularly amongst 'young people':

> [I]f the law is to protect and help young people, it must be a law that wins their respect as being just. I think that the respect of young people for the law, and the morality which it tries to uphold, is at present hindered by the feeling of young people that the law is really unjust. More still, young people are going to be moral if we present to them a version of morality which is Christian and rational, which can win their respect, and is not a kind of lopsided presentation of morality.[125]

Ramsey argued that it was necessary to adopt a notion of 'sin' that would not 'be rejected by the people of the new generation'.[126] Legislators, he warned, needed to moderate their discourse, using caution when referring to homosexuality as 'abominable behaviour' and not engage in a 'lopsided presentation of morality'.[127] While clinging to the notion of homosexuality as sin, Ramsey argued that the

---

122 Homosexual Law Reform Society, 'HLRS leaflet on the Wolfenden Report', Hall-Carpenter Archives (HCA/Grey1/11), 1958.
123 The Wolfenden Report recommended an increase in the maximum sentences for acts of buggery or gross indecency 'by a man over twenty-one with a person of or above the age of sixteen but below the age of twenty-one, in circumstances not amounting to indecent assault' (§ 91(c)) or 'by a person under twenty-one with a consenting partner of or above the age of sixteen' (§ 91(d)). For fuller details of the sentencing proposals see § 90–91 and Recommendation vii of Home Office, op. cit. Sentences for buggery and gross indecency were revised by S.3 Sexual Offences Act 1967.
124 HL Debate, 24 May 1965, c.662.
125 HL Debate, 28 October 1965, c.716.
126 Ibid.
127 Ibid.

younger generation were sceptical of a rhetoric being used in Parliament 'which quotes the Old Testament, which takes the line that sexual sins are apparently the worst of all sins, and that homosexual sins are invariably the worst sort of sins among sexual sins'.[128]

Arguments about the need to 'win the respect' of young people through 'Christian and rational' morality were fundamental in ensuring the careful and partial decriminalisation of male homosexual acts by the SOA 1967. The majority of parliamentarians, including the bishops, supported the SOA 1967 insofar as it did not repeal either the crime of buggery or gross indecency but rather decriminalised these acts only if they were done 'in private' between two consenting adult men.[129] The partial decriminalisation of homosexual acts was shaped by the primary concern to ensure that, as one Member of Parliament put it, '[w]hatever else we do, we cannot have homosexuals parading their homosexuality in public'.[130] Underpinning the objective of maintaining the social invisibility of homosexuality was a broad acceptance that homosexuality was antithetical to public, Christian morality. As the Bishop of Chichester, Roger Wilson, stated:

> I think we recognise the great issues of morality, and while we are not divided in our upholding of that morality, or in our desire to maintain it, we are deeply divided as to the ways in which we conceive this should be done. This has led to the most acute discussions in this House, and in the process of the passage of this Bill and all that preceded it, we have been through some agonising debates. Speaking from these Benches, I should like to say how deeply I, and others, have been aware of the depth of sincerity and concern, not only of those who have upheld this Bill but of those who have opposed it. For there is no division between us in our desire for the maintenance or the protection and upholding of that morality for the well-being of the community.[131]

---

128 Ibid.
129 S.1(1) Sexual Offences Act 1967. S.1(2) Sexual Offences Act 1967 specified that any homosexual act would not be treated as being done in private when 'more than two persons take part or are present' ('to deal with any possible danger of orgies developing', R. Jenkins, HC Debate, 3 July 1967, c.1453) or 'in a lavatory to which the public have or are permitted to have access, whether on payment or otherwise' (there were several unsuccessful amendments that sought to specify that homosexual acts should remain criminalised 'in a public park to which the public have or are permitted to have access', 'on any land or woodland to which the public can obtain access', 'in premises which either person uses by virtue of his employment', 'in a British Railways sleeping car' and 'in a prison cell', HC Debate, 3 July 1967, c.1429). The Bishop of St Albans, Edward Jones, had earlier been instrumental in encouraging the continuation of the criminalisation of all homosexual acts aboard merchant ships (HL Debate, 10 May 1966, c.617; enacted as S.2 Sexual Offences Act 1967), and parliamentarians unquestioningly supported provisions ensuring that homosexual acts remained offences in the armed forces (S.1(5) Sexual Offences Act 1967).
130 W. Rees-Davies, HC Debate, 3 July 1967, c.1439.
131 HL Debate, 21 July 1967, c.526.

At the point that male homosexual acts were partially decriminalised in England and Wales, Christian morality had been instrumental in fashioning legislation that continued to enforce the principle that homosexuality was both aberrant and abhorrent to 'the public'. As we explore in the next section, this Christian morality would be forcefully asserted to resist further legislative reform in the decades ahead.

The 'age of consent' debates

The SOA 1967 decriminalised homosexual acts in England and Wales between two men in private providing both parties had attained the age of 21 years. This minimum age for male homosexual acts, which reflected the then age of majority in the UK, was recommended by the Wolfenden Report which regarded it as 'the best criterion for the definition of adulthood'.[132] Ten years after the enactment of the SOA 1967, Lord Arran introduced a Bill into the Lords that proposed to lower the minimum age for male homosexual acts from 21 to 18 years[133] to reflect changes to the age of majority in England and Wales.[134] The Bill attracted strong opposition in the form of an amendment successfully moved by the Earl of Halsbury which proposed to decline the Bill a Second Reading 'in view of the growth in activities of groups and individuals exploiting male prostitution and its attendant corruption of youth, debasement of morals and spread of venereal disease'.[135] Opposition to lowering the minimum age for male homosexual acts remained strong in the Lords, and the use of the Parliament Acts 1911 and 1949 was eventually required to 'equalise' the minimum age for male homosexual acts with those set for heterosexual acts across the UK. In this section we examine the role of religion in both resisting and shaping legislative changes to the minimum age for homosexual acts in England in Wales.

The assertion of Christian morality: the Sexual Offences (Amendment) Bill 1977

Religious opposition to lowering the minimum age for male homosexual acts was central to halting the progress of the Sexual Offences (Amendment) Bill 1977. The Bishop of Birmingham, Laurence Brown, argued that he regarded 'homosexual acts as an undoubted deviation from the natural order, and in religious terms as contrary to the divine intention' and that a change in the age

---

132 Home Office, op. cit., § 71.
133 Sexual Offences (Amendment) Bill 1977, HL Debate, 3 March 1977, c.740.
134 The age of majority was lowered from 21 to 18 years in England and Wales by S.1 Family Law Reform Act 1969.
135 HL Debate, 14 June 1977, cc.13–14. The amendment was agreed 146-25 and three bishops (Birmingham, Carlisle and Norwich) voted with the majority. HL Debate, 14 June 1977, Division No.1.

of consent for homosexual acts would not be 'supported by those – and I think them still to be a majority – whose standard of personal conduct is derived from their Christian sympathies, if not from their clearly expressed convictions'.[136] Brown argued that lowering the minimum age would encourage homosexual practices with 'adolescents whose growth towards a stable heterosexual personality is still proceeding'.[137] This claim – that a higher minimum age for homosexual acts was necessary to avoid the corruption of youth by older men – was a stable trope in this and all other parliamentary debates regarding the age of consent between 1977 and 2000. However, although opposition to law reform relied upon a range of scientific and medical ideas about the dangers of homosexuality (see also Chapter 2), these were imbricated with and gained greater authority from assertions about the hegemony of 'Christian sympathies' in the population.

For example, when the Countess of Loudoun argued that lowering the age of consent would cause an 'infectious growth of this filthy disease' through the 'spreading of corruption and perversion among a new generation of young men and the younger boys in contact with them',[138] she asserted that the 'framework of our society is the teaching and example of Christ. He is our model. There can be no accord between homosexual activities and Christianity.'[139] Lord Stamp characterised the debate as a conflict between 'those who regard homosexuality as a sin before God, an abomination for which there can be no tolerance' and 'the gay liberationists, who glory in their proclivities and are out to proselytise and convert others'.[140] Lord Macleod of Fuinary similarly argued that the debate should be seen 'in terms of the Ten Commandments'[141] and that to lower the age of consent would be to '[give] up the god of our morality' and 'unseat the moral law'.[142] The Bishop of Norwich, Maurice Wood, summed up the mood of the majority of Peers by arguing that lowering the minimum age for homosexual acts would be both 'illiberal and cruel'[143] – illiberal because it 'takes away the liberty of our growing and senior adolescents [. . .] to go on developing in natural

---

136 HL Debate, 14 June 1977, c.32.
137 Ibid., c.33.
138 Ibid., cc.45–46.
139 Ibid., c.47.
140 In describing the 'spectrum' of attitudes in respect of 'the subject of the place of the homosexual in society', Lord Stamp closely associated the ideas and practices of the 'gay liberation movement' with paedophilia. He argued that 'gay liberationists' were 'towards the extreme end of the spectrum' but also at the 'end of the spectrum of sexual proclivity and deviation' were 'those, composed mainly, but not entirely of homosexuals [. . .] known as paedophiles [. . .] – the child lovers – who indulge in sexual practices with young children and whose increasing proselytising activities are closely related to the gay liberation movement'. HL Debate, 14 June 1977, cc.49–51.
141 HL Debate, 14 June 1977, c.55.
142 Ibid., c.57.
143 Ibid., c.65.

and harmonious psychological ways', and cruel because 'there is physical [and] moral danger' in homosexual relationships.[144]

In this debate about the minimum age for homosexual acts, appeals to Christian morality and values (argued to represent 'mainstream' views) were central to opposing any law reform beyond that achieved by the SOA 1967. As the Bishop of Birmingham, Laurence Brown, put it, '[w]e already have the Act of 1967 [and] enough is enough'.[145] Whereas religious intolerance of homosexuality was somewhat obscured in the SOA 1967 debates because of the Church of England's support for partial decriminalisation, the extent of religious hostility towards homosexuality was brought into focus in this debate. The assertion of Christian morality to halt legal reform should therefore not be characterised as a 'backlash' but rather as the continuation of established understandings about the dangers posed by homosexuality and the role of Christianity in mitigating these (by aiding the homosexual 'struggling against his inclination'[146]). Although arguments such as these depended upon a particular ontological construction of the homosexual which gained greater prominence in the latter half of the twentieth century – in which two types of male homosexuals were imagined: one the naïve, vulnerable and sexually immature young man, and the other the congenital homosexual who preys on him – they were underpinned by established ideas about sexual deviation in need of legally enforced restraint founded upon Christian moral values. Whilst the assertion of Christian morality in Parliament during the late 1970s and throughout the 1980s was shaped and enhanced by the ascendency of 'new right' politics,[147] it was promulgated within an established 'tradition' in which law relating to homosexuality reflected Christian concerns. This was fundamental in ensuring that no reform of the criminal law regulating male homosexual acts in England and Wales was achieved during this period.[148]

'Homophobia' and 'equality': the Criminal Justice and Public Order Act 1994

When the minimum age for male homosexual acts was next extensively debated in the UK Parliament, there had been broad social, cultural and legal changes in respect of homosexuality. Male homosexual acts had been partially decriminalised

---

144 Ibid.
145 Ibid., c.34.
146 Countess of Loudoun, HL Debate, 14 June 1977, c.47.
147 For a discussion of Christian morality and the 'new right' see: A.M. Smith, *New Right Discourses on Race and Sexuality: Britain, 1968–1990*, Cambridge: Cambridge University Press, 1994.
148 Changes were made by the Criminal Law Act 1977 to how the offences of gross indecency between men (S.13 Sexual Offences Act 1956) and procuring others to commit homosexual acts (S.4 Sexual Offences Act 1967) were triable in England and Wales but this did not alter the scope of regulation.

in Scotland[149] and in Northern Ireland,[150] and organisations campaigning for further legal equality were significantly more established.[151] The potential for a successful complaint in the European Court of Human Rights about statutory differences in the minimum age for homosexual and heterosexual acts[152] was a key factor in motivating an amendment to what became the Criminal Justice and Public Order Act (CJPOA) 1994 to lower the minimum age for homosexual acts. However, its sponsor, Edwina Currie MP, was also driven by ideological interests. In describing her ambition to end the 'enforced discrimination' of homosexuals in laws relating to sexual conduct, Currie played a key role in introducing a comparatively new social discourse into Parliament by describing the law as having an 'unpleasant homophobic nature'.[153] Central to Currie's advocacy of legal reform was a challenge to religious opposition to homosexuality:

> In this country there are [. . .] people who dislike, even abhor, homosexuality. They are entitled to campaign for those opinions. We have all been bombarded with St. Paul and Leviticus, and we have been accused of joining the forces of Satan. Such views are held with passionate sincerity – of course

---

149 S.80 Criminal Justice (Scotland) Act 1980. During parliamentary debates about the partial decriminalisation of male homosexual acts in Scotland a religious discourse about 'pastoral care', similar to that present in the Sexual Offences Act 1967 debates, was evident: 'The propositions are not particularly controversial. As far back as 1968 the General Assembly of the Church of Scotland went on record demanding the same change in the law. It is instructive to recall why the General Assembly called for the change. It recognised that so long as homosexual acts were a criminal offence homosexual men would inevitably be inhibited from coming forward and seeking the pastoral care of the Church.' R. Cook, HC Debate, 22 July 1980, c.286.

150 In 1978, the UK Government published a proposal for a draft Homosexual Offences (Northern Ireland) Order 1978, which would have partially decriminalised male homosexual acts in Northern Ireland. This failed to progress as the result of religious opposition and, compelled by the judgment of the European Court of Human Rights in *Dudgeon v the United Kingdom* (no. 7525/76, 22 October 1981, Series A no.45), partial decriminalisation was introduced by the Homosexual Offences (Northern Ireland) Order 1982. For a discussion, see: P. Johnson, *Homosexuality and the European Court of Human Rights*, Abingdon: Routledge, 2013.

151 From the 1970s gay and lesbian political organisations expanded rapidly, starting in 1970 with the reconstitution of the Homosexual Law Reform Society as the Sexual Law Reform Society and the founding of the Gay Liberation Front. By the 1990s the International Gay Association (now International Lesbian and Gay Association), Stonewall (established in 1989 to lobby against S.28 of the Local Government Act 1988, which we discuss in Chapter 6), and Outrage! existed. For a history of gay and lesbian political organisations during this period, see: S. Jeffrey-Poulter, *Peers, Queers and Commons: The Struggle for Gay Law Reform from 1950 to the Present*, London: Routledge, 1991.

152 *Wilde, Greenhalgh and Parry v the United Kingdom*, no. 22382/93, Commission decision, 19 January 1995.

153 HC Debate, 21 February 1994, c.75.

they are – but the people who hold them are not entitled to insist that their prejudices be written into British law.[154]

Currie's speech represented a decisive shift in Parliamentary debates about the regulation of homosexual sex because it challenged the previously unquestioned moral legitimacy of the Christian condemnation of homosexual acts. Whilst Currie's argument about the relationship between religious belief and the criminal law was not new – she asserted the same distinction between 'crime' and 'sin' made in the Wolfenden Report – her charge that religious arguments against homosexuality represented a form of unacceptable homophobia had rarely been made this strongly within parliamentary debates. While, as we discussed in the Introduction, the terms 'homophobia' and 'homophobic' first entered the parliamentary lexicon in 1986/7, use of the term was still comparatively rare and had never previously been linked so directly to religion in debates over sexual offences. There was no direct rebuttal of Currie's claim in the Commons and little subsequent reference was made to religion. When those who opposed a reduction in the minimum age for male homosexual acts relied upon religious arguments, these were directly challenged. For example, when Anthony Durrant MP cited a newspaper piece by the Archbishop of York, John Habgood, to argue against a reduction in the minimum age for male homosexual acts to 16 years,[155] this was directly challenged by Simon Hughes MP who argued that '[t]his is not a debate about what the Church teaches or about the Christian ethic'.[156] Other than a brief reference to the Apostles' view of the superiority of the 'normal sex act within the marriage vow' by Ian Paisley MP,[157] there was no further reference to religion in a debate that centred wholly on what Michael Alison MP referred to as 'the stage of crystallisation' when a 'homosexual orientation' is fully formed.[158] Although a majority of MPs were willing to accept the view, as expressed, for example, by Tony Blair MP, that 'being homosexual is not something that people catch, are taught or persuaded into, but something that they are' as a reason for reducing the minimum age for male homosexual acts to 18 years, there was insufficient support for a reduction to 16 years.[159]

---

154 Ibid., c.76.
155 Durrant argued that 'there is a distinction, rooted not only in [. . .] biological differences but in the belief that there are proper and improper uses for the human body' and that 'homosexuality in young men is neither to be treated as uncontroversial nor to be penalised beyond the age of maturity' (HC Debate, 21 February 1994, cc.87–88).
156 HC Debate, 21 February 1994, c.91.
157 Ibid., c.114.
158 Ibid., c.101.
159 A small majority voted against the reduction of 21 to 16 years by 307-280 (HC Debate, 21 February 1994, Division No.136) but a large majority supported a reduction to 18 years by 427-162 (HC Debate, 21 February 1994, Division No.137).

However, the absence of religious discourse evident in the Commons was not a characteristic of the CJPOA 1994 debates in the Lords. The Bishop of Lichfield, Keith Sutton, spoke at length about the important role of law in ensuring the existence of a Christian moral vision on human sexuality:

> The main point, if I may say so, that Christians will want to make is that the public debate in the press and in another place has focused too much on the question of age: the age of consent. That, with respect, is not the Church's focus. The Church has teaching about human sexuality and sexual relationships which applies to all ages. The kernel of our position here is that the Christian vision of human sexuality would stress that the greater the degree of personal intimacy, the greater should be the degree of personal commitment, the one to the other, of those involved. In the Christian view, the ideal context for intimate sexual relationships is the married love of man and wife. The criminal law therefore has a part, but only a limited part, to play in affirming and upholding a wider and richer humane moral vision [. . .] It is not right to criminalise activity unnecessarily, but I do not find the argument for equality in this area as between heterosexual and homosexual practices convincing or in the public interest.[160]

As well as reiterating the established Christian discourse that homosexuality is antithetical to a 'humane moral vision' of sexuality, Sutton also introduced a faith-based objection to law reform: an explicit Christian rejection of 'equality'.[161] This opposition to legal equality was founded upon, as the Archbishop of York, John Habgood, explained, the desire to ensure that the law continued to enforce the Christian view that heterosexual and homosexual sexual acts were not morally equivalent:

---

160 HL Debate, 25 April 1994, cc.433–434.
161 Sutton was reiterating a view that was expressed by the House of Bishops in *Issues in Human Sexuality: A Statement by the House of Bishops of the General Synod of the Church of England* (London: Church House Publishing, 1991). This report was the result of Resolution 64 of the 1988 Lambeth Conference that called upon all bishops of the Anglican Communion to produce a 'deep and dispassionate study of the question of homosexuality'. In the 1991 report the bishops argued: 'Heterosexuality and homosexuality are not equally congruous with the observed order of creation or with the insights of revelation as the Church engages with these in the light of her pastoral ministry' (p.40). This view reiterated the sentiment of the motion passed by the General Synod on 11 November 1987 by 403-8 that 'homosexual genital acts [. . .] fall short' of 'the biblical and traditional teaching on chastity and fidelity in personal relationships in response to, and expression of, God's love for each one of us'. This discourse rejecting the moral equivalence of heterosexuality and homosexuality found early expression in debates over the promotion of homosexuality by local authorities discussed in Chapter 6 (for example, Rhodes Boyson MP, HC Debate, 8 May 1987, cc.1002–1003) and teaching materials related to HIV transmission (for example, Lord Stoddart, HL Debate, 11 June 1992, c.1435).

> [A]re homosexuality and heterosexuality simply alternative and equivalent forms of sexuality or is there a difference between them which should somehow be represented in the law? We have inherited a long-standing belief that there is a difference. Much of this is rooted in Christian tradition [...] [T]here is something fundamental about our human nature which is safeguarded within the Christian tradition. It is a tradition which talks about the purpose of sex, which is procreational as well as relational. It is a tradition about the way in which we are made. It is a long-standing tradition about how human beings should relate to one another and where the limits should be drawn [...] I do not think that as a society we can simply say that homosexuality and heterosexuality are in all respects equivalent. Plainly they are not. Therefore, in our legislation we need in some way to define a norm. It seems to me that to have the small age difference which is represented by the figure 18 says something about society's acceptance of heterosexuality as the norm.[162]

Although Habgood also reiterated established concerns about the need to protect younger men from homosexuality – and from the risk of AIDS, which was an important part of these debates – his key argument was that it was necessary to retain differences between homosexual and heterosexual acts in the criminal law to reflect their inherent moral inequality. This was a view shared by Lord Jakobovits who argued that, as 'a member of the faith community [Judaism] that started the whole argument that we are debating today by ruling in its legislation that homosexual conduct was not only immoral but also illegal', he believed that the criminal law must 'give a signal to our society and to the world at large that we still want our children to be raised in an environment in which the difference between right and wrong is inculcated by teachers, by parents and certainly by ourselves'.[163]

Whilst the Lords ultimately voted in favour of reducing the minimum age for male homosexual acts from 21 to 18 years,[164] religious arguments against 'equality' were a vital means for resisting attempts to reduce the minimum age

---

162 HL Debate, 20 June 1994, cc.17–18.
163 Ibid., cc.38–39. Several other Peers also relied on religious discourse to oppose reform. The Duke of Norfolk stated that as 'a practising Roman Catholic' he believed 'homosexual acts to be morally wrong' (ibid., c.19); the Earl of Longford argued that, although he regarded 'all human beings as equal in the sight of God', homosexuals have 'a terrible handicap in life' and 'we must not pander to them' (ibid., c.26); and Baroness Young claimed, on behalf of 'very many members of the Church of England' that '[w]e are worried' and '[w]e should not be afraid to say that the normal is better than the abnormal' (ibid., c.27).
164 At Committee stage of the Criminal Justice and Public Order Bill 1994, the Lords voted 176-113 in favour of a reduction in the minimum age for male homosexual acts from 21 to 18 years. HL Committee, 20 June 1994, Division No.2.

to 16 years whilst avoiding the charge of 'homophobia'.[165] For example, Lord Orr-Ewing, who was given authority to speak on behalf of the Bishop of Chester, argued:

> The decisions on the age of consent will have such far-reaching effects on our society that it seemed right for them to be debated in your Lordships' House. A substantial body of opinion in the church and the country believes, *without homophobia*, that the lowering of the age of consent from 21 will result in moral damage to teenagers who are still developing to adult maturity. The argument of justice is flawed. It assumes equivalence between heterosexual and homosexual physical relationships. This is not so – either physically or Biblically.[166]

This form of denial that faith-based opposition to legal equality constitutes 'homophobia' has become a central trope of religious opposition to law reform and, as we explore in subsequent chapters, has underpinned efforts to resist legislative changes in respect of the adoption of children, education, employment, partnership rights and hate speech.

The CJPOA 1994 retained a range of legal inequalities between male homosexual and heterosexual sexual acts across the UK that were favoured by religious opponents of reform. Although the CJPOA 1994 partially decriminalised heterosexual buggery for the first time in England and Wales[167] and set the same minimum age of 18 years for both heterosexual and homosexual acts in private, buggery between men remained subject to stricter privacy requirements.[168] Other genital sexual acts between men (gross indecency) remained subject to a higher minimum age of 18 years across the UK in contrast to the minimum ages set for heterosexual acts. The CJPOA 1994 also extended partial decriminalisation

---

165 Peers opposing reform also made unsuccessful attempts to introduce further amendments to the Criminal Justice and Public Order Bill 1994. As we discuss in Chapter 2, one such amendment was moved by Baroness Ryder of Warsaw to create a 'Restriction on custody of children by homosexuals'. HL Debate, 12 July 1994, c.1770.
166 HL Debate, 19 July 1994, c.183. Our emphasis.
167 S.143 Criminal Justice and Public Order Act 1994. Heterosexual buggery had never been criminalised in Scotland (there was an unsuccessful attempt to partially criminalise it in 2000: HL Committee, 13 November 2000, c.65) but remained illegal in Northern Ireland under S.61–62 Offences Against the Person Act 1861 until its partial decriminalisation by S.19 Criminal Justice (Northern Ireland) Order 2003.
168 S.143(3) Criminal Justice and Public Order Act 1994 (amending S.12 Sexual Offences Act 1956) provided that all acts of buggery remained criminalised unless they took place 'in private', but in respect of an act of buggery by one man with another it reiterated the requirement of S.1(2) Sexual Offences Act 1967 that no act would be deemed to be 'in private' if more than two persons took part or were present, or it took place in a public lavatory.

of male homosexual acts to the armed forces and merchant ships[169] and prevented male homosexual acts in private from being prosecuted in Scotland under the common law of shameless indecency.[170] Therefore, although Currie's amendment was a key moment in introducing the emerging social rhetoric of sexual orientation equality to parliamentary debate about homosexual sex, religious opponents had helped shape the legislation to ensure that significant inequalities remained in respect of all male homosexual acts.

The triumph of equality over religion? The Sexual Offences (Amendment) Act 2000

Religious opposition to lowering the minimum age for male homosexual acts remained strong in the Lords when, in order to avoid an adverse ruling in the European Court of Human Rights,[171] there were several attempts to introduce legislation to equalise the minimum ages for homosexual and heterosexual acts. The first attempt, introduced as a backbench amendment to what became the Crime and Disorder Act (CDA) 1998,[172] was widely supported by MPs.[173] Although there was debate in the Commons about a statement by the House of Bishops[174] (supported by the Archbishop of Canterbury, George Carey) which set out the Church of England's opposition to an equal age of consent – because it 'would send a signal that homosexual practice is on a par with, and equal to, heterosexual relationships'[175] – there was little explicitly faith-based opposition to the amendment.[176] In the Lords, however, a motion was introduced by Baroness

---

169 S.146–147 Criminal Justice and Public Order Act 1994.
170 S.148 Criminal Justice and Public Order Act 1994.
171 In *Sutherland v the United Kingdom* (no. 25186/94, Commission report, 1 July 1997), the European Commission of Human Rights decided that maintaining a higher minimum legal age for male homosexual acts violated Article 8 taken in conjunction with Article 14 of the European Convention on Human Rights. Aware that a judgment by the European Court of Human Rights would almost certainly have reflected this decision, the UK Government requested that the applicants delay their complaint in light of its commitment to legislative reform. See: P. Johnson, *Homosexuality and the European Court of Human Rights*, op. cit.
172 A. Keen, HC Debate, 22 June 1998, c.754.
173 The Commons voted 336-129 in favour of the amendment to lower the minimum age for male homosexual acts to 16 years in England and Wales and Scotland, and 17 years in Northern Ireland. HC Debate, 22 June 1998, Division No.311.
174 BBC News, 'Church opposes lowering age of consent', 21 June 1998. Available online at http://news.bbc.co.uk/1/hi/uk_politics/116865.stm (accessed on 4 December 2013).
175 S. Bell, HC Debate, 22 June 1998, c.795.
176 In response to the support given by the Commons to a reduction in the minimum age for homosexual acts, the *Catholic Herald* (26 June 1998) stated its 'bewilderment' that no Catholic MP had opposed the amendment and described those in favour of legislative reform as 'those who voted to allow your child to have gay sex'.

Young to reject the amendment on the grounds that it represented the 'thin end of the wedge' that would 'lead to a demand for gay and lesbian marriages and for the right for such couples to adopt children'.[177] Although Young rejected the claim that her opposition to 'equality' and to recognising 'the moral equivalence between heterosexual and homosexual relationships'[178] was a 'religious Right-Wing plot',[179] religion (including a then uncommon reference to the religious sensibilities of a non-Judeo-Christian faith) was central to her opposing motion:

> I speak as an Anglican. However, I know that I have the support of Roman Catholics and members of the Welsh nonconformist Church. I was very grateful that the noble Lord, Lord Jakobovits, indicated his support for me. I have been approached twice by the secretary-general of the Moslem Council of Great Britain, representing 600 mosques, to say that the council is entirely in support of this proposal. And of course there are many others who have no religious convictions at all who also support what I am doing. I think we all greatly welcome the firm statement from the most reverend Primate of all England, the Archbishop of Canterbury, that he cannot support the reduction in the age of consent to 16.[180]

The Bishop of Winchester, Michael Scott-Joynt, also cited George Carey[181] when supporting Young's motion and advised Peers to be 'very wary indeed about deserting the wisdom in these matters not only of the Christian faith but of the other major faiths too'.[182] Lord Jakobovits stated that arguments made in favour of equality and against homophobia were designed to 'whitewash what is morally unacceptable to the vast majority of the citizens of this country and elsewhere'.[183]

177 HL Debate, 22 July 1998, c.939.
178 Ibid.
179 Ibid., c.936.
180 Ibid. There had been previous occasional reference to Muslims, Jews, Hindus, Sikhs and others in debates over the passage of Section 28 (see Chapter 6).
181 The Archbishop of Canterbury, George Carey, stated in *The Times* on 22 July 1998 that 'many people are viewing the issue [of the age of consent] as simply an "open and shut" matter about whether or not one is in favour of equalising the age at which the criminal law seeks to regulate sexual behaviour between consenting adults over the age of 16' and that 'this view is far too simple, and wilfully ignores important moral considerations'. Carey, reflecting views expressed by the House of Bishops, argued that legislation should be 'rooted in sound moral values' and any potential reform 'be looked at in the context of an overall vision of what we want a morally healthy society to look like'. He argued against 'accepting that homosexual acts for adolescent boys should in some way be endorsed by society'. Taking this 'broader perspective', Carey concluded: 'I remain opposed to the lowering of the age of consent and take some comfort from the fact that it seems that very many people in our land share my sense of unease.'
182 HL Debate, 22 July 1998, c.943.
183 Ibid., c.949.

Whilst the Bishop of Bath and Wells, Jim Thompson, disagreed with Young's motion and voted against it, he restated the long-standing argument that law reform was essential in discouraging the existence of a 'homosexual sub-culture' that limited 'efforts to prevent people from becoming gay'.[184] Young's motion was successful and ensured that the CDA 1998 did not lower the minimum age for male homosexual acts.[185]

When the Government subsequently introduced the bespoke Sexual Offences (Amendment) Bill 1999 which proposed to make reductions in the minimum age set across the UK for buggery and gross indecency in order to standardise the age at which homosexual and heterosexual acts were lawful – which received overwhelming support in the Commons[186] – Young again relied on familiar religious arguments to support an amendment to deny the Bill a Second Reading in the Lords for six months (an amendment designed to effectively end the Bill's parliamentary passage). Young cited support for her amendment from *inter alia* the Cardinal Archbishop of Westminster, 'the Moslem community in Great Britain' and 'the public'.[187] The Lords passed Young's amendment[188] but three of the seven bishops who voted in the division opposed it.[189] Justifying his opposition, the Bishop of Birmingham, Mark Santer, restated the argument that law reform was necessary to remove 'the stigma of criminality from young men who are involved in homosexual behaviour' and who 'are less likely to be able to find [help] if they know that their behaviour is labelled as criminal'.[190]

The Government introduced a subsequent Bill into the Commons in the next parliamentary session which again passed at Second and Third Readings by an overwhelming majority.[191] The Lords gave the Bill a Second Reading[192] but in Committee Baroness Young successfully tabled an amendment that proposed to reduce the age for male homosexuals acts of gross indecency to 16 years but retain

---

184 Ibid., c.954.
185 The Lords voted by 290-122 (with the bishops voting 6-3) to remove the amendment to the Crime and Disorder Bill 1998 that would have lowered the minimum age for male homosexual acts (as well as heterosexual acts of buggery in England and Wales) in the UK. HL Debate, 22 July 1998, Division No.4.
186 On Second Reading in the House of Commons of the Sexual Offences (Amendment) Bill 1999 it was agreed 313-130 to reduce the minimum age for male homosexual acts (as well as heterosexual acts of buggery in England and Wales) to 16 years in England and Wales and Scotland, and 17 years in Northern Ireland (although heterosexual buggery would have remained criminalised in Northern Ireland). HC Debate, 25 January 1999, Division No.46.
187 HL Debate, 13 April 1999, cc.652–653.
188 Amendment agreed 222-146, HL Debate, 13 April 1999, Division No.1.
189 The Bishops of Bath and Wells, Birmingham, and Oxford.
190 HL Debate, 13 April 1999, c.731.
191 Sexual Offences (Amendment) Bill 2000 passed by Commons at Second Reading 263-102 (HC Debate, 10 February 2000, Division No.71) and Third Reading 317-117 (HC Debate, 28 February, Division No.90).
192 HL Debate, 11 April 2000, cc.91–167.

the minimum age for buggery at 18 years.[193] Young emphasised that she introduced the amendment 'as a Christian' and again claimed support of diverse faith communities.[194] In response to the success of Young's amendment, the Government announced that the Bill would receive no further parliamentary time[195] and would be submitted for Royal Assent in compliance with the Parliament Acts 1911 and 1949.[196] The Christian Institute condemned the use of 'a draconian device intended to be used on matters of major national and constitutional significance'.[197]

The use of the Parliament Acts 1911 and 1949 was significant given that it represented only the sixth time that it had been used.[198] There is no doubt that its use was underpinned by a need for the UK to meet its commitments under the European Convention on Human Rights,[199] but it was driven by the ascendency of a discourse in the Commons in favour of sexual orientation equality. Although the Sexual Offences (Amendment) Act (SOAA) 2000 did not remove fundamental differences in the legal regulation of male homosexual and heterosexual acts (which we address in the next section), proponents argued that it was 'based on the principle of equality before the law'.[200] The SOAA 2000 therefore represented the first successful 'discursive displacement' of religious opposition to homosexuality by the assertion of a counter-discourse organised around the principle of equality.[201] As such, the SOAA 2000 was a significant evolution of the relationship between law, religion and homosexuality. It marked

---

193 The House divided 205-144, with the bishops voting 4-4. HL Committee, 13 November 2000, Division No.1.
194 HL Debate, 13 November 2000, c.64.
195 HL Debate, 23 November 2000, cc.947–951.
196 Speaker's Statement, HC Debate, 30 November 2000, c.1137. As a result of S.1 Sexual Offences (Amendment) Act 2000, in England and Wales the minimum age for homosexual and heterosexual acts of buggery was reduced to 16 years and the minimum age for male homosexual acts of gross indecency was also reduced to 16 years. In Scotland the minimum age for male homosexual acts was reduced to 16 years. In Northern Ireland the minimum age for male homosexual acts was reduced to 17 years (although, because heterosexual acts of buggery remained criminalised until their partial decriminalisation by Criminal Justice (Northern Ireland) Order 2003, this did not create equality in the minimum age for buggery) and this was subsequently further reduced to 16 years for all heterosexual and homosexual acts by the Sexual Offences (Northern Ireland) Order 2008.
197 The Christian Institute, 'Why the Parliament Acts should not be used on the Sexual Offences (Amendment) Bill', 2000. Available online at www.christian.org.uk/htmlpublications/protectgirls.htm (accessed on 4 December 2013).
198 Previous uses of the Parliament Act 1911 had been in respect of the Government of Ireland Act 1914, Welsh Church Act 1914 and Parliament Act 1949. Parliament Acts 1911 and 1949 had been used in respect of the War Crimes Act 1991 and the European Parliamentary Elections Act 1999.
199 *Sutherland v the United Kingdom*, op. cit.
200 J. Straw, HC Debate, 10 February 2000, c.432.
201 G.C. Spivak, *In Other Worlds: Essays in Cultural Politics*, New York: Meuthen, 1987.

a decisive break from the long-established socio-legal formulation that the Christian antipathy to male same-sex sexual acts should be expressed through the criminal law. As we explain in the next section, this necessitated discursive shifts by religious opponents who wished to further resist law reform orchestrated in the name of equality.

The disappearance of religion? The decriminalisation of male homosexual acts

The offences of buggery and gross indecency, along with other homosexual related offences, were repealed in England and Wales by the Sexual Offences Act (SOA) 2003.[202] This legislative reform was driven by the need to meet obligations under the European Convention on Human Rights[203] to ensure that the 'criminal law should not treat people differently on the basis of their sexual orientation'.[204] A key feature of parliamentary debates surrounding the SOA 2003 is that those opposing the wholesale repeal of male homosexual offences from English law did not explicitly invoke religion. Religious organisations outside of Parliament, such as the Christian Institute, were vocal in publicly opposing the repeal of male homosexual offences on the basis of 'moral and medical differences between penetration of the vagina and penetration of the anus'.[205] However, in Parliament those who had so explicitly deployed religious arguments when opposing a reduction in the minimum age for male homosexual acts now muted reference

---

202 In respect of England and Wales, the Sexual Offences Act 2003 repealed *inter alia* the offences of buggery (S.12 Sexual Offences Act 1956), gross indecency (S.13 Sexual Offences Act 1956), solicitation by men (S.32 Sexual Offences Act 1956) and procuring others to commit homosexual acts (S.4 Sexual Offences Act 1967). In respect of Northern Ireland, the Sexual Offences Act 2003 repealed the offences of buggery (S.61–62 Offences Against the Person Act 1961) and gross indecency (S.11 Criminal Law Amendment Act 1885) as well as provisions relating to homosexual offences contained in the Homosexual Offences (Northern Ireland) Order 1982 (although Art.9 still makes reference to 'premises resorted to for homosexual practices' in respect of brothels, mirroring S.6 Sexual Offences Act 1967 in England and Wales). However, the Criminal Justice (Northern Ireland) Order 2003 continued to partially criminalise buggery (Art.19) and criminalise 'assault with intent to commit buggery' (Art.20) – both gender-neutral offences – as well as criminalising 'indecent assault on a male' (Art.21). These offences were repealed by the Sexual Offences (Northern Ireland) Order 2008. In respect of Scotland, all homosexual offences were repealed by the Sexual Offences (Scotland) Act 2009.
203 For a discussion, see: P. Johnson, *Homosexuality and the European Court of Human Rights*, op. cit.
204 *Setting the Boundaries: Reforming the Law on Sex Offences, Volume I*, London: Home Office, 2000, p.101.
205 The Christian Institute, 'Sex Offences Review: Response by the Christian Institute', 2001.

to religion in their opposition. Recognising that religious discourse was potentially displaceable by pro-equality and anti-homophobia discourses, religious opponents adopted a different strategy of opposition.

This strategy involved the deployment of arguments about 'public morality' to oppose the wholesale repeal of homosexual offences. Although this can be viewed as one example of an endemic moral authoritarianism about sex at the start of the twenty-first century,[206] it also represents a reactivation of an older discourse about homosexuality in which, as we showed above, claims about public morality were based on unspoken assumptions about the hegemony of Christian values and the threat of homosexuality to these. The focus for opposition to law reform was on the repeal of the provision relating to male homosexual acts in public lavatories contained in the SOA 1967.[207] Although the Government had included the new offence of 'sexual activity in public' in the Sexual Offences Bill 2003 – which would have criminalised any individual who intentionally engaged in sexual activities in a public place knowing that they could be seen by a non-participating party – Baroness Noakes claimed that this 'legitimises what is known as "cottaging"; that is sex between homosexuals in a public lavatory provided that it is in a cubicle and hence not seen'.[208] On this basis, Noakes subsequently encouraged the removal of the proposed 'sexual activity in public' offence from the Bill[209] and successfully included the bespoke offence of 'sexual activity in a public lavatory'[210] that was retained by the Commons and enacted in the SOA 2003.[211]

Although parliamentary debates about this offence included none of the religious discourse present in previous debates to justify its inclusion, it provided a touchstone for parliamentarians with established records of opposing homosexual law reform on religious grounds. In making it a criminal offence for a person to engage intentionally in sexual activity in a lavatory to which the public or a section of the public has access, the SOA 2003 – although written in gender-neutral terms – gives expression to a deliberate wish to regulate male homosexual activity.[212] During debate, Peers repeatedly juxtaposed the 'offensive public

---

206 J. Phoenix and S. Oerton, *Illicit and Illegal: Sex, Regulation and Social Control*, Cullompton: Willan Publishing, 2005.
207 S.1(2)(b) Sexual Offences Act 1967. Male homosexual acts remained an offence if they took place 'in a lavatory to which the public have or are permitted to have access, whether on payment or otherwise'.
208 HL Debate, 13 February 2003, c.779.
209 HL Debate, 19 May 2003, cc.586–588.
210 The House divided 133-95 in favour of the amendment. HL Debate, 9 June 2003, Division 1.
211 S.71 Sexual Offences Act 2003. Identical provisions are contained in Art.75 Sexual Offences (Northern Ireland) Order 2008. The offence does not apply in Scotland.
212 For a longer discussion, see: P. Johnson, '"Ordinary folk and cottaging": law, morality and public sex', *Journal of Law and Society* 34, 2007, 520–543.

nuisance of homosexuals'[213] with the 'general public sentiment which is that public lavatories are not places for sexual activity'.[214] 'Ordinary people',[215] 'decent, law-abiding communities',[216] 'the vast majority of people',[217] 'doctors, parents',[218] 'all right-thinking people'[219] and 'ordinary folk'[220] were invoked in support of the regulation of the 'anathema'[221] of male homosexual acts in public lavatories. The SOA 2003 debates demonstrate the continuation of both the moral preoccupation with and fear of male homosexual acts in the public sphere that was present in the SOA 1967 debates. Peers incited and reiterated a heteronormative discourse about 'cottaging' to demark it from 'conventional' sex – both public and private – and as an activity that is beyond the threshold of what can be considered socially acceptable behaviour. In doing this, the justification for the offence reiterated long-standing ideas about homosexual men as promiscuous deviants in need of specific regulation by the criminal law.

The parliamentary debates surrounding the public lavatory offence in the SOA 2003 are significant for two main reasons. First, although championed by Peers who had relied on religious rhetoric in previous debates to oppose sexual orientation equality,[222] explicit invocations of religion were conspicuously absent from moral arguments made about homosexual sex. Although the Christian Institute had argued in favour of a specific offence dealing with male homosexual acts in public lavatories with explicit reference to Christianity,[223] no use of these arguments was made during parliamentary debates (in contrast to, as we discuss in Chapter 2, the extensive citation of literature produced by the Christian Institute during debates relating to the Adoption and Children Act 2002). Furthermore, no bishop participated in any debate about the offence or voted in the relevant division.[224] The second key feature of these debates is that supporters

---

213 Baroness Blatch, HL Debate, 13 February 2003, c.789
214 Baroness Noakes, HL Debate, 19 May 2003, c. 577.
215 Baroness Noakes, HL Debate, 13 February 2003, c.779.
216 Baroness Blatch, HL Debate, 9 June 2003, c.69.
217 Baroness Noakes, HL Debate, 9 June 2003, c.66.
218 Lord Hylton, HL Debate, 9 June 2003, c.71.
219 Lord Fitt, HL Debate, 9 June 2003, c.72.
220 Lord Clarke of Hampstead, HL Debate, 9 June 2003, c.74.
221 Lord Fitt, HL Debate, 9 June 2003, c.72.
222 For example, Lady Saltoun of Abernethy, who had previously referred to Christianity when supporting provisions in the Criminal Justice and Public Order Act 1994 to allow a homosexual act to constitute grounds for discharge from the armed forces (HL Debate, 20 June 1994, c.89), made no reference to religion in her support for the offence (HL Debate, 19 May 2003, c.582).
223 The Christian Institute, 'Legalising sexual activity in public toilets: how the Sexual Offences Bill effectively legalises a major public nuisance', 2003. Available online at www.christian.org.uk/pdfpublications/sex_in_public_toilets.pdf (accessed on 4 December 2013).
224 HL Debate, 9 June 2003, Division No.1.

of the offence more carefully and skilfully negotiated the ascendent equality discourse in respect of sexual orientation. This was achieved in two ways: first, through an explicit rejection of the idea that the offence was homophobic, and, second, through the assertion that it did not discriminate against homosexual men. For instance, Dominic Grieve MP 'put [. . .] on the record because concern has been expressed that the provision was an expression of a return to homophobic fears; it is not',[225] and MPs rejected any claim that the provision was discriminatory and would have a disproportionate impact on (homosexual) men. Yet the consequences of the offence are that it is almost exclusively enforced in respect of male homosexual acts[226] and is a barrier for individuals applying for a disregard of previous convictions or cautions for now repealed homosexual offences.[227] Therefore, a provision that was supported by religious opponents of sexual orientation equality continues to subject male homosexual acts to specific legal regulation.

Conclusion

In this chapter we have examined the changing relationship between law and religion in respect of the regulation of homosexual sex. We have shown that although this relationship has been subject to considerable alteration, religion exerted a strong influence on shaping law relating to homosexual sex in the twentieth century. Whilst our analysis shows a decline amongst legislators in the invocation and acceptance of faith-based arguments for regulating homosexual sex, it also shows the development of a strategic response by religious opponents to this change. The nature of parliamentary discourse changed drastically between debates over the SOAA 2000 (which evidenced high levels of religious opposition) and the SOA 2003 (which showed an absence of religious rhetoric). The SOA 2003 debates show that many established opponents of sexual orientation equality who had hitherto relied on religious rhetoric in Parliament omitted references to religion when arguing for the retention of specific statutory provision designed to regulate male homosexual acts in public. This sublimation of religion by opponents of law reform represents a strategic discursive transformation in response to the ascendency of the sexual orientation equality agenda. The justifications for the inclusion of the 'sexual activity in a public lavatory' offence in the SOA 2003 can be seen as emblematic of an approach in which familiar and long-standing faith-based arguments about homosexual sex are often presented without explicit reference to their religious foundations. This strategy is a means of obscuring the long but now problematic association between Christianity and the regulation of homosexual sexual acts. However, although religious arguments

---

225 HC Debate, 15 July 2003, c.191.
226 P. Johnson, '"Ordinary folk and cottaging": law, morality and public sex', op. cit.
227 S.92(3)(b) Protection of Freedoms Act 2012.

and rhetoric disappeared from the last parliamentary debates about adult homosexual sex, this has not been the case in respect of all of the other substantive issues we examine in subsequent chapters of the book. For example, as we show in the next chapter, religious discourse has remained a fundamental feature of debates about childhood, parenting and processes of family formation.

Chapter 2

The boundaries of the family

Religion and same-sex parenting

In this chapter we examine the role of religion in debates over two pieces of legislation that bear directly on the ability of same-sex couples to engage in legally recognised practices of parenting: the Adoption and Children Act (ACA) 2002 and the Human Fertilisation and Embryology Act (HFEA) 2008. The legal reforms benefiting same-sex couples created by the ACA 2002 and the HFEA 2008 were subject to concerted religious opposition within Parliament and beyond, including campaigns involving religious groups such as the Christian Institute, Christian Action Research and Education (CARE) and the Catholic Children's Society. This opposition was based not only on the practical implications of the legal changes (the new routes created for same-sex couples to be jointly recognised as the parents of children – something not possible before the ACA 2002) but also their symbolic significance. A number of religious opponents argued strenuously that the reforms would have widespread negative social consequences because they undermined the materially and symbolically privileged legal position of heterosexual marriage and the mother–father model of parenting. In making their arguments, some religious opponents deployed a range of long-standing discourses about the dangers posed to children by exposure to homosexuality (which had featured prominently in debates over homosexual offences, as we discussed in Chapter 1). However, in recognition that moral and religious arguments about the dangers of homosexuality to children could no longer be taken to be 'rhetorically self-sufficient'[1] – that is, in need of no real explanation or defence – religious opponents of reform also sought to utilise 'scientific' evidence to bolster their claims about the negative consequences of gay and lesbian parenting for the welfare of children. Despite this blending of both familiar and newer discursive strategies, efforts to block or significantly dilute the reforms ultimately failed.

---

1 M. Summers, 'Rhetorically self-sufficient arguments in Western Australian parliamentary debates on lesbian and gay law reform', *British Journal of Social Psychology* 46, 2010, 840.

This chapter provides a critical analysis of these failed efforts on the part of religious opponents of homosexual law reform. We consider these failures highly significant for two key reasons. First, prior to the ACA 2002 debates, representations of homosexuals as threats to children served as a powerful resource to justify the legal regulation of male homosexual sex and the exclusion of gay men and lesbians from a range of rights and protections. The declining influence of this stigmatising discourse in Parliament represented a significant diminishment of the discursive repertoire available to religious opponents of homosexual law reform. Although the argument that homosexuals posed a danger to children maintained legitimacy and authority amongst some parliamentarians (as evidenced by the narrow margin of their defeat in Parliament, particularly in relation to the ACA 2002), they were robustly challenged by counter-discourses which ascribed positive, if sometimes qualified, moral value to same-sex couples seeking to become legally recognised parents of children. Second, and relatedly, the awareness by religious opponents of the obvious weakening of once reliable arguments instigated a need for new discursive strategies capable of opposing law reform. As illustrated in debates over the HFEA 2008, religious opponents, when confronted with the likely failure of their efforts to block reform, frequently resorted to claims about the growing marginalisation of religion within the public sphere and the undermining of their religious freedoms by the advancement of sexual orientation equality. Although these discourses have significantly shaped a number of other aspects of law reform (as we detail in subsequent chapters), their influence proved limited within the context of debates over same-sex parenting. As we show throughout this chapter, religion's power to delimit the boundaries of legitimate 'family' has significantly abated.[2]

Before providing an analysis of debates over the ACA 2002 and HFEA 2008, however, we first excavate one almost entirely forgotten parliamentary episode from the mid-1990s during which religious arguments were marshalled in an attempt to criminalise the care of children by homosexuals (representing a potential new form of criminalisation that would have impeded the ability of gay men and lesbians to form families and participate in the life of communities). This episode serves as a reminder of how unsettled basic questions remained about the rights of homosexuals to even have close contact with children – let alone assume parental responsibility for them – just eight years prior to the adoption reforms of the ACA 2002.

---

2 It should be stressed that a two-parent model of legal parentage (whether female/male, female/female or male/male) remained hegemonic in debates over both Acts. More radical proposals, such as to allow the naming of more than two parents on birth certificates to reflect both 'genetic' and 'social' parents, were alluded to only rarely (for example, see: Baroness O'Neill of Bengarve, HL Debate, 21 November 2007, c.858; Baroness Barker, HL Debate, 21 November 2007, c.861) and not seriously debated.

The Ashbourne–Ryder amendment

During debates over the wide-ranging Criminal Justice and Public Order Act 1994, Baroness Ryder of Warsaw (Sue Ryder, founder of the eponymous charity) moved an amendment to make it a criminal offence 'for a homosexual man or woman, other than the natural parent, to have the care or custody of a child under the age of eighteen'.[3] It was proposed that offenders would face a custodial sentence of up to six months, a level-five fine[4] or both. Although both Ryder and Lord Ashbourne (who authored the amendment) acknowledged that the amendment's wording 'may not be perfect',[5] they stressed that it gave the Government an important opportunity to state publicly its position on parenting by homosexuals. Lord Ashbourne explained:

> I hope that the Government will state [. . .] that the welfare and best interests of a child are never served by any order as a result of which a child is placed in a homosexual household. The Lord Jesus Christ said: 'If anyone causes any of these little ones, who believe in me, to sin ... it would be better for him to have a large millstone hung around his neck and to be drowned in the depths of the sea'. That quotation comes from Matthew, chapter 18, verse 6. I bear that warning very much in mind.[6]

Ryder similarly made religion central to her explanation for moving the amendment: 'The reason that I and my supporters take this view is that the Bible makes it very clear that it is unrighteous for a so-called homosexual couple to be given the care and custody of a child.'[7] Ryder claimed that the amendment was 'to safeguard children [and] not intended as an attack on those with homosexual tendencies'.[8]

Baroness Cumberlege,[9] who provided the Government's response, expressed 'great sympathy with the intentions behind this amendment'[10] and stated that Ashbourne and Ryder should 'be applauded'.[11] However, Cumberlege urged no support on the grounds that the wording was problematic, particularly its presumption that a 'homosexual' could be clearly defined. Additionally, she argued, it allowed no flexibility for 'very rare and exceptional cases'[12] when judges

---

3   Amendment 153A, Criminal Justice and Public Order Bill 1994. HL Debate, 12 July 1994, c.1770.
4   Level five is the highest level on the standard scale of fines for summary offences.
5   Baroness Ryder, HL Debate, 12 July 1994, c.1771.
6   HL Debate, 12 July 1994, c.1771.
7   Ibid., c.1779.
8   Ibid.
9   Baroness Cumberlege identifies publicly as Roman Catholic (*Catholic Herald*, 1 May 2009, p.11).
10 HL Debate, 12 July 1994, c.1776.
11 Ibid., c.1779.
12 Ibid., c.1778.

might view placement of a child in the care of a homosexual as the only reasonable and just course of action. Nevertheless, Cumberlege stated that she understood why it 'could appear an attractive amendment'.[13] With the amendment gaining only limited support, and given the Government's stated opposition, Ryder withdrew it while issuing a firm warning that she intended to pursue the matter further. There is no record in Hansard of Ashbourne or Ryder having made a similar proposal in the Lords again.

The significance of this now obscure episode rests not in any particular legislative outcome; rather, it serves as a reminder of the challenges faced (particularly in the House of Lords) by those who would later seek to reform adoption law. Although by the mid-1990s Ryder recognised that an open 'attack' on homosexuals was unlikely to be broadly palatable, she felt no compunction about deploying a biblical justification for criminalising homosexuals who cared for children to whom they were not biologically related in order to 'safeguard' minors. While not speaking in religious terms herself, Cumberlege offered her party's praise of the amendment's intentions, offering legitimacy to the claim that gay men and lesbians presented a safeguarding risk to children (but not a risk that required new legislation, given existing child protection measures). The Ashbourne–Ryder episode illustrates that while the deployment of religiously inflected objections to adult homosexual relationships required careful navigation – due to their increasing discursive displacement that we discussed in Chapter 1 – there remained significant disquiet amongst parliamentarians about the nature of non-heterosexual people's relationships with children. This disquiet remained in evidence during debates over the ACA 2002. However, in contrast to the approach of Ryder and Ashbourne in 1994, which seemingly assumed that claims regarding the harmful nature of children's exposure to homosexuals needed little explanation or defence beyond the sureties of religious morality, religious opponents of the ACA 2002 sought to offer more systematic and 'scientific' evidence of the harms of parenting by same-sex couples than that provided by scripture or popular prejudice. In the next section, we explore both the discursive strategies of religious opponents of adoption reform and the counter-discourses deployed by its supporters.

The contested moralities of same-sex parenting: the Adoption and Children Act 2002

It has been lawful for single people to become adoptive parents in England and Wales since the Adoption of Children Act 1926.[14] Prior to the ACA 2002, however, unmarried couples (and, hence, all same-sex couples) were prevented

---

13 Ibid., c.1779.
14 However, the practices of adoption agencies and the courts have not necessarily supported adoptions by non-heterosexuals. M. Owen, *Novices, Old Hands and Professionals: Adoption*

from adopting children jointly, and nor was it possible for a child to be adopted by the unmarried partner of that child's parent.[15] The ACA 2002 made changes in England and Wales[16] to allow for adoption by a 'couple'[17] (rather than a 'married couple', as required by the Adoption Act 1976) defined to include either 'a married couple' or 'two people (whether of different sexes or the same sex) living as partners in an enduring family relationship'.[18] The ACA 2002 also allows for second-parent adoptions by the partner of a child's parent.[19]

The process of formulating what would become the ACA 2002 took place at a time when religious opposition had recently played an important role in preventing the repeal of Section 28 (see Chapter 6), which characterised same-sex couples and families as 'pretended family relationships'. As such, when focused discussions of adoption law commenced with the *Prime Minister's Review: Adoption*,[20] there was little cause for optimism by supporters of gay law reform that any changes would benefit non-heterosexual couples.[21] Press accounts and discussions of parenting by same-sex couples in this period almost invariably highlighted the sharp condemnation of religious groups of efforts to legitimise 'gay adoption'.[22] The public comments of leading figures such as Jack Straw MP

   by Single People, London: British Association for Adoption and Fostering, 1999. On the position of the English courts, see: P. Britton, 'The rainbow flag, European and English law: new developments on sexuality and equality', *Indiana International & Comparative Law Review* 8, 1997–8, 261–316.
15 Since the Adoption Act 1976, a practice developed whereby one partner in a same-sex couple would be granted an adoption order, and the other partner would subsequently apply for a joint residence order which grants parental authority (but which is not equivalent to legal parenthood). See: L. Yeatman, 'Discrimination and the children of gay parents', Paper presented at the 4th World Congress of Family Law and Children's Rights, 20–23 March 2005.
16 Similar provisions were not made in Scotland until the Adoption and Children (Scotland) Act 2007. On 18 October 2012, the High Court of Justice in Northern Ireland declared that Art.14–15 of the Adoption (Northern Ireland) Order 1987, which restrict eligibility to adopt to married couples and single people, unjustifiably discriminate against unmarried partners and civil partners (*Northern Ireland Human Rights Commission, Re Judicial Review* [2012] NIQB 77). The Court of Appeal in Northern Ireland dismissed an appeal on 27 June 2013 ([2013] NICA 37) and on 22 October 2013 the Supreme Court of the United Kingdom refused permission to appeal the Court of Appeal's decision. Consequently, unmarried couples, including same-sex couples, are now eligible to be considered as adoptive parents in Northern Ireland.
17 S.50 Adoption and Children Act 2002.
18 S.144(4) Adoption and Children Act 2002.
19 S.51(2) Adoption and Children Act 2002 allows an application for an adoption order to be made by the 'partner' (as defined in S.144(7)) of the parent of the child to be adopted.
20 Performance and Innovation Unit, *Prime Minister's Review: Adoption*, 2000.
21 See J. Roll, 'The Adoption and Children's Bill', House of Commons Research Paper 01/33, 23 March 2001.
22 V. Clarke, 'What about the children? Arguments against lesbian and gay parenting', *Women Studies International Forum* 24, 2001, 555–570.

(then Home Secretary) similarly did little to suggest that a change of position was imminent. As Straw explained: 'I'm not in favour of gay couples seeking to adopt children because I question whether that is the right start in life. We should not see children as trophies.'[23]

When the Government introduced the Adoption and Children Bill 2001 into the Commons, it maintained the position of the Adoption Act 1976, which permitted only married couples to adopt jointly. This decision was defended 'on the grounds that adoption by a married couple was more likely to provide the stability and security that the child needed because married couples have made a joint, publicly recognised, legal commitment to each other'.[24] However, at Report stage, amendments were introduced to the Bill by a backbench member, David Hinchliffe MP, to permit adoption by both unmarried heterosexual and homosexual couples. The late introduction of these amendments is credited in part to pressure from children's charities. Although most Catholic adoption agencies and the Catholic Children's Society expressed strong objections,[25] the British Association of Adoption and Fostering and numerous other children's charities campaigned for the changes (the Children's Society, the major Church of England charity involved with adoption, indicated its support for widening the adoption pool to unmarried couples,[26] having previously lifted a ban on adoption

---

23 BBC Radio 4, *Today*, 4 June 1998. This was requoted by many opponents of reform: for example, Baroness Young, HL Debate, 10 June 2002, c.33. In a leaked memo written in April 2000 (just prior to the publication of the adoption review), Prime Minister Tony Blair indicated that 'the family' constituted one of the key issues on which Labour was viewed as weak 'partly due to [. . .] gay issues' and adoption was one 'entirely conventional' area where Labour should seek to build its family credentials. *BBC News*, 'Full text of Blair memo', 17 July 2000. Available online at http://news.bbc.co.uk/1/hi/uk_politics/836822.stm (accessed on 4 December 2013).
24 J. Smith, HC Special Standing Committee, 29 November 2001, c.383.
25 Concerns were expressed during the debates regarding how Catholic adoption agencies would be affected by reforms to the eligibility criteria, given their policy of discriminating against homosexuals. At the time, several supporters of reform stressed their belief that nothing about the reforms should prevent the work of Catholic agencies (for example, Baroness Gould of Potternewton, HL Debate, 16 October 2002, c.888). Discrimination against same-sex couples was prohibited by the Equality Act (Sexual Orientation) Regulations 2007, although Reg.15 provided a temporary exception (until the end of 2008) for voluntary adoption and fostering agencies that met the requirements of being an organisation relating to religion or belief (as specified by Reg.14(1)). A prohibition on discrimination by agencies under contract from a public authority was maintained in the Equality Act 2010. See Chapter 3 on religious exceptions to equality. On the impact of the Equality Act 2010 on adoption agencies, see: R. Sandberg, *Law and Religion*, Oxford: Oxford University Press, 2011, pp.125–126. At the time of writing, Catholic adoption agencies in England have closed or dropped 'Catholic' from their titles. A Leeds-based agency, Catholic Care, which sought the right to continue to discriminate against same-sex couples, failed in its legal challenge. *Catholic Care (Diocese of Leeds) v Charity Commission for England and Wales* [2012] UKUT 395 (TCC).
26 Bishop of Oxford, HL Debate, 10 June 2002, c.46.

or fostering by single gay men and lesbians in 1999[27]). Adoption charities lobbied the Government to increase the size of the adoption pool, with some groups providing anecdotal evidence that same-sex couples were willing to parent children who had proven difficult to place otherwise, such as older children or children with certain disabilities.[28] Due to this lobbying and backbench pressure, the Government allowed a free vote on the issue as a matter of 'conscience'. One Member who opposed reform expressed openly that 'many of us have been heavily lobbied [. . .] by all manner of Christian family organisations and the politically correct social worker brigade'.[29]

The issue of eligibility criteria for adoptive parents was to become 'perhaps the most politically contentious issue in the Bill'.[30] Jonathan Shaw MP stated that a full debate over reforms to the eligibility criteria was only possible because the legislation had been introduced soon after a general election: 'If an election had been pending, we would have all vied for the chance to show which party was the most family friendly.'[31] The amendment to remove the marriage requirement from the Adoption and Children Bill 2001 succeeded by a large majority in the Commons, despite opposition from many Conservatives.[32] However, the House of Lords provided much stronger resistance, amending the Bill to restrict adoption exclusively to married couples.[33] During ping pong, the Commons disagreed with the Lords' amendment after further debate.[34] When the Bill was returned to the Lords, an attempt to insist on restricting adoption to married couples failed by a narrow margin.[35]

In the sections that follow, we provide an analysis of the discourses deployed by religious opponents of reform and the counter-discourses articulated by supporters. We first examine how the overriding framing of the debate around

27 The Archbishop of Canterbury, Justin Welby, was sharply critical of this decision by the Children's Society at the time. Then a parish priest, Welby urged his parish 'to review its decision to support them'. J. Bingham, 'Archbishop of Canterbury opposed gay sex and adoption', *Daily Telegraph*, 8 March 2013.
28 For example, Lord Hunt of Kings Heath quoted evidence from the Fostering Network. HL Committee, 11 July 2002, c.251. See also L. Yeatman op. cit.; C. Ball, 'The Adoption and Children Act 2002: a critical analysis', *Adoption & Fostering* 29, 2005, 6–17.
29 T. Loughton, HC Debate, 16 May 2002, c.997.
30 Earl Howe, HL Committee, 11 July 2002, c.227.
31 HC Debate, 29 October 2001, c.707.
32 The House divided 288-133. HC Debate, 16 May 2002, Division No.244. There was a further attempt to change the wording of the amendments to grant eligibility to unmarried heterosexual couples but not same-sex couples, and although this found wide support, it was defeated by 174-301. HC Debate, 20 May 2002, Division No.246.
33 The House divided 196-162. HL Debate, 16 October 2002, Division No.1. Only the Bishops of Chelmsford and Winchester voted (both with the majority) in the division.
34 The House divided 344-145. HC Debate, 4 November 2002, Division No.345. Labour members were given a free vote, while Conservative members had a whip imposed.
35 The House divided 184-215. HL Debate, 5 November 2002, Division No.1. The five present Lords Spiritual divided 3-2 in favour of a requirement for marriage.

issues of child welfare provided opportunities for religious opponents to invoke discourses of child harm while simultaneously providing grounds for supporters of reform to characterise opposition as 'immoral'. We then explore the common 'scientific' justifications that were deployed by religious opponents of reform (in lieu of overtly religious discourse) to attempt to lay claim to the position of 'rationality'. Finally, we demonstrate the symbolic significance accorded to the debates by religious opponents, who stressed that heterosexual married couples must maintain a privileged position in law compared with unmarried couples (and especially same-sex couples). While claims about the need to preserve the unique status of marriage were actively contested, notions of the superiority of heterosexual marriage were only partially displaced in the debates. As we show, even staunch supporters of law reform relied on arguments that the married mother–father family was the preferred site for the raising of children.

Religion and child welfare

The particular character of the adoption debate in England and Wales at the turn of the twenty-first century necessitated that any struggle over adoption by unmarried (including same-sex) couples would be waged on the terrain of child welfare and rights. The Government faced a number of pressing challenges related to the supply of willing adoptive parents which contributed to setting England and Wales on an unusual trajectory of reform compared to many other European states.[36] The trajectory of England and Wales contrasts with that of Belgium, Denmark, France, the Netherlands, Norway, Portugal and Sweden, all of which provided some form of legal recognition for same-sex relationships prior to enacting legislation allowing same-sex couples to adopt. Yeatman suggests that this is partially attributable to important differences in national rhetoric and policy priorities in relation to adoption. For example, in the Netherlands (where far fewer children were taken into care and made available for adoption than the UK), the emphasis of the adoption debate was more focused on 'fulfilling a desire of childless [couples] to have children' than on 'the need to find good homes for children of unsuitable parents'.[37] In contrast, the dominant policy priority in the UK in the 1990s/2000s concerned the urgent need to widen the pool of willing adopters for the large numbers of children growing up in care.[38] Much of the debate therefore focused on the 'rights' of children to be raised in stable environments, with both opponents and supporters of reformed eligibility criteria repeatedly stressing that 'the welfare of the child'[39] must be the main priority of

---

36 L. Yeatman, op. cit.
37 L. Yeatman, op. cit., 2.
38 In the UK, most children who are available for adoption have been taken into care by the state rather than being the children of unmarried mothers (which was the dominant pattern in the middle decades of the twentieth century). See C. Ball, op. cit.; L. Yeatman, op. cit.
39 For example: Bishop of Manchester, HL Debate, 10 June 2002, c.79.

any law reform. The urgency of the calls for wide-ranging reforms to the adoption process helped produce a discursive environment in which it was possible for legislation to be enacted that permitted adoptions by same-sex couples prior to both the repeal of Section 28 (see Chapter 6) and the creation of civil partnership (see Chapter 4).[40] Adoption reform was achieved in part through the displacement and reworking of once dominant 'moral' arguments which insisted that the protection of child welfare required the shielding of children from the influence of homosexuals. We focus on the contested nature of claims regarding child welfare and their relationship to conceptions of religion and morality below.

In contrast to parliamentary debates over homosexual offences (see Chapter 1), the discourses of child harm invoked in debates over adoption reform focused less on the alleged vulnerability of children to homosexual predation (although these claims were not entirely absent) and more on assertions about the need for children to receive parenting that reflected the 'natural' gendered order. This was supported by research evidence purporting to demonstrate that parenting by same-sex couples had deleterious effects on children. A number of religious opponents stressed that their objections were consistent not only with wider public opinion but also with the UK's international treaty obligations under the 1967 European Convention on the Adoption of Children (which permitted only married people and single people to adopt).[41] One of the most common charges made during debates was that those who favoured adoption reform were seeking to privilege the desires of adults over the well-being of children. As Baroness Young argued, 'the needs of the child are not being treated as paramount in these considerations. The argument has become about the rights of adults.'[42] This alleged privileging of adult desire resonated with long-standing discourses regarding the narcissism of gay lifestyles (it recalls, for instance, Jack Straw's previously quoted insinuation that prospective gay and lesbian adoptive parents sought children as 'trophies').

The emphasis on discourses of child welfare and rights provided a means for religious opponents to articulate objections to homosexuality that were less

---

40 Provisions enabling adoption by same-sex couples in the Adoption and Children Act 2002 were not commenced until 2005.
41 For example: Baroness O'Cathain, HL Debate, 16 October 2002, c.882. As a result of the Adoption and Children Act 2002, the UK in 2005 had to partially denounce the European Convention on the Adoption of Children which stated that the 'law shall not permit a child to be adopted except by either two persons married to each other, whether they adopt simultaneously or successively, or by one person' (CETS No.058, Art.6.1). In 2011, the European Convention on the Adoption of Children (Revised) entered into force and now provides that contracting states are 'free to extend the scope of this Convention to same sex couples who are married to each other or who have entered into a registered partnership together' as well as to 'couples who are living together in a stable relationship' (CETS No.202, Art.7.2).
42 HL Debate, 10 June 2002, c.32.

obviously rooted in a straightforward disgust for, or impulse to regulate, homosexual practice. This form of discourse allowed opponents of adoption by same-sex couples to challenge the alleged prioritisation of 'equality' over the more fundamental need to promote child welfare whilst, at the same time, reinscribing notions of the superiority of the heterosexual married family form. For example, as the Bishop of Chelmsford, John Perry, argued:

> [T]here is a deep unease among many people in the public domain about the possibility that cohabiting, and especially same-sex, couples might be granted the legal right to adopt a child. Like many noble Lords, I have had more letters about this issue than any other, including hunting! The Judaeo-Christian ethic clearly emphasises that it is within the context of the committed heterosexual relationship of marriage that the paramount interests of the child are best served. All of us emphasise that it is the children who must be our paramount concern and that has emerged repeatedly throughout the debate. Children are not pawns or trophies. They need and deserve to be cared for and nurtured ideally within a home environment in which the complementarity of the sexes is expressed by a male and female parent. Having children is one of the three purposes of marriage, universally recognised by all the Christian Churches. The intention is for parents to be as committed to the nurture of their children as they are committed to each other as husband and wife. The 'pick and mix' family, now so often advocated, where any configuration of adults will do, is a clear rejection of the very Judaeo-Christian beliefs which pioneered adoption and fostering in the United Kingdom.[43]

Although Perry's argument made recourse to claims of a national 'Judaeo-Christian ethic', he did not articulate a specific religious objection to homosexuality. Rather, he sought to situate this Christian ethic at the historical root of British adoption and fostering practice, arguing that it prioritised the well-being of children in ways that calls to recognise the 'pick and mix' family failed to do. For Perry, claims about the superiority of heterosexual marriage as a context for child rearing were treated as rhetorically self-sufficient, leaving silent the assumption that same-sex adoption had potentially damaging consequences.

Perry, however, was amongst only a small number of parliamentarians who made Christianity central to the ACA 2002 debates. Many other opponents and sceptics of adoption reform avoided direct reference to religious principles in favour of citing the evidence base surrounding the impacts of parenting by same-sex couples on child development and welfare. Typical in this regard was the Bishop of Manchester, Christopher Mayfield, who eschewed any direct reference

---

43 HL Debate, 16 October 2002, c.888.

to Christian morality or heritage when questioning whether same-sex relationships could be considered of 'equal worth' as a context for raising children:

> Too often casual talk has suggested overmuch emphasis in popular minds on the interests of adults, on the alleged 'rights' and 'freedoms' of adults, rather than on the interests and needs of children [. . .] It is with the welfare of children in mind that I wish to express some concerns about the status of prospective adopters. OK, that will be unpopular and I shall wait to be told that I am prejudiced and that I am immoral. I can hear all that. I should confess that I have a vested interest, having been married for 39 years. Tut, tut [. . .] The best interests of children are served by enabling them to live and grow in a loving and stable environment. In speaking, I am conscious that today there is considerable pressure to equalise all relationships – female and female, female and male, male and male – and to regard all relationships as being of equal worth. But for all the understandable pressure to equalise relationships, I still want to ask: are the different types of relationship not only equal, but of equal worth? [. . .] [T]hat is not to say that some cohabiting couples, whatever their gender, may not offer better loving care than some married couples [. . .] So while not wanting to deny the fact that single people and people of the same gender sometimes can offer better care than those who are heterosexually married, we ought to proceed with some care when thinking about where the best care lies rather than simply going, as it were, for any option that is around.[44]

For Mayfield, while calls for legal equality were 'understandable', they did not necessitate that all relationships be accorded equal social worth. However, Mayfield's speech illustrates a growing recognition by many religious opponents of homosexuality in Parliament that the deployment of 'traditional' Christian views on marriage was vulnerable to the growing strength of 'equalities' discourses (which we discuss in greater detail in Chapter 3). This is evident in Mayfield's pre-emptory remark about the potential for his argument to be characterised as 'prejudiced' and 'immoral'.

The discourse of children's welfare and rights that pervaded the ACA 2002 debates provided grounds on which supporters of reform could advance counter-claims. Many proponents of reform challenged the moral authority of religious speakers who attempted to situate their objections within the moral framework of child welfare. This was accomplished by drawing upon the national adoption debate that had been initiated by a pressing need to find homes for children who seemed destined to spend their lives in foster homes or institutional care. In the relatively uncommon instances when supporters of reform invoked a personal religious identity, this was almost invariably done to challenge the attempted

---

44 HL Debate, 10 June 2002, cc.79–81.

monopolisation of the 'religious' and 'moral' perspective on child welfare by some religious conservatives. For example, Baroness Goudie challenged the 'so-called' Christian motivations of those who opposed adoption reform:

> The [reform of the eligibility criteria] puts the needs of children at the centre of the adoption process and I hope it will speed up the adoption system, of which I have had personal experience at every level, to provide permanent, secure and loving families for children who cannot live with their birth family. As a Christian and practising Catholic, I am appalled at the opposition to the [reforms] by CARE, the so-called Christian Action, Research and Education charity.[45]

Seeking to rework the child welfare arguments put forward by religious opponents of reform, Lord Alli issued a direct moral challenge to the forces of 'Christian intolerance' who, he argued, sought 'to hijack this debate':

> You have a moral obligation to those children in institutional care and you will have to make a case to them as to why you wish to deny them access to loving homes. If you cannot do that, or your arguments run short, I hope that this House will stand up, not for the rights of unmarried couples, gay couples, or even for the rights of married couples, but for the children who need a loving, caring home. This is indeed a debate about morality – a complex morality – but more importantly, it is about the needs of children [. . .] It is absurd that there are children without homes and couples who want to adopt them [. . .] The [reform of the eligibility criteria] has a strong sense of moral purpose and I hope that petty intolerance will not stand in its way.[46]

In attempting to 'make a case' of the kind demanded by Alli and others, opponents of adoption reform sought to marshal a range of 'evidence' about the negative impacts of same-sex parenting. We turn to this intersection between religious and scientific argument in the next section.

Religion and the 'evidence' of homosexual parenting

A key tactic of religious opponents of reform was to insist that homosexual parenting could be the subject of dispassionate and reasoned debate not rooted in 'moral bias'. Earl Howe, for example, argued:

> [O]n Report, amendments were accepted by the Government that would allow unmarried and same-sex couples to adopt jointly. We shall want to

---

45 Ibid., c.78.
46 Ibid., cc.68–69.

revisit that decision in Committee, not as part of some moral crusade in favour of marriage or against other forms of relationship, but because we believe on the evidence available that couples who are married provide the best chance of permanence and stability for adopted children. If the interests of the child are to be paramount, surely that must be an area which we examine with detachment and without moral bias.[47]

Opponents of reform drew extensively on resources made available through an organised campaign led by the Christian Institute and its supporters. These resources sought to cast 'scientific' doubt on the fitness of gay and lesbian couples to adopt children based on two related factors: first, the alleged brevity and instability of same-sex relationships, which risked introducing further insecurity into the lives of already vulnerable children; and, second, the long-term impact of same-sex parenting on children, including their future prospects, relationships with other children and processes of gender identity formation. Parliamentarians often cited statistics provided in reports and press releases prepared by the Christian Institute, including Patricia Morgan's *Children as Trophies? Examining the Evidence of Same-Sex Parenting*.[48] Morgan's report, which had been circulated amongst and obviously read by many opponents of reformed eligibility criteria, made a number of claims regarding the characteristics of 'homosexual culture' and its potential influences on children. Morgan reviewed research undertaken on the nature of gay and lesbian families, dismissing as statistically unrepresentative ethnographic and longitudinal studies based on interview data that purported to show children prospering in gay and lesbian households. Morgan's report particularly sought to discredit research by Susan Golombok and colleagues that argued that same-sex parenting is not detrimental to children's development.[49]

Morgan insisted that the only type of evidence relevant to adoption reform was from studies in which the sexual orientation of parents was analysed as a 'causal' variable within scientifically controlled designs.[50] This echoed the rhetoric expressed by the Christian Institute in its memorandum to Parliament, which argued that the evidential standard necessary to allow adoption by same-sex parents was 'clinical research' that showed no adverse affects on children.[51] Given that no such clinical studies of adoption and same-sex parenting existed, the case for changing the law, in Morgan's view, could not be safely made. The report

---

47 Earl Howe, HL Debate, 10 June 2002, c.105.
48 P. Morgan, *Children as Trophies? Examining the Evidence of Same-Sex Parenting*, Newcastle-upon-Tyne: The Christian Institute, 2002.
49 For example: S. Golombok and F. Tasker, 'Children in lesbian and gay families: theories and evidence', *Annual Review of Sex Research* 5, 1994, 73–100; S. Golombok and F. Tasker, 'Do parents influence the sexual orientation of their children? Findings from a longitudinal study of lesbian families', *Developmental Psychology* 32, 1996, 3–11.
50 P. Morgan, op. cit., p.50.

recited familiar claims about the links between homosexuality and paedophilia, while also drawing on anecdotal evidence to characterise gay and lesbian cultures as pervaded by alleged 'paedophobia', or a fear of children: 'Most male homosexuals have little interest in children [and] the lesbian community is not supportive of mothers.'[52] Thus, in Morgan's analysis, those gay men and lesbians who sought to adopt were unlikely to make successful parents.

The data compiled by Morgan and the Christian Institute were referenced repeatedly by opponents of reforming the eligibility criteria. Andrew Selous MP, a member of the Conservative Christian Fellowship, for example, was one of many opponents of reform to cite statistics that featured prominently in the Morgan report:

> I wholly abhor any form of homophobia; I want no truck with that. However, a Department of Health-funded study found that the average length of a close homosexual relationship is only 21 months. Is not that deeply worrying as regards the lifetime of commitment needed for a damaged child?[53]

Lord Brennan similarly attempted to characterise Christian opposition to reform as motivated by concerns based on the evidence about the impacts of gay parenting rather than on religious intolerance.[54] Furthermore, Brennan argued that those supporting reform, and not those opposing it, were motivated by 'sentiment' and irrationality:

> I am a Christian. If I disagree, I hope that that does not make me an intolerant Christian. If I think that it is too soon, if ever, to allow gay couples to adopt, I hope that my carefully considered and honestly held views will be respected in the same measure as I respect a contrary view, even if I disagree with it [. . .] What is the evidence, not simply from this country but from any other, that a child brought up by a same sex couple will not be adversely affected or, alternatively, will be beneficially affected? I know of no

---

51 The Christian Institute, Memorandum submitted to the Special Standing Committee on the Adoption and Children Bill, 28 November 2001.
52 P. Morgan, op. cit., pp.109–110.
53 HC Debate, 4 November 2002, c.34. The statistic Selous cites is based on the Morgan report's interpretation of the following study: F.C.I. Hickson, P.M. Davies, A.J. Hunt, P. Weatherburn, T.J. McManus and A.P.M. Coxon, 'Gay men as victims of nonconsensual sex', *Archives of Sexual Behaviour* 23, 1994, 281–294. The research was funded by the Medical Research Council and the Department of Health. The statistic was challenged by several speakers, who provided alternative readings of the research and questioned its methods and sample: for example, E. Harris, HC Debate, 4 November 2002, cc.56–57.
54 See also Lord Astor of Hever's declaration in the same debate that Christian opposition to reform does not make one an 'intolerant Christian'. HL Debate, 10 June 2002, c.73.

such evidence. I have carefully read the paper by Dr Golombok. It is only a year or two old. The study cohort was very small and no responsible commentator could regard it as a definitive base for saying that there is no effect. We simply do not know [. . .] I respect and have voted in this House for the rights of homosexuals,[55] but I refuse to vote for a principle which affects children on the basis of any sentiment about those rights.[56]

A number of religious opponents of reform acknowledged that in certain instances same-sex couples could make excellent parents,[57] but argued that the balance of 'statistical evidence' suggested that adoption by a gay couple was likely to be *worse* for a child's welfare than being raised in institutional or foster care. As the Bishop of Winchester, Michael Scott-Joynt, argued:

> The statistical evidence is only too strong that, notwithstanding the rates of marriage breakdown, heterosexual relationships short of marriage are much less secure and much more prone to dissolution than are marriages. Same-sex relationships are more so still [. . .] My reading of the slight research evidence that exists about the effects on children of parenting by same-sex couples and letters that I have received from people with first-hand experience of those effects, as parents or as social workers and other specialists, make me doubt the regularly made claim that children are unlikely to suffer damage if they are brought up by a same-sex couple. Indeed, the probabilities seem to me to lie the other way.[58]

Given the intense intermingling of moral-religious arguments and statistical evidence that characterised opposition to adoption reform, supporters of reform devoted considerable time to both offering alternative interpretations of the available 'evidence' and challenging the logic that social scientific studies could provide a fair basis on which to make categorical distinctions about eligibility to adopt. Jacqui Smith MP, who had previously defended the Government's unwillingness to support reform, later decried how the ACA 2002 debate was being dominated by 'dogma backed up by dodgy statistics'.[59] Lord Adebowale criticised the use of statistical 'risk management' as a basis for making distinctions

---

55 Lord Brennan voted with the minority to reject an amendment to the Sexual Offences (Amendment) Bill 2000 that sought to maintain a higher 'age of consent' for acts of buggery. HL Committee, 13 November 2000, Division No.1. See Chapter 1 for a discussion.
56 Lord Brennan, HL Debate, 10 June 2002, cc.97–98.
57 For example, the Bishop of Manchester expressed with reluctance that adoption by a same-sex couple should be permissible as a last resort. HL Debate, 10 June 2002, cc.79–82.
58 HL Debate, 16 October 2002, cc.873–874.
59 HC Debate, 4 November 2002, c.96

about adoption eligibility between classes of people, noting that 'on the basis of the statistics on marriage and sustained partnerships [. . .] poor people would not be allowed to adopt'.[60] The Bishop of Oxford, Richard Harries, rejected the statistical interpretations of several of his fellow Lords Spiritual, instead quoting favourably from the same body of research that was lambasted by the Christian Institute and its supporters.[61] Harries, while affirming that the Church of England was 'fully committed to marriage', also questioned 'whether we really support the institution of marriage by making adoption more difficult for unmarried couples'.[62] The need to protect marriage, however, was central to arguments used by some religious opponents of reform for whom defending the symbolic status of heterosexual marriage became seemingly more important than the welfare of individual children in need of adoption.

Religion and the symbolic politics of marriage

Many opponents characterised the ACA 2002 reforms as a conscious attempt to diminish heterosexual marriage as a social institution. As the Bishop of Winchester, Michael Scott-Joynt, argued:

> I continue to believe that a responsibility lies on government to sustain the unique, particular position of marriage as the fundamental reference point for family life and adult relationships and to withstand the pressure to equate other couple relationships with it. I am in no doubt that the effect of this [reform of the eligibility criteria] in its present form will be to contribute to the undermining of marriage.[63]

Additionally, opponents asserted that the reforms would provide an indirect mechanism for same-sex relationships to gain recognition in law. The ACA 2002 debates took place at a time when discussions about the introduction of a 'partnership registration scheme'[64] were preliminary and far from certain (for a discussion, see Chapter 4). Such was the concern that the ACA 2002 would give legal standing to same-sex relationships that the explanatory notes were written to clarify that the definition of 'couple' provided in the ACA 2002[65] 'applies solely

---

60 HL Committee, 11 July 2002 c.245.
61 HL Debate, 10 June 2002, cc.47–48. The quotation appears in the longitudinal study: S. Golombok, 'New families, old values: considerations regarding the welfare of the child', 1998. Available online at http://claradoc.gpa.free.fr/doc/191.pdf (accessed on 4 December 2013).
62 HL Debate, 10 June 2002, c.47.
63 HL Debate, 16 October 2002, c.873.
64 For example: Lord Hunt of Kings Heath, HL Debate, 16 October 2002, c.917.
65 S.144(4) Adoption and Children Act 2002.

for the purposes of this act'.[66] This assurance did little to appease opponents who viewed the debates as an opportunity to engage in a form of symbolic politics regarding the nature of marriage and family in British society.

Opponents of adoption reform acknowledged that their efforts to block it, even if successful, would do nothing to change the fact that many children would be adopted into and raised in the households of same-sex couples (only potentially maintaining a disincentive for those couples who would not pursue adoption unless they were legal equals in the process). The importance of the social symbolism of the reform was therefore frequently stressed as much as any practical consequences for children. For example, the Bishop of Manchester, Christopher Mayfield, concluded his lengthy intervention in the ACA 2002 debates by offering limited support for adoption by same-sex couples in rare circumstances while stressing that the law must explicitly ascribe a preferred social status to heterosexual marriage:[67]

> I recognise that different types of relationship can satisfy different adult needs. I have friends who are lesbian and homosexual. Individual adults find a way of relating and not relating to other adults. Such differences are to be understood and welcomed. But I am afraid that I remain convinced [. . .] that if children are to have the best chance of thriving – I stress my use of the word 'best' rather than 'only' – then they need the security of loving and stable relationships that are publicly and legally recognised by the state, and that offer both female and male role models [. . .] I believe that Her Majesty's Government have a continuing duty to support the notion that, while different kinds of relationships can be of value to the individuals involved in them, offering friendship, support and so forth, we should continue to accord marriage a special status among all the other important and valuable relationships that exist. Normally a married couple should be the first choice of context in which to place a child for adoption. However, this is not to say that ultimately it would be inappropriate to place people in need of love and care with those who are not married [. . .] or may be couples of the same gender.[68]

Others went further than Mayfield, arguing that the principle of denying joint adoption to same-sex couples should apply even in situations when it was clear that the child's best interests would be served by such an adoption. This is well illustrated in an exchange between Julian Brazier MP (a prominent member of the Conservative Christian Fellowship) and Jonathan Shaw MP:

---

66 Adoption and Children Act 2002, *Explanatory Notes*, § 344.
67 His speech, given much of its negative tone, was misinterpreted by a number of other parliamentarians to be decisively against any reform of the eligibility criteria, but a close reading reveals otherwise. He ultimately did not vote in the relevant divisions.
68 HL Debate, 10 June 2002, c.81.

> Jonathan Shaw: Let us take a situation in which two gay men were fostering a child who had all kinds of different challenges, and it was felt that the best people to look after that child for the rest of its life were those two individuals. Would the hon. Gentleman deny that child the opportunity to be adopted by those two people?
> Julian Brazier: I am afraid that on the basis of the arguments that I have put forward, my answer would be yes. I do not, however, see any reason why one of those people should not adopt the child. I should have made it clear when I answered the question of my hon. Friend the Member for Buckingham earlier that my first choice for adoption would always be a married couple. I accept the principle of the occasional gay adoption, but only when there is no one else available.[69]

Brazier voiced no specific objection to one partner in a same-sex couple adopting a child, but he insisted that the adopter's partner should not be given the legal status of 'parent' despite the disadvantages for both the couple and the child.[70]

The ACA 2002 debates served to expose the prevalence of heteronormative understandings of marriage and family even amongst many supporters of adoption by same-sex couples. A number of supporters of the reforms, for example, stressed that they continued to view marriage as 'special' and deserving priority in law, public policy and social esteem. Speaking for the Government, Lord Hunt of Kings Heath stressed that the Government still viewed 'marriage' as the best arrangement for child rearing:

> Noble Lords have raised the question of and strength of marriage. They will know that the Government support the concept of marriage, both politically and financially. They recognise that marriage is the surest foundation for raising children and that it remains the choice of the majority of people in the country. But they also recognise that not all children are born to parents who are married. We must face up to the changing nature of this country and make our dispositions accordingly.[71]

Lord Alli, the first 'out' gay Peer in Parliament and also a self-identified Muslim,[72] similarly stated his belief that (heterosexual) married couples could legitimately be prioritised over other prospective adopters:

---

69 HC Debate, 4 November 2002, c.77.
70 As noted previously, in these situations it had been common for the other partner to apply for a joint residence order, which confers parental responsibility. However, as explained by Yeatman, these orders have potentially significant disadvantages compared with adoption orders. They can be terminated with comparative ease, and 'the order does not carry with it any responsibility for maintenance of a child on the breakdown of a relationship nor for inheritance under intestacy rules'. L. Yeatman, op. cit., 4.
71 HL Debate, 10 June 2002, c.108.
72 Lord Alli did not, however, invoke this identity explicitly in these debates, although he would do so in subsequent debates over homosexual law reform.

> What is best for those children? I ask those who oppose the extension of adoption of children to unmarried couples to think again. I do not care if this House puts unmarried couples and same-sex couples to the back of the adoption queue. Let married couples have priority, if that is what your Lordships want. But we must face reality, because there is no adoption queue. There is no queue of couples waiting to adopt these children. Until there is, it is simply immoral – and I choose my words carefully – that these children are being brought up in an institution when there are loving couples willing to adopt them.[73]

Alli was subsequently quoted selectively several times by religious opponents of reform as evidence of broad support for the principle that heterosexual marriage should remain privileged in adoption law.

The intensity of the pro-marriage discourse in Parliament produced an unusual discursive shift amongst a small number of parliamentarians with well-known conservative moral views. These parliamentarians felt compelled to challenge the seeming willingness to prioritise the symbolic defence of marriage over child welfare. For example, Lady Saltoun of Abernethy – who had previously opposed both the repeal of Section 28 and equalisation of the age of consent, and would subsequently speak against same-sex marriage – argued that although adoption by homosexual couples is not 'in any way the optimum',[74] she would support legislation even with the reformed eligibility criteria because its overall aim was 'not about propping up the institution of marriage, but about getting these wretched children out of care and into families'.[75]

Although attempts to block the reform of the eligibility criteria ultimately failed, the nature of the moral-religious rhetoric which characterised the debates raised concerns for some Conservative Party members who feared that the party's complicity with (and active promulgation of) this rhetoric adversely affected public perceptions of it.[76] Robert Key MP retrospectively explained his decision to defy the Tory three-line whip on a key Commons vote in terms of the need to:

> be quite clear that we are not a European-style Christian Democrat Party with party lines on moral and religious issues; nor are we a US-style

---

73 HL Debate, 10 June 2002, c.68. In a subsequent debate, Lord Alli also quoted favourably from comments by Lady Saltoun of Abernethy: 'Well, something funny happened to me in Grand Committee. I found myself in agreement with the noble Lady [...] "I do not believe that adoption by an unmarried couple or a homosexual couple is in any way the optimum. However, the alternative to adoption in the case of a child who has been in care is so infinitely worse than adoption into a home which is less than ideal that I believe that the risk is justified."' HL Debate, 16 October 2002, cc.874–875.
74 HL Committee, 11 July 2002, c.232.
75 Ibid., c.238.
76 See also: M. McManus, *Tory Pride and Prejudice: The Conservative Party and Homosexual Law Reform*, London: Biteback Publishing, 2011.

Republican Party with deep dependence on some branches of Christianity. The Conservative Party is a secular party. And I am a Christian who on issues such as adoption will exercise my judgment.[77]

This intervention notwithstanding, the Conservative Party's relationship with 'moral and religious issues' was far from settled at the time the ACA 2002 was enacted. Nor did religious opposition (certainly not limited to the Conservative Party) to further reforms in relation to same-sex parenting dissipate. Many of the discourses deployed during the ACA 2002 debates regarding child welfare would be reactivated to oppose reforms made by the HFEA 2008. However, in the HFEA 2008 debates, which we examine below, there was a greatly enhanced emphasis on how homosexual law reform had become emblematic of the marginalisation of religion in British society.

The marginalisation of religion? The Human Fertilisation and Embryology Act 2008

Although there had been many prior instances of same-sex couples accessing fertility services in the UK, the HFEA 2008 addressed what many considered to be discriminatory provisions that impeded the ability of same-sex couples to access fertility services on an equal basis with opposite-sex couples or to be jointly recognised as parents of children from donated gametes or embryos. The HFEA 2008 was designed to amend the legal framework established by the Human Fertilisation and Embryology Act (HFEA) 1990, which regulates the use of embryos created outside of a woman's body, the use of donated gametes and the storage of gametes. The need for changes to the HFEA 1990 was recognised in light of both new scientific developments and the rapidly changing social and legal context of the UK – including the increased acceptance of 'non-traditional' family forms and the passage of sexual orientation equalities legislation (see Chapter 3). Interest by religious groups in what would become the HFEA 2008 was intense given that the proposed amendments involved issues that were understood to have far-reaching religious and ethical implications. These included the use of embryos for research purposes, the creation of human admixed embryos (embryos containing both human and animal matter), the selection of embryos to create 'saviour siblings' (children conceived to provide stem cells to sick older siblings), the upper time limit at which women could legally seek abortions, and reforms intended to benefit same-sex couples who sought access to fertility services regulated by the legislation.[78]

---

77 R. Key, 'Why I rebelled', *BBC News*, 21 February 2003. Available online at http://news.bbc.co.uk/1/hi/uk_politics/2409987.stm (accessed on 4 December 2013).
78 See: S. Kettell, 'Did secularism win out? The debate over the Human Fertilisation and Embryology Bill', *Political Quarterly* 80, 2009, 67–75.

The provisions of the HFEA 2008 most directly related to same-sex couples involved two specific types of reforms. First, the HFEA 2008 removed a condition in the *licensing provisions* of the HFEA 1990 that required clinicians, before providing treatment, to consider the child's 'need [. . .] for a father' as part of an assessment of the welfare of the planned child and any other children who would be affected by the birth. The HFEA 2008 replaced this with a gender-neutral requirement to consider 'the need [. . .] for supportive parenting'.[79] The HFEA 1990 had never directly prevented female couples from accessing fertility services (although an attempt led by Lady Saltoun of Abernethy to criminalise the implantation of an embryo in any unmarried woman had failed in the Lords by a single vote[80]). Female couples often sought to fulfil the licensing condition by assuring service providers that a nominated male relative or friend would serve as an active role model in the life of the child (although cases of fertility services being refused to female couples as a result of the licensing provision were also cited during debates).[81] Even though many female couples had successfully

---

79 S.14(2)(b) Human Fertilisation and Embryology Act 2008. This amends S.13(5) of the Human Fertilisation and Embryology Act 1990 which on enactment read: 'A woman shall not be provided with treatment services unless account has been taken of the welfare of any child who may be born as a result of the treatment (including the need of that child for a father), and of any other child who may be affected by the birth.' A fuller history of the debates over S.13(5) Human Fertilisation and Embryology Act 1990 can be found in: R. Lee and D. Morgan, *Human Fertilisation and Embryology: Regulating the Reproductive Revolution*, London: Blackstone, 2001. S.13(5) Human Fertilisation and Embryology Act 1990 was also subjected to extensive socio-legal analysis after its enactment. For example, see: J. McCandless and S. Sheldon, '"No father required"? The welfare assessment in the Human Fertilisation and Embryology Act 2008, *Feminist Legal Studies* 18, 2010, 201–225.

80 The amendment sought to criminalise 'placing an embryo in an unmarried woman'. It failed by a vote of 60-61 in the House of Lords. HL Committee, 6 February 1990, Division No.1. In the words of its author, Lady Saltoun of Abernethy, the amendment was designed 'to prohibit the provision of AID [artificial insemination from donor] to unmarried women, lesbian couples or unmarried couples' (c.788). Moral anxieties about the use of fertility treatment by unmarried women were earlier clearly evident in the 1984 report of a Committee of Inquiry led by Mary Warnock. M. Warnock, *Report of the Committee of Inquiry into Human Fertilisation and Embryology*, London: HMSO, 1984.

81 The extent to which the licensing condition presented a significant barrier as opposed to merely a psychological disincentive was in fact a contested point during the debates. Alan Johnson MP, then Secretary of State for Health, asserted that the change was primarily so that lesbian couples would not feel that the law was treating them unequally: 'the need for a father has never adversely affected any gay or lesbian couple going through the process' (HC Debate, 12 May 2008, c.1071). Others challenged this claim, including most vocally Evan Harris MP, who provided evidence (HC Debate, 12 May 2008, c.1071) that eligibility criteria used in the National Health Service (NHS) were being influenced by the licensing condition (although the deletion of 'the need for a father' would not have directly compelled the NHS to change its own eligibility criteria). He also introduced correspondence from fertility and family lawyer Natalie Gamble in which she discussed instances of her clients being refused treatment due to the licensing provisions (HC Debate, 20 May

accessed services, the licensing provision was viewed by some as producing potential psychological barriers for female couples who wished to pursue fertility services, as well as being symbolically discriminatory and insulting to the women involved in the process. The Government also feared that lesbian couples wary of potential discrimination would opt to use unregulated means of securing sperm and insemination with incumbent health risks.[82] The second pertinent reform created by the HFEA 2008 relates to the *status provisions* which now 'recognises same-sex couples as legal parents of children conceived through the use of donated sperm, eggs or embryos' and allows same-sex couples to be named as the parents on the birth certificates of children conceived through assisted means.[83] These provisions therefore had practical significance for male couples entering into surrogacy arrangements as well as female couples.

Religious opposition to the Human Fertilisation and Embryology Act 2008

The reforms to both the licensing provisions and the status provisions were subject to organised campaigns of religious opposition both inside and outside Parliament (although the licensing provisions had considerably more time devoted to debate than the status provisions).[84] Religious discourse in Parliament regarding the reforms created by the HFEA 2008 should be viewed as part of a much longer

---

2008, c.202). In 2013, the National Institute for Health and Care Excellence (NICE) issued guidance recommending that female couples be offered access to fertility services. National Institute for Health and Care Excellence, *Fertility: Assessment and Treatment for People with Fertility Problems*, NICE Clinical Guidance 156, February 2013.

82 For a discussion, see: J. McCandless and S. Sheldon, op. cit.

83 E. White, 'Human Fertilisation and Embryology Bill: what happened?', House of Commons Library, Standard Note SN/SC/4886, 11 November 2008. For female couples, the female partner of the gestational mother can now be named as the other 'parent' on a birth certificate when one of the couple conceives through insemination by a donor or in-vitro fertilisation (S.42 Human Fertilisation and Embryology Act 2008 makes provision for women in civil partnerships, and S.43 for female couples who are not civil partners). These provisions were commenced on 6 April 2009. In the case of male couples, where one partner provided gametes to a surrogate, the couple can apply for a parental order, after which (if granted) a new birth certificate listing both men as parents will be issued (S.54 Human Fertilisation and Embryology Act 2008). This change came into effect on 6 April 2010. For a broader discussion of the legal significance of the changes to the status provisions, see: J. McCandless and S. Sheldon, 'The Human Fertilisation and Embryology Act (2008) and the tenacity of the sexual family form', *The Modern Law Review* 73, 2010, 175–207.

84 This was in large part due to the extensive number of issues covered in the Human Fertilisation and Embryology Bill. Complaint was rife throughout the debates that the timetable was too rushed and that certain issues were not properly debated, including the status provisions.

narrative arc extending back to the earliest debates in Parliament about the use of reproductive technologies. Debate in Parliament in 1984 over the 'Warnock Report'[85] had obvious religious overtones, and unease about the potential for reproductive technologies to be exploited by homosexuals was a clear feature of the multifaceted anxieties that were expressed about the new familial possibilities engendered by science. In the debates of this period, parliamentarians drew a distinction between adoption (constructed as a noble enterprise) and the use of reproductive technologies (often constructed as selfish, particularly when sought by unmarried couples) and this was underpinned with the claim that 'children are God-given, not man-made'.[86] This conceptual distinction was similarly prominent in debates over the (narrowly defeated) effort to criminalise implantation of an embryo in any unmarried woman in 1990:

> [T]he Committee may consider that lesbian couples should not be eligible to receive AID or in vitro fertilisation services. Some people argue that since it is legal, and often desirable, for single women, and even men, to adopt children, it should also be legal for them to have AID, but there is a great difference between placing a child who already exists with a single person when that child would otherwise be brought up in an institution, and deliberately creating a child to be brought up in circumstances which must be less than ideal.[87]

Given these and other long-standing religious concerns about reproductive technologies, when the Government in 2007 drafted its proposed amendments to the HFEA 1990 it consulted closely with religious groups and sought their views in multiple ways. This included a special Evening Forum where invited 'faith groups or others with particular ethical perspectives' were able to provide evidence that was subsequently included in the report of the Joint Committee on the draft of the legislation.[88] Representatives of religious groups in attendance were exclusively Christian, although invitations had been extended to the Muslim Council, the Muslim Doctors and Dentists Association, and the Office of the Chief Rabbi. Mounting religious opposition to reform was widely noted in the media, with, for example, the *Daily Telegraph* running the headline 'Christian fundamentalists fighting spiritual battle in Parliament' (although religious opposition was not limited to fundamentalist Christian groups).[89] Concerted opposition to

---

85   M. Warnock, op. cit.
86   J. Knight, HC Debate, 23 November 1984, c.566.
87   Lady Saltoun of Abernethy, HL Committee, 6 February 1990, c.788.
88   Joint Committee on the Human Tissue and Embryos (Draft) Bill, *Human Tissue and Embryos (Draft) Bill, Volume I: Report*, 1 August 2007, pp.92–104. The Bill would later be retitled the Human Fertilisation and Embryology Bill to make its connection to the HFEA 1990 more explicit.
89   D. Modell, 'Christian fundamentalists fighting spiritual battle in Parliament', *Daily Telegraph*, 17 May 2008.

the reforms involved several familiar organisational actors including CARE and the Christian Institute. A number of Conservative MPs who had sought to partially distance themselves from religious conservatism in the years after the ACA 2002 – by, for example, voting for reforms including the Civil Partnership Act 2004 and the Equality Act (Sexual Orientation) Regulations 2007 – realigned themselves with religious efforts to block the removal of barriers to parenting faced by same-sex couples. For example, Iain Duncan Smith MP (and David Smith MP, Labour) introduced an amendment that sought to retain the 'need for a father' in the licensing provision with the addition of 'and a mother' but the amendment failed on a free vote despite overwhelming Conservative support.[90]

Opposition from the Church of England was more systematic and united in parliamentary debate than during the passage of the ACA 2002. Whereas Baroness Blatch could remark in debates over the ACA 2002 that 'we can all select our favourite bishop to make our case'[91] – in recognition of the internal divisions amongst the Lords Spiritual – the Bishops' Bench was unified during debates over licensing and status provisions. In a key division in the Lords, five bishops supported an unsuccessful attempt to require service providers to consider the need for 'support by a father and mother' before providing fertility services (the margin of defeat in the Lords was larger than in divisions over adoption reform in 2002).[92] The Archbishop of York, John Sentamu, made a lengthy and much-referenced intervention in the debates during which he devoted his attention almost exclusively to defending the licensing provision in the HFEA 1990 while largely bypassing issues of abortion, human–animal hybrid embryos, and the selection of embryos to produce saviour siblings (issues which were attributed substantial religious significance by others). The Church of England's Mission and Public Affairs Council made a written submission opposing the changes to the licensing provisions, as did the Catholic Bishops' Conference of England and Wales, the Church and Society Council of the Church of Scotland, the Free Church of Scotland and the Brethren Christian Fellowship.[93]

---

90 The House divided 217-292. HC Debate, 20 May 2008, Division No.197. Only 12 of 156 Conservative MPs opposed the amendment. In the same debate, an amendment failed that sought to amend the licensing provision to require consideration of 'supportive parenting and a father or male role model'. The House divided 222-290. HC Debate, 20 May 2008, Division No.198.
91 HL Debate, 5 November 2002, c.599.
92 HL Debate, 21 January 2008, Division No.3. The House divided 93-165, with the Archbishop of York and the Bishops of Chester, Manchester, St Albans, and Winchester voting with the contents. The amendment was tabled by Baroness Deech, Lady O'Cathain and Lord Lloyd of Berwick.
93 Joint Committee on the Human Tissue and Embryos (Draft) Bill, *Human Tissue and Embryos (Draft) Bill, Volume II: Evidence*, 8 August 2007, The Stationery Office. In contrast to debates over same-sex marriage (see Chapter 4), no formal submissions were made by 'liberal' religious groups such as the Quakers or Unitarians.

The symbolism of fatherhood and the 'truth' of genetic heritage

Similar to the debates over the ACA 2002, opponents expressed concerns about child welfare and the symbolic significance of the proposed reforms. Mirroring discourse used during the ACA 2002 debates, opponents stressed that a concern for 'equality' must not supersede the more pressing imperative to act in the best interests of children. As Baroness Deech, former chair of the Human Fertilisation and Embryology Authority, argued:

> The [reforms] will ensure non-discrimination between family units and persons, at the expense, it could be argued, of the welfare of the child. After all, British law still rightly discriminates against underage, polygamous and incestuous unions, so why should the family welfare of a child not be considered before the mother undergoes IVF?[94]

In a similar fashion to the ACA 2002 debates, statistics and research evidence were deployed extensively regarding the long-term impacts of same-sex parenting for children. However, in recognition that the HFEA 1990 licensing provision did not directly prevent lesbian couples from accessing fertility services (and thus had limited practical significance for child welfare), arguments for preserving the language of fatherhood in the provision emphasised its overriding 'symbolic value'. As Gary Streeter MP stressed, '[a]lthough the practical implications [of reform] are slight [. . .] we must accept that [. . .] its symbolic magnitude should not be underestimated'.[95] To remove the licensing requirement relating to fathers would, Iain Duncan Smith MP argued, 'send a powerful signal to everyone involved that fathers no longer matter'.[96] To make such a change would be detrimental, Baroness Deech argued, 'at a time when many of them feel undermined as providers and parents, contrary to government policy in the field'.[97] The Bishop of St Albans, Christopher Herbert, similarly stressed the law's symbolic function:

> What does the omission [of language regarding the importance of fathers] signal? I travel quite often by public transport. Like the rest of your Lordships, I am bombarded with announcements. A man with a megaphone tells me that I am to keep my belongings with me at all times and that I must not smoke. I wonder what would happen if an announcement came across every station in London which said, 'In the interests of equality, people are reminded that children do not necessarily need fathers'.[98]

---

94 HL Debate, 8 November 2007, cc.211–212.
95 HC Debate, 12 May 2008, c.1109.
96 Ibid., c.1079.
97 HL Debate, 19 November 2007, c.674.
98 HL Debate, 21 January 2008, cc.70–71.

Although efforts to retain the reference to the need for fathers in the licensing provisions failed, the intensity of the family values rhetoric from religious opponents (combined with negative coverage in the right-wing press over the effort 'to sideline Dads'[99]) impelled the Government to modify its approach to reform. Originally, the Government sought simply to repeal the language requiring consideration of the need for a father from the HFEA 1990. At Report stage in the Lords – largely in response to religious opposition and as a gesture towards recognising the importance of 'family' – the Government inserted a requirement to consider the 'need [. . .] for supportive parenting' as an aspect of child welfare.[100]

Despite the limited time given over to debate on the status provisions, a number of religious opponents also intervened to object to changes affecting the identification of parents on birth certificates.[101] It was argued that to not include the genetic father on the birth certificate was 'grotesque and unpleasant'.[102] Or, as the Bishop of Newcastle, Martin Wharton, argued in milder terms: 'to have two women, or, indeed for that matter, two men on a birth certificate as parents is a very odd way to put things'.[103] Although the national registration of births only commenced in 1837, the birth certificate was constructed by many opponents of reform as a document preserving an incontestable 'truth' that would be undermined if it named same-sex parents: 'If the well-being of the child is a key principle, and if truthfulness is a key principle, then above all we have to be honest'.[104] Naming same-sex couples on birth certificates, it was argued, would promote sexual orientation equality at the expense of denying children knowledge of their 'origins' and infringing their rights.[105] As the Archbishop of York, John

---

99 The *Sun*, 'Fear over law to sideline Dads', 19 May 2008.
100 S.14(2)(b) Human Fertilisation and Embryology Act 2008.
101 Issues related to the status provisions did, however, feature prominently in written evidence provided to Parliament. For example, see: Joint Committee on the Human Tissue and Embryos (Draft) Bill, op. cit.
102 Lord Elton, HL Debate, 21 November 2007, c.842.
103 HL Debate, 21 November 2007, c.841.
104 Bishop of Newcastle, HL Debate, 21 November 2007, c.841.
105 Issues concerning a child's right to know its genetic heritage, of course, do not arise solely, or even primarily, in the context of children of same-sex couples. Unmarried women can choose to omit the name of the father when registering a birth, with children having no means of learning the identity of their genetic father. Many married women name their husbands on the birth certificates of children fathered by other men, without the child or husband ever knowing. In cases where couples have used donated sperm obtained through licensed channels, children can request to learn the identity of the donor when they reach age 16 years. This process is set out in the Human Fertilisation and Embryology Authority (Disclosure of Donor Information) Regulations 2004. Additionally, claims that birth certificates are repositories of truth miss the complex issues related to the attribution of motherhood, whereby motherhood is attributed in UK law to gestational mothers even if the egg is donated from another woman. For a discussion of gestational versus genetic motherhood in surrogacy, see: J. McCandless and S. Sheldon, 'The Human Fertilisation and Embryology Act (2008) and the tenacity of the sexual family form', op. cit.

Sentamu, postulated: 'Supposing that a child wants to know, "Who is my dad?", and is told "Don't ask such questions. It is discriminatory. We are your supporting parents." A child will not be satisfied. A child will want to know.'[106]

Equalities and the morality of conception by assisted means

During debates over the ACA 2002, supporters of adoption reform actively contested arguments about the potential harms of adoption by same-sex couples by mobilising representations of the moral worthiness of same-sex couples who sought to adopt hard-to-place children. In contrast, arguments in favour of the reformed licensing and status provisions of the HFEA 2008 rested more narrowly on claims for equality and fairness to prospective gay and lesbian parents who, it was argued, were 'normal' people seeking the same access to services as heterosexual couples.[107] For example, Lord Darzi of Denham, speaking for the Government, justified the reforms as necessary for consistency 'with the wider government policy of promoting equality'.[108] Religious opponents sought to challenge this equality discourse by evoking tropes about the narcissistic and self-indulgent nature of lesbians and gay men who would seek to produce children through the use of reproductive technologies. Same-sex couples were represented as seeking to privilege their own desires at the expense of children who would potentially be denied the truth of their origins or not provided with parenting that evinced 'gender complementarity'. The Church of England's Mission and Public Affairs Council asserted that the calculus of children's rights differed from the adoption debate because:

> [b]ringing the care of an adoptive home to a needy child is a wholly different circumstance to deciding in advance to use IVF technology to bring into the world a child who will, 'by design', never have a father (or mother, in the case [of] gay men commissioning a child by IVF surrogacy) [...] It sends the signal that everyone has a right to a child and this 'right' over-rules consideration of that child's welfare. If discrimination is the issue here, we feel the greater discrimination is in ensuring that a child will never have any

---

106 There is evidence that lesbian mothers are more likely to share information about the identity of the father than heterosexual single mothers: see J. McCandless and S. Sheldon, '"No father required"? The welfare assessment in the Human Fertilisation and Embryology Act 2008', op. cit.
107 McCandless and Sheldon suggest that the government portrayed 'equality' issues as secondary to the health issues. J. McCandless and S. Sheldon, '"No father required"? The welfare assessment in the Human Fertilisation and Embryology Act 2008', op. cit., p.208. Although this was perhaps evident in discussions before the formal introduction of the Bill, equality issues were foregrounded by a large number of speakers on both sides of the debate and, in our view, were far from secondary.
108 HL Debate, 21 January 2008, c.55.

chance of knowing a father, rather than in saying that gay couples have an automatic right to have a child. We consider that the child's right not to be deliberately deprived of having a father is greater than any right of a gay couple to commission a child by IVF. The prior protection in law should be afforded to those with the greater vulnerability – the children yet to be born.[109]

The desire of same-sex couples for children was portrayed as an extension of consumption-orientated gay lifestyles that privileged the self over other considerations. The Archbishop of York, John Sentamu, warned against this in a lengthy intervention concerning the 'individualistic consumerism' of the 'wannabe parent':

> There is an unhealthy theme of rampant indifference at the heart of [these reforms], rooted in a consumerist mentality in which the science that allows something to happen is transformed into the right to have it. The 'cogito ergo sum' of Descartes – 'I think therefore I am' – becomes the consumerist mantra, 'I shop therefore I am' or 'Tesco ergo sum'. The competing individualist arias of 'I, I, I' and 'me, me, me' provide the mood music for an individualism that posits the right of a wannabe parent over the welfare of a child. This virus of individualistic consumerism which informs a rights-based mentality is alien to those of us who come from another place – Africa – where they say, 'I am because we are: I belong therefore I am'. The laws that are passed in this your Lordships' House are more than mere regulation. The law is a statement of public policy. This is not about messages which are sent out about what is or is not acceptable in terms of family arrangements, but more fundamentally about the roles of parents, and in particular the need for a father where possible.[110]

In deploying this form of rhetoric, some religious opponents of adoption reform actively sought to shield themselves from an association with 'homophobia'. As Claire Curtis-Thomas MP (who converted to Roman Catholicism after her election as a Labour MP) argued:

> The rights of adults are paramount in the proposals before us [. . .] A child is to be treated as a mere commodity, where someone can opt to become the other parent simply by giving notice. That child product, like a washing machine, can be registered by two mothers as parents on the birth certificate.

---

109 Joint Committee on the Human Tissue and Embryos (Draft) Bill, *Human Tissue and Embryos (Draft) Bill, Volume II: Evidence*, op. cit., p.322.
110 HL Debate, 19 November 2007, c.707.

There are genuine religious concerns, and plenty of biblical passages support the family. They should not be constantly devalued or perceived as old fashioned. It is not old-fashioned homophobia to support the traditional family. I oppose unjustified discrimination against homosexuals, but I must protect the traditional notion of a family [. . .] It is the simple assertion of the rights of a child.[111]

Curtis-Thomas' recourse to theology was rare in the HFEA 2008. Her awareness that 'religious concerns' were 'constantly devalued' reflected the broad marginalisation of religious rhetoric in these debates. Religious opponents repeatedly complained that their views were belittled in the public sphere as well as in Parliament. They argued that supporters of the reforms were 'abusing' those who spoke as Christians,[112] subjecting religious speakers to disdainful 'grins on faces',[113] and attacking the 'free speech' rights of religious people.[114] One MP questioned 'why my vote or opinion should carry less weight than those of others because it has a base of faith, nor why any reference that I should make to God in that context should be considered bizarre'.[115] A key characteristic of religious opposition to the reforms of the HFEA 2008 was a defensiveness and anxiety about religion's role in the British public sphere and its loss of moral authority to delimit the boundaries of legitimate 'family'. For John Sentamu, the reforms demonstrated 'just how far the severance [of law, religion and morality] has gone and its unintended consequences' for child welfare and understandings of the gendered ordering of the family.[116]

Conclusion

Whereas Chapter 1 demonstrated the declining authority of religious discourse to regulate private homosexual sex, this chapter has documented the waning power of religious discourse regarding homosexuality to shape family law. Despite considerable religious opposition, the reforms of the ACA 2002 and HFEA 2008 created new and more straightforward routes for same-sex couples to share joint parental responsibility for children. Debates over the ACA 2002 marked an

---

111   HC Debate, 12 May 2008, c.1134.
112   I. Robinson, HC Debate, 20 May 2008, c.213. Her comments were in response to Chris Bryant MP, who had warned that parliamentarians must not 'start to impose our understanding of what is normal or natural on others' and quoted the biblical injunction 'Judge not that ye be not judged'. HC Debate, 20 May 2008, c.213. Bryant has publicly identified himself as a 'heterodox' Christian. See: S. Moss, 'Chris Bryant: "I don't think of myself as a gay MP"', The *Guardian*, 18 March 2010.
113   I. Robinson, HC Debate, 20 May 2008, c.213.
114   A. Burt, HC Debate, 12 May 2008, c.1143.
115   Ibid., c.1144.
116   HL Debate, 19 November 2007, c.705.

important development in parliamentary discourse about homosexuality. For the first time, lesbian and gay men were frequently accorded explicit moral value and social worth for their efforts to establish relationships with children and young people. This represents a significant discursive shift given the prevalence of tropes of the homosexual as a sexual predator evident in earlier parliamentary debates about the minimum age for male homosexual acts. Although such tropes still featured in some religious discourse deployed by those opposing reform, their use was significantly diminished. Whilst many supporters of adoption reform reinscribed notions of the superiority of heterosexual marriage as a context for raising children – depicting same-sex couples as capable parents but regarding them as adopters of last resort – discourses regarding the dangers that homosexuals posed to children were robustly challenged. Many religious opponents of the reforms created by both the ACA 2002 and HFEA 2008 seemingly recognised the reality that arguments about the dangers to children of homosexuality had lost their rhetorical self-sufficiency. As a result, during debates over the HFEA 2008, religious opponents often resorted to claims of religious discrimination and inequality to resist law reform. In the next chapter, we focus on this discourse of religious discrimination and disadvantage in parliamentary debates, emphasising its use in securing religious exceptions in sexual orientation equality legislation.

Chapter 3

Religious exceptions from sexual orientation equality

In this chapter we consider the influence of religion in shaping legislation designed to protect sexual minorities from discrimination in the areas of employment and the provision of goods and services. Such legislation has become increasingly common in a number of jurisdictions where governments have introduced new statutory provisions or amended existing laws in an attempt to promote greater social equality in respect of sexual orientation.[1] Our analysis in this chapter focuses on three pieces of UK legislation that have extended protection from discrimination on the basis of sexual orientation: the Employment Equality (Sexual Orientation) Regulations 2003; the Equality Act 2006; and the Equality Act 2010. There has been some scholarly analysis of the extent and implications of a 'clash' between religion and homosexuality created by the enforcement of this legislation.[2] In this chapter our focus is on the ways in which religious groups and individuals have sought to limit the scope of sexual orientation equality law and secure exceptions from it. We examine the discursive strategies employed to encourage the inclusion of bespoke provisions in legislation to afford religious organisations exceptions from law prohibiting discrimination on the grounds of sexual orientation. In the first part of the chapter we focus on legislation relating to employment, before going on to consider goods, services, facilities and premises.

Employment equality and religious exceptions

Until 2003, the UK Parliament had not enacted any legislation that prohibited discrimination on the grounds of sexual orientation in employment.[3] Although the Human Rights Act 1998 gave domestic effect to Article 14 of the European

---

1 For example, by May 2013, 39 European states had enacted national legislation to prohibit sexual orientation discrimination in employment, and 27 had done so in respect of the provision of goods and services. ILGA-Europe, *Rainbow Map (Index) May 2013*.
2 For example: C.F. Stychin, 'Faith in the future: sexuality, religion and the public sphere', *Oxford Journal of Legal Studies* 29, 2009, 729–755.

Convention on Human Rights, this provided limited protection from discrimination in the area of employment.[4] In this section we consider the Employment Equality (Sexual Orientation) Regulations (EESOR) 2003 which, for the first time, established a legal framework for ensuring equal treatment in the sphere of employment in respect of sexual orientation.[5] The EESOR 2003 made it unlawful to discriminate on grounds of sexual orientation in employment and vocational training by prohibiting direct discrimination,[6] indirect discrimination,[7] victimisation[8] and harassment.[9] The EESOR 2003 was enacted as secondary legislation in order to meet the requirements of Council Directive 2000/78/EC of the European Union relating to equal treatment in employment and occupation.[10]

---

3   Previous attempts to enact anti-discrimination legislation relating to sexual orientation in employment had failed in the UK Parliament. For example, Jo Richardson MP unsuccessfully introduced provisions in the Sex Equality Bill 1983 (HC Debate, 9 December 1983, c.586) and Baroness Turner of Camden made three failed attempts in the Sexual Orientation Discrimination Bill 1995 (HL Debate, 13 June 1995, c.1640), Sexual Orientation Discrimination Bill 1995/1996 (HL Debate, 11 December 1995, c.1102) and Sexual Orientation Discrimination Bill 1998 (HL Debate, 13 May 1998, c.1080). There was considerable hostility to Turner's Bills on the basis that it was for 'those who are gay or of a different sexual orientation [...] to take care that they do not ostensibly, willingly and arbitrarily offend those with whom they work' (Lord Arran, HL Debate, 5 June 1998, c.645) and that the proposed legislation would cause 'great concern to some Christian and other religious charities which do not believe that homosexuality is compatible with Christian or other faith beliefs' (Bishop of Wakefield, HL Debate, 5 June 1998, c.649).
4   Although Article 14 of the European Convention on Human Rights (ECHR) prohibits discrimination in respect of the rights contained in the ECHR, its application in relation to discrimination on the grounds of sexual orientation in employment (as well as in the provision of goods and services) has been limited by both the substantive scope of ECHR rights and their restriction to public authorities. The European Court of Human Rights has never upheld an Article 14 complaint relating to sexual orientation discrimination in employment, but has issued judgments in respect of discrimination in the provision of services such as public housing. See: P. Johnson, *Homosexuality and the European Court of Human Rights*, Abingdon: Routledge, 2013.
5   The Employment Equality (Sexual Orientation) Regulations 2003 applied to England, Wales and Scotland from commencement on 1 December 2003; similar provisions in the Employment Equality (Sexual Orientation) Regulations (Northern Ireland) 2003 commenced on 2 December 2003 and remain in force.
6   Reg.3(1)(a) Employment Equality (Sexual Orientation) Regulations 2003.
7   Reg.3(1)(b) Employment Equality (Sexual Orientation) Regulations 2003.
8   Reg.4 Employment Equality (Sexual Orientation) Regulations 2003.
9   Reg.5 Employment Equality (Sexual Orientation) Regulations 2003.
10 Council Directive 2000/78/EC of 27 November 2000 establishing a general framework for equal treatment in employment and occupation, Official Journal L 303, 02/12/2000 P. 0016–0022. The stated purpose of the Directive was to 'lay down a general framework for combating discrimination on the grounds of religion or belief, disability, age or sexual orientation as regards employment and occupation, with a view to putting into effect in the Member States the principle of equal treatment'.

When the Government published the first draft of the EESOR in October 2002, as part of a wider *Equality and Diversity* consultation,[11] it contained an 'exception for genuine occupational requirement' which allowed an employer to treat individuals differently on the grounds of sexual orientation if 'being of a particular sexual orientation is a genuine and determining occupational requirement' and 'it is proportionate to apply that requirement in the particular case'.[12] The exception was included to enable employers to specify sexual orientation as an occupational requirement during the recruitment, promotion, transferring and training of employees. The Government deemed this exception appropriate in meeting the requirements of European Union law.[13] The same exception for a genuine occupational requirement was simultaneously inserted into existing anti-discrimination legislation relating to race,[14] new legislation relating to religion or belief,[15] and subsequently included in legislation relating to age.[16]

Following the publication of the first draft of the EESOR 2003, several religious organisations expressed concerns that the genuine occupational requirement exception would not allow them sufficient scope to exclude homosexuals from employment. For example, the Christian Institute argued:

> Under the regulations it is only possible to discriminate on the basis of sexual orientation if that is a genuine occupational requirement. It will be very difficult for a religious employer to show that they *need* a heterosexual for the job.[17]

The Christian Institute's advice to Christian organisations was that the genuine occupational requirement exception could be used to exclude homosexuals from employment if employers specified that a requirement of employment was that employees model Christian behaviour and therefore be either celibate or married. However, the Christian Institute recognised that whilst the 'requirement to be celibate discriminates equally against homosexuals, heterosexuals and bisexuals',

---

11 Department for Trade and Industry, *Equality and Diversity: The Way Ahead*, 2002.
12 Reg.7 Employment Equality (Sexual Orientation) Regulations 2003, draft published for consultation on 22 October 2002.
13 Article 4.1 of Council Directive 2000/78/EC states: 'Member States may provide that a difference of treatment which is based on a characteristic related to any of the grounds referred to in Article 1 shall not constitute discrimination where, by reason of the nature of the particular occupational activities concerned or of the context in which they are carried out, such a characteristic constitutes a genuine and determining occupational requirement, provided that the objective is legitimate and the requirement is proportionate.'
14 Reg.7 Race Relations Act 1976 (Amendment) Regulations 2003.
15 Reg.7 Employment Equality (Religion or Belief) Regulations 2003.
16 Reg.8 Employment Equality (Age) Regulations 2006.
17 I. Leigh and C. Hart, *Implementing the EU Employment Directive*, Newcastle: The Christian Institute, 2003, p.23.

the 'requirement to be married indirectly discriminates against homosexuals since they cannot marry, though presumably a bisexual could'.[18] The Christian Institute advanced faith-based objections to the aims of the EESOR 2003 that had existed since the establishment of Council Directive 2000/78/EC. Baroness Young, for example, had argued that the Directive was a 'great cause for concern to religious people' and represented 'another nail in the coffin of the whole Judaeo-Christian basis of our society'.[19] At the point that the draft EESOR 2003 was published, therefore, there was existing hostility to both its aims and scope amongst religious organisations and individuals.

The Church of England and the sexual orientation exception

The Church of England's response to the draft EESOR 2003 sought to widen the scope of the exception for genuine occupational requirement in respect of sexual orientation. The Archbishops' Council stated that 'it is crucial that they [the EESOR 2003] do not encroach on the freedom which all religious organisations must have to set and enforce their own conduct rules in relation to those who work for and represent them' and prevent 'them from conscientiously applying their own sincerely held doctrines and beliefs on moral issues'.[20] The Church of England strongly urged the Government to include in the EESOR 2003 the following specific exception relating to religion:

> Nothing in [...] these Regulations shall render unlawful *anything* done for the purposes or in connection with an organised religion so as to comply with the doctrines of the religion or avoid offending the religious susceptibilities of a significant number of its followers.[21]

This proposed wording drew upon and widened the existing religious exception for sex discrimination in respect of the employment of ministers of religion.[22] The Church of England's request was incorporated in modified form into the final draft of the EESOR 2003 that was placed before Parliament in May 2003. Regulation 7(3) of the EESOR 2003 provided an exception in respect of the discrimination provisions relating to applicants and employees if an employer satisfied a three-limb test: first, that any employment be for the 'purposes of an organised religion'; second, that a requirement 'related to sexual orientation' be applied either to 'comply with the doctrines of the religion' or 'to avoid conflicting with

18 Ibid. This was prior to same-sex marriage being made lawful by the Marriage (Same Sex Couples) Act 2013.
19 HL Debate, 30 June 2000, c.1189.
20 Church of England, 'Equality and diversity: Church of England response to DTI consultation document', Archbishops' Council, 23 January 2003.
21 Ibid. Our emphasis.

the strongly held religious convictions of a significant number of the religion's followers'; and, third, that either 'the person to whom that requirement is applied does not meet it' or 'the employer is not satisfied, and in all the circumstances it is reasonable for him not to be satisfied, that that person meets it'.[23]

The wording of the Church of England's proposed exception and the wording of regulation 7(3) of the EESOR 2003 show some differences, but it meets the Church of England's request that it be granted a wider margin to apply a requirement on the grounds of sexual orientation than that permitted by the genuine occupational requirement exception (which was enacted as regulation 7(2) of the EESOR 2003[24]). Regulation 7(3) allowed an exception for an 'organised religion' (subsequently interpreted not to encompass 'all religious organisations' as hoped for by the Church of England[25]) when it applies a requirement 'related to sexual orientation'. Regulation 7(3) is therefore wider in scope than the genuine occupational requirement exception because it extends beyond 'being' of a particular sexual orientation to cover other 'related' aspects.[26] Regulation 7(3) also omitted the provision, found in the genuine occupational requirement exception, that the application of any sexual orientation requirement be 'proportionate'. As we examine later in this chapter, the framework which regulation 7(3) of the EESOR 2003 introduced to enable differences in treatment by organised religions on the grounds of sexual orientation was retained, in slightly modified form, in the Equality Act 2010.[27]

22 S.19 Sex Discrimination Act 1975. The Church of England's proposed exception drew on the wording of this section prior to its amendment by Reg.20(1) Employment Equality (Sex Discrimination) Regulations 2005.
23 Reg.7(3) Employment Equality (Sexual Orientation) Regulations 2003. These exceptions applied to: arrangements made for determining who to offer employment; refusing employment; the promotion, transfer or training of an existing employee; the dismissal from employment.
24 Reg.7(2) Employment Equality (Sexual Orientation) Regulations 2003 retained the original proposed exception that was applicable when 'being of a particular sexual orientation is a genuine and determining occupational requirement' and 'it is proportionate to apply that requirement in the particular case'. Reg.7(2) also had an explanation written into it to enable its use by an organised religion.
25 Richards J confirmed that 'for purposes of an organised religion' has a narrower scope than 'for purposes of a religious organisation' and that, for example, 'employment as a teacher in a faith school is likely to be "for purposes of a religious organisation" but not "for purposes of an organised religion"'. *R (Amicus) v Secretary of State for Trade and Industry*, [2004] EWHC 860 (Admin), § 116.
26 In *R (Amicus) v Secretary of State for Trade and Industry*, op. cit., Richards J did not elaborate on the meaning of 'related to sexual orientation' beyond confirming that it included sexual behaviour, but stated that the overall scope of Reg.7(3) Employment Equality (Sexual Orientation) Regulations 2003 was narrow. However, see our discussion below of *Reaney v Hereford Diocesan Board of Finance* (Cardiff Employment Tribunal, 17 July 2007, 1602844/2006) which confirmed that Reg.7(3) was not limited to the employment of clergy.
27 Sch.9 Pt.1 Para.2 Equality Act 2010.

The exact process by which the Church of England's proposed exception was included in regulation 7(3) of the EESOR 2003 is obscure. Because the EESOR 2003 was secondary legislation and did not undergo full parliamentary scrutiny in either House, there is no definitive documentary evidence relating to the decision to include it. However, parliamentarians in both Houses, as well as the High Court, concluded that the Government included regulation 7(3) because of the representation made by the Church of England.[28] Some evidence of this exists in the form of witness statements made by representatives of the Department of Trade and Industry (DTI) to the Joint Committee on Statutory Instruments (JCSI) during an examination of the EESOR 2003. For example, DTI witnesses explained that they had met with Church representatives and, as a result, amended the EESOR 2003:

> The churches, in relation to the draft Regulations on which we consulted last, pointed out that there was an omission which was causing them difficulty and, after much consideration and discussion with them to work out what the Directive would enable us to do and where the Regulations should cover it, we decided that the Regulation should be changed to take account of that.[29]

DTI evidence also shows that although the Government incorporated specific exceptions for organised religions in the EESOR 2003, 'the churches still felt that we had not gone anywhere near far enough in the provision that we drafted'.[30]

Although the DTI evidence to the JCSI makes reference to 'the churches' in explaining the inclusion of regulation 7(3) of the EESOR 2003,[31] a subsequent letter from the Secretary General of the General Synod and the Archbishops' Council, William Fittall, to the JCSI suggests that the Church of England was instrumental in encouraging its inclusion. Fittall stated that the Church of England had requested the additional exception (beyond that offered by the genuine occupational requirement exception) because without it 'it would not in practice be open to faith communities to defend successfully the application of a marriage or abstinence policy against a discrimination claim by arguing that the

---

28 Richards J held that 'Regulation 7(3) was not included in the detailed draft regulations originally published for the purposes of consultation. It was added as a result of representations from the Churches, including in particular, it would seem, the Archbishops' Council of the Church of England.' *R (Amicus) v Secretary of State for Trade and Industry*, op. cit., § 90.
29 Joint Committee on Statutory Instruments, Minutes of Evidence, 3 June 2003, Q.36.
30 Ibid.
31 Lord Sainsbury of Turville later stated that representation was made by 'the Archbishops' Council of the Church of England, the Catholic Bishops' Conference of England and Wales, the Muslim Council of Great Britain and the Baha'i Community of the UK. Many other representations supported this view'. HL Written Answer, 1 July 2003, c.96.

requirement was about behaviour rather than mere orientation'.[32] The inclusion of the wording 'related to sexual orientation' in regulation 7(3), which allows a requirement to be applied to cover sexual behaviour, precisely meets the Church of England's demand that it should be given 'freedom to determine what requirements in relation to *sexual behaviour* should apply' (such as a prohibition on sex outside of marriage) '*even though this might otherwise constitute direct or indirect discrimination in relation to sexual orientation*'.[33]

Parliamentary acceptance of the employment exception

When the EESOR 2003 was considered in Parliamentary Committee, Evan Harris MP called the inclusion of the religious exception 'astonishing' because it was 'supported only by the Church of England in a confused way and wholeheartedly by the Christian Institute and CARE [Christian Action Research and Education]'.[34] Harris joined Edward Leigh MP in voting against the EESOR 2003 on the basis that both MPs, despite holding diametrically opposed views on the role of sexual orientation anti-discrimination legislation, agreed that regulation 7(3) was a 'dog's dinner' that satisfied neither religious opponents nor those seeking employment protection for sexual minorities.[35] When the EESOR 2003 was laid before the Lords, Lord Lester of Herne Hill unsuccessfully moved a motion inviting the Government to withdraw it and amend regulation 7(3) because it was 'both unnecessary and unlawful'.[36] Lester argued it was unlawful because it licensed discrimination beyond that allowed by Council Directive 2000/78/EC and 'will remain effective as a sweepingly broad exemption clause apparently permitting a religious body to refuse to employ not a priest but a cleaner or messenger because of their sexuality'.[37]

One of the strategies employed in Parliament by religious opponents of the EESOR 2003 to ensure the inclusion of regulation 7(3) was to argue that the exception did not relate to homosexuality. The Bishop of Blackburn, Alan Chesters, for example, stated that regulation 7(3) addressed 'genuine issues of religious liberty' because it related to 'some posts and orders where, irrespective of sexual orientation, be it heterosexual or homosexual, the requirement remains for marriage or abstinence'.[38] Chesters argued that regulation 7(3) was not the result of 'Downing Street [having] caved in to the prejudices of extreme religious

---

32 W. Fittall, 'Letter to Joint Committee on Statutory Instruments from the Secretary General of the General Synod and the Archbishops' Council', 9 June 2003.
33 Ibid. Our emphasis.
34 HC Committee, 17 June 2003, c.36.
35 Ibid., c.44.
36 HL Debate, 17 June 2003, c.755.
37 Ibid.
38 Ibid., cc.758–759.

organisations' and that it was 'emphatically not about pandering to prejudices'.[39] Although there was opposition to regulation 7(3),[40] there was no direct challenge to it (or to the Church of England's desire for it) on the grounds that it was anti-gay or homophobic. Rather, the issue of homosexuality remained unaddressed in a debate that focused on the extent to which 'religious communities may preserve their distinctive character' in respect of marriage and celibacy.[41] While Lord Alli explicitly condemned the bishops for using 'the privilege that they enjoy [in] law-making, [to use] the civil law as a means of exempting themselves or their religion from the norms and values of civil society', he made no explicit reference to homosexuality.[42] The debate instead remained focused on what the Church of England described as the need to protect 'religious organisations from litigation which would in effect be challenging the application of their own doctrines and beliefs within their own internal structures'.[43]

The tactic of focusing parliamentary debate on the extent to which organised religions can exercise doctrine and belief to impose marital and celibacy requirements on employees followed the line of argument initially proposed by the Christian Institute. In focusing on sexual behaviour in relation to marriage, religious opponents were able to make opaque their central concern about employing homosexuals. This was decisive in ensuring the inclusion of regulation 7(3) in the EESOR 2003, which effectively provided a bespoke exception to allow organised religions to realise an ambition to discriminate against homosexuals. The Lesbian and Gay Christian Movement called regulation 7(3) an 'odious provision'[44] and UNISON General Secretary, Dave Prentis, stated that it meant that 'equality stops at the church gates'.[45] A consequence of the legislation has been the creation of a hierarchy in equality law – continued by the Equality Act 2010 which we discuss later in the chapter – whereby organised religions are afforded a wider exception from anti-discrimination provisions relating to sexual orientation (as well as sex, transsexuality, marital or civil partnership status,[46] and

39 Ibid., c.759.
40 The Bishop of Worcester likened the potential use of the exceptions in Reg.7(3) to the discrimination practised by far-right political parties such as the British National Party (HL Debate, 17 June 2003, cc.770–771) and Lord Alli argued that it 'feels more like a provision dreamed up by the Taliban than one suitable for a mature democracy' (HL Debate, 17 June 2003, c.766).
41 Bishop of Worcester, HL Debate, 17 June 2003, c.771.
42 HL Debate, 17 June 2003, c.766.
43 W. Fittall, op. cit.
44 Lesbian and Gay Christian Movement, Press Release, 'LGCM deplores Employment Regulations', 9 May 2003. Available online at www.sarmiento.plus.com/equality/lgcm.html#note (accessed on 4 December 2013).
45 D. Prentis, cited in S. Sarmiento, '*Church Times* op-ed article for issue of 18 July [2003], draft last revised 8 July'. Available online at www.sarmiento.plus.com/equality/ctarticle.html (accessed on 4 December 2013).
46 These employment requirements ('to be of a particular sex'; 'not to be a transsexual person'; 'not to be married or a civil partner'; 'not to be married to, or the civil partner

religion or belief[47]) than those available to other employers. As we explore below, this hierarchy also exists (although more acutely drawn in respect of sexual orientation) as a result of religious exceptions from law prohibiting discrimination in the provision of goods and services.

Goods, services, facilities, premises and religious exceptions

In 2004 the UK Government announced its intention to extend then existing laws prohibiting discrimination in the provision of goods, services, facilities and premises on the grounds of race[48] to cover religion and faith.[49] This ambition was realised in the Equality Bill 2005. During the passage of the Bill through Parliament a number of attempts were made to amend it to extend the discrimination protections to cover sexual orientation. For example, Baroness Turner of Camden argued that 'while provision is made to provide protection against discrimination in these areas on grounds of religion or belief, no such provision is made for gay and lesbian people'.[50] The Government attempted to resist making this provision.[51] However, the Lords successfully included in the Equality Act (EA) 2006 a section that placed a requirement on government to create a statutory instrument to prohibit discrimination and harassment on the grounds of sexual orientation.[52] There was significant religious concern about and opposition to this. The Bishop

---

of, a person who has a living former spouse or civil partner'; or 'relating to circumstances in which a marriage or civil partnership came to an end') are grouped with sexual orientation in the exception for organised religions in Sch.9 Pt.1 Para.2 Equality Act 2010 which we discuss below.

47 Reg.7(3) Employment Equality (Religion or Belief) Regulations 2003 provided an exception (in addition to the genuine occupational requirement) 'where an employer has an ethos based on religion or belief and, having regard to that ethos and to the nature of the employment or the context in which it is carried out [. . .] being of a particular religion or belief is a genuine occupational requirement for the job'. This exception was incorporated in Sch.9 Pt.1 Para.3 Equality Act 2010. The exception does not apply only to 'organized religions' but to '[a] person [. . .] with an ethos based on religion or belief [. . .] applying in relation to work a requirement to be of a particular religion or belief'.
48 S.20 Race Relations Act 1976.
49 Home Office Press Release, 'Strengthening protection against religious discrimination', 302/2004, 28 September 2004.
50 HL Committee, 11 July 2005, c.891.
51 Baroness Scotland explained the Government's reluctance in the following way: [t]he issue is not one of principle; it is [. . .] one of method and timing'. HL Committee, 13 July 2005, c.1196.
52 Amendments moved and accepted without division by Lord Alli (HL Debate, 9 November 2005, cc.627–637) and Lord Lester of Herne Hill (HL Debate, 9 November 2005, cc.677–679) created Pt.3 Equality Act 2006 which provides for regulations to be made in Great Britain (S.81) and Northern Ireland (S.82). An Early Day Motion had been tabled in the Commons which also called 'on the Government to extend the protections for

of Newcastle, Martin Wharton, argued that although he welcomed 'the principle of non-discrimination on the grounds of sexual orientation and its extension into the areas of goods, services, facilities and premises', he had 'one concern' about the 'interface between the right not to be discriminated against on the one hand and the right to freedom of religion on the other'. Wharton argued that because this was a 'complex and sensitive matter' requiring 'a careful balancing exercise', it necessitated that the Government 'engage in early discussions with the Churches and other faith communities on how their interests can be reflected in the provisions'.[53] Wharton's concern with the interests of faith communities was expressed more firmly by Baroness O'Cathain, who opposed the provisions because they gave 'no guarantees of proper religious protections, which means that there could be alarming problems for Churches and religious organisations'.[54] Lord Stoddart also opposed the provision on the grounds that:

> these laws will [. . .] presumably apply to people providing a couple of rooms for bed and breakfast [. . .] It may very well be that the person providing bed and breakfast has religious objections to people living as lesbians or homosexuals. In that case, she will presumably be criminalised if she refuses to give them a room overnight. I would like to know about that, for example, because we are talking about ordinary people now, not great hotel chains or other, larger, establishments.[55]

The concern with the impact of the law on 'ordinary people' who offer commercial services from premises in which they live was a key feature of religious opposition to the legislation. Whereas the religious opposition to same-sex marriage that we discuss in the next chapter focused on maintaining the spatial exclusion of homosexuality from sacred spaces, religious opposition to equality legislation was concerned with maintaining boundaries between homosexuality and private and domestic dwellings.

As a consequence of the EA 2006 the Government issued a consultation document on discrimination on the grounds of sexual orientation in respect of goods, services, facilities and premises in which it stated that it had no intention to make exempt 'activities that are provided by an organisation related to religion or belief, or by a private individual who has strongly held religious beliefs, where the sole or main purpose of the organisation offering the service is commercial'.[56]

---

religious groups, in respect of discrimination in the provisions of goods, facilities and services, to lesbians and gay men' (710, 10 October 2005).
53 HL Debate, 9 November 2005, c.630.
54 Ibid.
55 Ibid., c.631.
56 Women and Equality Unit, *Getting Equal: Proposals to Outlaw Sexual Orientation Discrimination in the Provision of Goods & Services*, 2006, § 3.35.

The Government stated that any religious exceptions would be 'limited to activities closely linked to religious observance or practices that arise from the basic doctrines of a faith'.[57] The Government's original intention, therefore, was to provide religious organisations with a narrower exception than that provided in respect of religion or belief in Part 2 of the EA 2006.[58] This provoked considerable hostility from religious organisations. The Catholic Bishops' Conference of England and Wales, for example, argued that the proposed exceptions were 'too limited' because for 'Catholic organisations the goods and services they may provide, and the manner in which this is done, will often be as much a manifestation of doctrinal beliefs as matters of religious observance and practice'.[59] They complained that 'there appears to be little recognition in the consultation document of the difference between *homophobia* and a conviction, based on religious belief and moral conscience, that homosexual practice is wrong'.[60] The Catholic Bishops' Conference 'urge[d] the Government to consider incorporating into the new [regulations] exceptions to cover these which broadly parallel those in Part Two of the Equality Act'.[61] The Church of England made the same demand:

> [I]t is not right to seek to draw the exemptions for religious bodies as narrowly as proposed [. . .] Rather, we believe that the regulations should include exemptions for religious bodies in terms no less wide than the exemptions contained in Part 2 of the Equality Act in relation to discrimination on grounds of religion or belief.[62]

As a result of these objections and recommendations from religious organisations, the Government included in the two statutory instruments that gave effect to the

---

57 Ibid., § 3.33.
58 S.57 Equality Act 2006 provided an exception from provisions relating to discrimination on the grounds of religion and belief. This allowed an organisation relating to religion or belief to exercise restrictions relating to membership, participation in activities, the provision of goods, facilities and services, and the disposal or use of premises, if imposed 'by reason of or on the grounds of the purpose of the organisation' or 'in order to avoid causing offence, on grounds of the religion or belief to which the organisation relates, to persons of that religion or belief'. The Government's original proposal was not to extend this wide exception in respect of sexual orientation.
59 Catholic Bishops' Conference of England and Wales, ' "Getting equal" – proposals to outlaw sexual orientation discrimination in the provision of goods and services: a submission to the DTI consultation from the Catholic Bishops' Conference of England & Wales', June 2006.
60 Ibid.
61 Ibid.
62 Church of England, ' "Getting equal" – consultation on proposals to outlaw sexual orientation discrimination in the provision of goods and services: a Church of England response', June 2006.

sexual orientation provisions in the EA 2006 an exception that mirrored the exception relating to religion or belief.[63] Although discrimination was prohibited on the grounds of sexual orientation in the provision of goods, facilities and services,[64] the disposal or management of premises,[65] and initially included protection in Northern Ireland from harassment,[66] religious organisations were given a significant exception. We discuss these two instruments below.

Religious opposition to harassment protection for sexual minorities: the Equality Act (Sexual Orientation) Regulations (Northern Ireland) 2006

When the UK Government issued the Equality Act (Sexual Orientation) Regulations (Northern Ireland) (EASORNI) 2006 it included a wide exception for 'organisations relating to religion or belief' in respect of discrimination on the grounds of sexual orientation. The exception applies to 'an organisation the purpose of which is [. . .] to practice', 'advance', or 'teach the practice or principles of a religion or belief', or 'to enable persons of a religion or belief to receive any benefit, or to engage in any activity, within the framework of that religion or belief', and which is not 'an organisation whose sole or main purpose is commercial' or related to education.[67] It enables such an organisation to restrict 'membership of the organisation', 'participation in activities undertaken by the organisation or on its behalf or under its auspices', 'the provision of goods, facilities and services in the course of activities undertaken by the organisation or on its behalf or under its auspices', or 'the use or disposal of premises owned or controlled by the organisation [. . .] in respect of a person on the ground of

---

63 The exceptions relating to sexual orientation contained in Reg.16 Equality Act (Sexual Orientation) Regulations (Northern Ireland) 2006 and Reg.14 Equality Act (Sexual Orientation) Regulations 2007 are substantially the same as the exceptions relating to religion and belief in S.57 Equality Act 2006, although there are some subtle differences. For example, the requirement that a restriction be imposed 'in order to avoid causing offence, on grounds of the religion or belief to which the organisation relates' in the exception relating to religion and belief differed from the requirement that a restriction be imposed 'so as to avoid conflicting with the strongly held religious convictions of a significant number of the religion's followers' in the exception relating to sexual orientation. This distinction is maintained in England and Wales and Scotland by the Equality Act 2010 which we discuss below.
64 Reg.5 Equality Act (Sexual Orientation) Regulations (Northern Ireland) 2006; Reg.4 Equality Act (Sexual Orientation) Regulations 2007.
65 Reg.6 Equality Act (Sexual Orientation) Regulations (Northern Ireland) 2006; Reg.5 Equality Act (Sexual Orientation) Regulations 2007.
66 Reg.3(3) Equality Act (Sexual Orientation) Regulations (Northern Ireland) 2006.
67 Reg.16(1)–(2) Equality Act (Sexual Orientation) Regulations (Northern Ireland) 2006.

his sexual orientation'.[68] A restriction is permitted 'if it is necessary to comply with the doctrine of the organisation' or 'so as to avoid conflicting with the strongly held religious convictions of a significant number of the religions followers'.[69]

Despite this wide exception, there remained considerable religious opposition to the introduction of the legislation. Although the EASORNI 2006 was introduced in the Westminster Parliament – as a consequence of the suspension of the Northern Ireland Assembly – a Private Member's Motion in the Northern Ireland Transitional Assembly called upon the Government to withdraw the regulations and leave them to be determined by the Northern Ireland Assembly upon restoration.[70] Much of the support for this motion focused on the 'unfair and discriminatory' treatment of Christians in the regulations.[71] A similar argument was made in the Lords by Lord Morrow when he moved a motion that the EASORNI 2006 be annulled because of the threat it posed to 'religious liberty':

> They make it possible for homosexual activists to sue people who disagree with a homosexual lifestyle because of their religious beliefs. Bed and breakfast owners and Christian old people's homes will be sued for not giving a double bed to homosexual civil partners. Wedding photographers will be made to pay compensation for not taking bookings for civil partnership ceremonies. Christians in business could even be sued for sharing their faith with customers. Worst of all, they require religious organisations to choose between obedience to God and obedience to the state.[72]

The focus of this opposition to the EASORNI 2006 was on protecting the 'conscientious objection' of individual Christians (rather than religious organisations) in order that they could withhold the provision of services to homosexuals on the grounds of religious belief.[73]

A significant aspect of this opposition to the EASORNI 2006 was hostility to the inclusion of the harassment provision, which regulated 'unwanted conduct

---

68 Reg.16(3) Equality Act (Sexual Orientation) Regulations (Northern Ireland) 2006.
69 Reg.16(5) Equality Act (Sexual Orientation) Regulations (Northern Ireland) 2006.
70 Northern Ireland Transitional Assembly, 11 December 2006, Motion proposed by J. Donaldson. The Motion was negatived by a tied vote of 39-39.
71 J. Shannon, Northern Ireland Transitional Assembly, 11 December 2006.
72 HL Debate, 9 January 2007, c.180.
73 The protection of conscientious objection is a long-standing argument made by religious opponents of anti-discrimination legislation in respect of sexual orientation. For advocacy of this argument, see: R.F. Duncan, 'Who wants to stop the church: homosexual rights legislation, public policy, and religious freedom', *Notre Dame Law Review* 69, 1993/94, 393–445. For a critique, see: C.F. Stychin, 'Closet cases: "conscientious objection" to lesbian and gay legal equality', *Griffith Law Review* 18, 2009, 17–38.

which has the purpose or effect of (a) violating [...] dignity; or (b) creating an intimidating, hostile, degrading, humiliating or offensive environment'.[74] No such provision existed in respect of discrimination on the grounds of religion or belief in the provision of goods and services,[75] and religious opponents argued that its extension to cover sexual orientation would create significant inequalities.[76] Furthermore, the harassment provision was argued to have 'major implications for religious liberty and freedom of speech' because 'if church membership were denied to a homosexual and the minister explained in orthodox, theological terms the religious belief that justified the denial, it would be open to the person to bring a claim for harassment'.[77] This claim was also made in the Commons Delegated Legislation Committee:

> It is one thing to serve a homosexual person a cup of coffee in a Christian bookshop – it is no problem at all, and Christians are glad to serve anyone – but quite another if he can sue someone for harassment because they explain the Gospel while serving the coffee, because of the environment that they are in.[78]

---

74 Reg.3(3) Equality Act (Sexual Orientation) Regulations (Northern Ireland) 2006. The harassment provision was not originally intended to form part of these regulations. The original consultation document issued by the Office of the First Minister and Deputy First Minister (*Getting Equal: Proposals to Outlaw Discrimination on the Grounds of Sexual Orientation in the Provision of Goods and Services in Northern Ireland*, July 2006) stated: 'On the basis of the complex arguments put forward we are minded to accept that it is not appropriate to legislate for harassment within these regulations.' However, following the consultation, the Northern Ireland Office included the provision, arguing: 'The Government listened carefully to the representations made by respondents on the inclusion of harassment in the Regulations. As a result the Government amended the proposals to include harassment provisions' (*Analysis of Responses to the Consultation on Getting Equal: Proposals to Outlaw Discrimination on the Ground of Sexual Orientation in the Provision of Goods, Facilities and Services in Northern Ireland*).
75 The Equality Bill 2005 did originally contain a provision on harassment on the grounds of religion or belief but this was removed in the Lords (HL Debate, 9 November 2005, Division No.1). S.47 Equality Bill 2005 as introduced prohibited harassment on grounds of religion or belief if it has the purpose or effect of either violating dignity or creating an intimidating, hostile, degrading, humiliating or offensive environment. The Lords rejected this largely because of fears that 'such a provision, wide and uncertain as it is, could be used to strike at religious organisations and their practices from outside the faith communities' (Bishop of Newcastle, HL Debate, 9 November 2005, c.657).
76 J. Donaldson argued in the Transitional Assembly of Northern Ireland: 'There is no religious harassment law in Northern Ireland with respect to the provision of goods, facilities and services, yet harassment laws on sexual orientation have been inserted into these regulations. That is completely inconsistent with the declared aim of creating equality of protection for all categories of persons' (11 December 2006).
77 Lord Morrow, HL Debate, 9 January 2007, c.181.
78 D. Simpson, HC Committee, 17 January 2007, c.4.

The Joint Committee on Human Rights agreed, stating that the harassment provision could create an 'interference with freedom of religion and belief [...] because explanations of sincerely held doctrinal beliefs might be perceived as violating a person's dignity or creating an offensive environment'.[79] Opponents of EASORNI 2006 were therefore successful in persuading some parliamentarians that both the inclusion of the harassment provision and the inadequacy of the religious exceptions could, as Lord Moran put it, mean that 'the regulations may be used to discriminate against those who deeply believe that homosexual activity is morally wrong'.[80]

In response to the EASORNI 2006 several religious organisations sought to challenge it through judicial review.[81] The High Court of Justice in Northern Ireland rejected the applicants' complaints about the discrimination provisions but set aside the harassment provision. Although Weatherup J cited several reasons for his decision in respect of the harassment provision – the absence of proper consultation, the extended reach of the harassment provisions beyond that of discrimination and statutory harassment law, the wider definition of harassment than that appearing in the European Directive,[82] and the concerns of the Joint Committee on Human Rights – a key factor determining his judgment was his acceptance that regulating harassment on the grounds of sexual orientation in respect of goods, services, premises and facilities had negative consequences for religious freedom:

> The outlawing of harassment in relation to race, religion and gender involves interference with freedom of speech and a fair balance of rights has been sought to be achieved by permitting interference with such freedom of speech on the ground of the rights of others not to be subject to harassment on the basis of gender or race or religious belief. However in outlawing harassment on the ground of sexual orientation the competing right may not only be the right to freedom of speech but may in addition be the right to manifest a religious belief. Where the exercise of the right to freedom of speech also involves the manifestation of a religious belief there will be an added basis on which to seek to justify the action. This provides an added consideration in the case of sexual orientation that may not apply in relation to harassment on the grounds of gender, race or religious belief.[83]

---

79 House of Lords and House of Commons Joint Committee on Human Rights, *Sixth Report of Session 2006–07 on Legislative Scrutiny: Sexual Orientation Regulations*, 28 February 2007, § 58.
80 HL Debate, 9 January 2007, c.189.
81 The Christian Institute, the Reformed Presbyterian Church in Ireland, the Congregational Union of Ireland, the Evangelical Presbyterian Church of Ireland, the Association of Baptist Churches in Ireland, the Fellowship of Independent Methodist Churches and Christian Camping International (UK) Limited.
82 Council Directive 2000/78/EC.
83 *An Application for Judicial Review by The Christian Institute and Others*, High Court of Justice in Northern Ireland Queen's Bench Division [2007] NIQB 66, § 42.

The reasoning of Weatherup J shows the use of a particular equalities hierarchy in order to distinguish sexual orientation from other protected characteristics and thereby justify more limited protection on this ground. Weatherup J reiterates the argument made by religious opponents in Parliament that a faith-based objection to particular sexual orientations has a special status because it involves not simply a form of expression but the manifestation of religious belief. This form of reasoning legitimises the view that religious believers require exceptions from anti-discrimination law relating to sexual orientation because of their need to manifest their religion through expressions about homosexuality. Furthermore, it endorses the view that curtailing the manifestation of faith-based hostility to homosexuality amounts to a form of discrimination. This mandates a problematic equality hierarchy, encouraged by religious opponents of sexual orientation equality legislation, in which sexual orientation is positioned beneath other protected characteristics because of a recognised need for religious believers to condemn homosexuality (we discuss this in further detail in Chapter 5).

The threat to religious liberty: the Equality Act (Sexual Orientation) Regulations 2007

Religious opposition to the harassment provision of the EASORNI 2006 was responsible for its omission from the Equality Act (Sexual Orientation) Regulations (EASOR) 2007, which covered the rest of the UK. However, even without the harassment clause, there was considerable religious opposition to the EASOR 2007 in Parliament, where it was described as 'an assault on the freedom of conscience of millions of our fellow citizens'.[84] Much of the parliamentary debate focused on the impact of the EASOR 2007 on religious adoption agencies (see Chapter 2) and education in schools (see Chapter 6), but there was also intense concern about the effect of the legislation on all those with 'Christian principles' involved in the provision of goods and services. This was repeatedly articulated through the example of 'religious bed and breakfast owners' but also through examples of other commercial service providers:

> If a website designer who has Christian principles is asked to design a website promoting gay sexual relations – about which, I wish to make clear, there is nothing illegal – and he wishes to say, 'Sorry, I do not want to do that', the way in which the regulations are drafted mean that he will be breaking the law. Until this House cottons on to the extent to which that marks a profound change between tolerance and enforcing a new form of orthodoxy, we will fail to grapple properly with the problems that the regulations pose.[85]

---

84 G. Howarth, HC Committee, 15 March 2007, c.6.
85 D. Grieve, HC Committee, 15 March 2007, cc.28–29.

Whilst the EASOR 2007 provided the same wide exception for religious *organisations*[86] as that included in the EASORNI 2006, religious opponents repeatedly argued that religious *individuals* should not be subject to the 'orthodoxy' of sexual orientation equality.

The essence of religious opposition to the EASOR 2007 was the claim that it threatened religious, but specifically Christian, liberty to 'promulgate the view that homosexuality is sinful or wrong'.[87] The claim that the EASOR 2007 threatened religious liberty underpinned a closely fought but ultimately unsuccessful amendment in the Lords that proposed the rejection of the legislation.[88] Speaking in support of that amendment, Baroness O'Cathain stated that it was 'profoundly dangerous of the Government to decide to use the law to force religious believers to change their beliefs'[89] and evidence that the Government had 'taken the view that gay rights trump religious rights'.[90] O'Cathain argued that the EASOR 2007 would ultimately 'ride roughshod' over religious freedom and destroy 'tolerance or diversity' in society.[91] The result, she argued, would be a violation of religious liberty and conscience:

> A Christian printer would be quite content to print materials for people who happen to be gay, but would not want to print the *Gay Times*, or leaflets promoting gay marriage. That is a crucial distinction which Christians make, but which the regulations will not permit. Others are allowed to carry on in business and keep their freedom of conscience intact: a staunch socialist can refuse to print a Tory election leaflet; a vegetarian printer can refuse to print flyers for his local butcher; and a pacifist can refuse to print a sales brochure for an arms manufacturer.[92]

Although O'Cathain gave expression to (and perhaps drew upon) similar claims being made by a number of organisations outside of Parliament, such as the Lawyers' Christian Fellowship,[93] her argument did not convince legislators that gay rights were trumping religious rights. This is perhaps because O'Cathain's argument is logically problematic insofar as none of the examples given (the

---

86 Reg.14 Equality Act (Sexual Orientation) Regulations 2007.
87 L. Burt, HC Committee, 15 March 2007, c.27.
88 Baroness O'Cathain, HL Debate, 21 March 2007, c.1296. The amendment was rejected by 122-168, but three Lords Spiritual (Southwell and Nottingham, Winchester, and York) voted in favour of it. HL Debate, 21 March 2007, Division No.1.
89 HL Debate, 21 March 2007, c.1297.
90 Ibid., c.1298.
91 Ibid., c.1297.
92 Ibid., c.1298.
93 Lawyers' Christian Fellowship Public Policy Unit, 'Submission in response to the consultation of the Women and Equality Unit', May 2006.

socialist, pacifist or vegetarian) relate to protected characteristics defined in equality law, and therefore any provider of commercial services, including a Christian printer, could withhold a service for these reasons. Furthermore, the requirements placed upon service providers by the EASOR 2007 were equivalent to those then existing in respect of other protected characteristics such as race[94] or sex.[95] O'Cathain's argument, that sexual orientation equality is limiting religious freedom, therefore only makes sense if it is accepted that there is a 'special relationship' between religion and sexual orientation (like the vegetarian has with meat, or the pacifist has with arms) which makes it absolutely essential for individual Christians to be able to restrict the provision of goods and services to homosexuals. Because the EASOR 2007 regarded such restriction as discrimination, the Bishop of Southwell and Nottingham, George Cassidy, complained that it meant 'the right to freedom of religion is being treated as of lesser weight than other human rights'.[96] Or, as the Archbishop of York, John Sentamu, argued:

> the Government are venturing down an unconsidered path through the establishment of a new hierarchy of rights. Rather than levelling the playing field for those who suffer discrimination [...] this legislation effects a rearrangement of discriminatory attitudes and bias to overcompensate and skew the field the other way.[97]

This argument is problematic because the EASOR 2007 extended protection from discrimination on the basis of sexual orientation in a similar way to that extended to religion or belief by the EA 2006.[98] In this sense, those providing goods, facilities or services to the public were *equally* required not to discriminate on the grounds of sexual orientation or religion and belief. Again, the law only appears 'skewed' if one accepts the commonly made claim that religious believers have a fundamental need to practise intolerance towards homosexuals. As we have shown, it has been the persuasiveness of that claim that has encouraged the inclusion of the exceptions in equality law that single out religious organisations for specific and additional benefits.

The claim that the EASOR 2007 discriminates against people on the basis of religion and belief and forces them to act against their consciences was central to the complaint advanced by the litigant in *Ladele v The London Borough of Islington*.[99] In its judgment the Court of Appeal held that a local authority was entitled to compel a registrar, Ms Ladele, to officiate at the registration of same-sex civil partnerships even though she objected on the grounds of religious belief because of:

---

94 S.20 Race Relations Act 1976.
95 S.29 Sex Discrimination Act 1975.
96 HL Debate, 21 March 2007, c.1302.
97 Ibid., c.1309.
98 S.46 Equality Act 2006.
99 *Ladele v The London Borough of Islington* [2009] EWCA Civ 1357.

the relatively limited circumstances in which it is permissible to discriminate against anyone on grounds of sexual orientation because of one's religious belief: those circumstances are essentially limited to the membership and operation of 'organisations relating to religion or belief', which plainly does not cover performing civil partnership unions, which is self-evidently a secular activity carried out in a public sphere under the auspices of a public, secular body.[100]

The European Court of Human Rights also subsequently rejected a complaint brought by Ms Ladele and another applicant who claimed that requiring them to provide services to homosexuals when they had a religious objection to homosexuality violated rights protected under Article 9 (freedom of thought, conscience and religion) and Article 14 (prohibition of discrimination) of the European Convention on Human Rights.[101] However, two judges in the European Court of Human Rights dissented from the majority in respect of Ms Ladele's complaint. In their partly dissenting opinion, Judges Vučinić and De Gaetano argued that although Ms Ladele had complained of religious discrimination, the broader issue at stake was one of freedom of conscience.[102] These judges compared Ms Ladele's refusal to be involved in the administration of the civil partnership registration of same-sex couples with forms of conscientious objection that have 'in the past all too often been paid for in acts of heroism, whether at the hands of the Spanish Inquisition or of a Nazi firing squad'.[103] Vučinić and De Gaetano argued that the failure of Ms Ladele's employers to protect her conscientious objection, which was a manifestation of her 'deep religious conviction and beliefs', was the result of a 'blinkered political correctness' which favoured 'gay rights' over 'fundamental human rights'.[104] Vučinić and De Gaetano therefore promulgated a hierarchy of rights in which the freedom to discriminate against homosexuals, when the outcome of a 'deep religious conviction' or 'conscientious objection', is regarded as more 'fundamental' than the right to be free of discrimination based on sexual orientation. It remains to be seen whether in the UK (and elsewhere) religious opponents of anti-discrimination legislation relating to goods, services, facilities and premises in respect of sexual orientation can advance the conscientious objection argument made by Vučinić and De Gaetano to further the scope for individual-level exceptions.

100 Ibid., § 70.
101 *Eweida and Others v the United Kingdom*, nos. 48420/10, 59842/10, 51671/10 and 36516/10, 15 January 2013.
102 Ibid., Joint Partly Dissenting Opinion of Judges Vučinić and De Gaetano.
103 Ibid., § 3.
104 Ibid., § 5.

Resisting greater equality and defending exceptions: religious opposition to the Equality Act 2010

The Equality Act (EA) 2010 is a significant piece of legislation that both consolidated existing equality legislation and introduced new measures.[105] A fundamental element of the EA 2010 was the introduction of a single public sector equality duty which requires public authorities, in the exercise of their functions, to 'eliminate discrimination, harassment, victimisation', 'advance equality of opportunity between persons' and 'foster good relations between persons' in respect of all of the protected characteristics specified by the EA 2010.[106] In the consultation that preceded the EA 2010, the proposal to extend the public sector equality duty to include sexual orientation produced the greatest number of overall responses and very strong objection from Christian groups.[107] Examples of this included the Catholic Parliamentary Office who argued that, in light of a 'promotion of the equivalence of homosexual and heterosexual lifestyle which has been strangely negligent of considering the different health implications', it was 'prudent and advisable' not to include sexual orientation within a single equality duty[108] (opposition was also expressed by the Church of England[109]). These objections again demonstrated that some religious opponents regarded sexual orientation and religion to be in a competitive relationship. For example, although also opposing the extension of the single public sector equality duty to religion or belief, religious opponents 'made clear that they would nevertheless argue for extension to include religion or belief, if the decision was made to extend the duty to include sexual orientation'.[110] Whilst religious opposition to the single public sector equality duty was unsuccessful, religious opponents, as we discuss below, did succeed in resisting a number of proposed changes to equality law that would have benefited sexual minorities.

---

105 In respect of sexual orientation equality, the Equality Act 2010 revoked the Employment Equality (Sexual Orientation) Regulations 2003 and the Equality Act (Sexual Orientation) Regulations 2007. The Employment Equality (Sexual Orientation) Regulations (Northern Ireland) 2003 and Equality Act (Sexual Orientation) Regulations (Northern Ireland) 2006 remain in force.
106 S.149(1) Equality Act 2010. The protected characteristics are: age; disability; gender reassignment; marriage and civil partnership; pregnancy and maternity; race; religion or belief; sex; sexual orientation.
107 HM Government, *The Equality Bill – Government Response to the Consultation*, July 2008, Cm. 7454.
108 Catholic Parliamentary Office: An Agency of the Bishops' Conference of Scotland, 'A framework for fairness: proposals for a single equality bill for Great Britain: a response', September 2007.
109 Church of England, 'A framework for fairness: proposals for a single equality bill for Great Britain, a Church of England response by the Archbishops' Council', 4 September 2007.
110 HM Government, op. cit., § 2.44.

Retaining religious employment exceptions

When the Equality Bill 2008/09 was introduced to Parliament it reproduced in largely similar form the employment exception for organised religions included in the EESOR 2003. However, the exception differed from the EESOR 2003 in two key ways. The first difference was the inclusion of a proportionality test that would have required an organised religion to show that applying a requirement related to sexual orientation was a 'proportionate means' of complying with the doctrines of religion or avoiding conflict with the strongly held religious convictions of a significant number of a religion's followers.[111] The second difference was the inclusion of a definition of the form of employment for which the requirement could be applied: specifically, work that involved 'leading or assisting in the observation of liturgical or ritualistic practices of the religion, or promoting or explaining the doctrine of the religion (whether to followers of the religion or to others)'.[112] Some scholars have argued that this definition would have narrowed the scope of the exception and, as a result, reversed the decision in *Reaney v Hereford Diocesan Board of Finance*[113] in which an employment tribunal deemed the post of Diocesan Youth Officer to fall within it.[114] However, this is far from conclusive since in *Reaney* the employment in question, which was to 'co-ordinate and to encourage and to promote church based youth organisations', was deemed to fall within 'that small number of posts outside of the clergy' to which the phrase 'organised religion' applies.[115] The proposed amendment can therefore be interpreted as reinforcing the decision in *Reaney* that the exception is applicable to work that involves promoting or explaining the doctrine of religion.

The Catholic Church and the Church of England objected to these proposed amendments on the grounds that they represented a 'distinct tightening of the law'[116] and 'a substantial narrowing of the present exemption'.[117] The Archbishop of York, John Sentamu, argued that the amendments narrowed the religious exception and failed 'to reflect the way in which members of the church and many other religious groups understand their faith to be the bedrock of their lives':

---

111   Sch.9 Pt.1 Para.2(5)–(6) Equality Bill 2009 as introduced 27 April 2009. As we detailed above, no proportionality test was included in Reg.7(3) Employment Equality (Sexual Orientation) Regulations 2003.
112   Sch.9 Pt.1 Para.2(8)(a)–(b) Equality Bill 2009 as introduced 27 April 2009.
113   *Reaney v Hereford Diocesan Board of Finance*, op. cit.
114   R. Sandberg, *Law and Religion*, Cambridge: Cambridge University Press, 2011, p.121.
115   *Reaney v Hereford Diocesan Board of Finance*, op. cit., § 102.
116   R. Kornicki, Parliamentary Co-ordinator, Catholic Bishops' Conference, HC Committee, 9 June 2009, c.68.
117   W. Fittall, Secretary-General, General Synod of the Church of England, HC Committee, 9 June 2009, c.69.

At the height of the floods in Cumbria, I visited Cockermouth, Workington and Keswick. A major part of the relief effort in those places was being carried out by Churches Together, with Christ Church, Cockermouth, as the hub of the activity. The church had been converted into a relief centre and the rector, Reverend Wendy Sanders, and members of the churches did outstanding work which made a huge difference to the whole relief programme. They were, of course, providing help and care to all people, regardless of faith or no faith. How would the Bill classify this activity? Would it come under 'liturgical or ritualistic practices' or 'explaining the doctrine of the religion'?[118]

The Archbishop of York's example obfuscates whether he would seek to exercise an exception based on sexual orientation in the context of offering aid to victims of natural disasters, but his wish to maintain the maximum scope to do so is clear. That wish was endorsed in the Lords when Peers approved amendments tabled by Baroness O'Cathain to remove the proportionality requirement and the definition of employment from the Bill.[119] O'Cathain argued that this did not represent 'special pleading for the churches [because] the principle of exemptions is widely accepted, not just for religion'.[120] However, the retention of the exception largely in the form enacted in the EESOR 2003 to allow organised religions to apply a requirement related to sexual orientation (as well as in respect of sex, transsexuality, and marital or civil partnership status) without reference to proportionality means that religion has a unique status in the EA 2010.[121] Organised religions retain special and bespoke provisions that allow wider scope for discrimination (albeit in respect of a narrow range of posts) than that available to other employers under exceptions relating to general occupational requirements.[122]

118   HL Debate, 15 December 2009, c.1433.
119   HL Committee, 25 January 2010, c.1211. The House divided 216-178 in favour of omitting the proportionality requirement from the Bill, with eight Lords Spiritual voting with the majority. HL Debate, 25 January 2010, Division No.1. The House divided 177-172 in favour of omitting the definition of employment from the Bill, with eight Lords Spiritual making a crucial contribution in voting with the majority. HL Debate, 25 January 2010, Division No.3.
120   Ibid., c.1212.
121   Sch.9 Pt.1 Para.2 Equality Act 2010. Somewhat confusingly, the *Explanatory Notes* for the Equality Act 2010 (§ 790–791) state that the exception only applies when a requirement is applied in a 'proportionate way'. This contrasts with the language used in Sch.9 Pt.1 Para.2 where there is no reference to proportionality. It is notable, however, that Sch.9 Pt.1 Para.3 Equality Act 2010, which provides an exception for a person 'with an ethos based on religion or belief' to apply 'in relation to work a requirement to be of a particular religion or belief', does specify that a person must demonstrate that the 'requirement is a proportionate means of achieving a legitimate aim'. This reflects the proportionality requirement that was previously included in Reg.7 Employment Equality (Religion or Belief) Regulations 2003.
122   Sch.9 Pt.1 Para.1 Equality Act 2010.

Attempts to widen goods, services, facilities and premises exceptions

The exception provided to religious organisations to permit lawful discrimination on the grounds of sexual orientation in respect of goods, services, facilities and premises in the EA 2010 mirror those first enacted in the EASOR 2007.[123] During the passage of the EA 2010 there were attempts by religious opponents to widen the scope of the exception. In Commons Committee, religious opponents unsuccessfully attempted to remove from the exception the requirement that a religious organisation not be 'an organisation whose sole or main purpose is commercial'[124] in order to allow 'commercial religious bodies to benefit from exceptions covering [...] sexual orientation'.[125] A further unsuccessful amendment sought to ensure that premises belonging to religious organisations – such as church halls – would not be classified as 'solely and mainly' commercial and therefore benefit from the exception. This may have been motivated by a concern about the interpretation of the scope of the exception advanced by Stonewall Chief Executive, Ben Summerskill, who stated that 'as long as the church is letting out the premises in general, the exemption does not apply'[126] – a view also endorsed by the Solicitor-General.[127] Yet, this interpretation ignores that the exception specifies that it is the purpose of the organisation that must be solely or mainly commercial (not the activity) and therefore a church is able to exercise the exception when letting out a part of its premises. The guidance issued with the EA 2010 confirms this:

> A Church refuses to let out its hall for a Gay Pride celebration as it considers that it would conflict with the strongly held religious convictions of a significant number of its followers. This would not be unlawful sexual orientation discrimination.[128]

However, for some religious opponents the exception for religious organisations was still not wide enough. In Lords Committee, Lord Mackay of Clashfern unsuccessfully attempted to include provision for individuals with a 'genuine conscientious objection' to withhold any goods or service because they have a 'fairly orthodox view' on homosexuality.[129] The Bishop of Chichester, John Hind, leant support to the principle of the amendment, arguing that religious beliefs 'inform our public attitudes and behaviour as citizens' and that attempts to 'privatise belief' demonstrated a 'profoundly dangerous tendency'.[130] Regardless

---

123 Sch.23 Para.2 Equality Act 2010.
124 Sch.23 Para.2(2) Equality Act 2010.
125 J. Mason, HC Committee, 2 July 2009, c.653.
126 HC Committee, 2 June 2009, c.46.
127 V. Baird, HC Committee, 2 June 2009, c.46.
128 Equality Act 2010, *Explanatory Notes (Revised Edition)*, August 2010, § 996.
129 HL Committee, 13 January 2010, cc.591–592.
130 Ibid., c.600.

of the failure of these attempts to widen the religious exception to cover individual belief, the EA 2010 reproduced the wide scope available to religious organisations to lawfully discriminate on the grounds of sexual orientation in respect of the provision of goods, services and facilities, and the use of premises.

Further religious opposition to protection from harassment on the grounds of sexual orientation

During consultation on the EA 2010, Christian groups had again opposed the extension of harassment protection on the grounds of sexual orientation and, as a consequence, the Government announced that it had decided not to 'extend protection against harassment outside work, on grounds of sexual orientation or religion or belief, because we do not see evidence of a real problem'.[131] As a consequence, the EA 2010 does not contain any protection from harassment outside of employment on the grounds of sexual orientation. For example, whilst the EA 2010 prohibits a service-provider from harassing a person requiring the service or a person to whom the service-provider provides the service,[132] and states that a person must not do anything that constitutes harassment in the exercise of a public function that is not the provision of a service to the public or a section of the public,[133] it states that sexual orientation and religion or belief are not relevant protected characteristics.[134] Similarly, although the EA 2010 prohibits harassment in the disposal of premises,[135] it also states that sexual orientation and religion or belief are not relevant protected characteristics.[136] When opposing the extension of harassment to cover sexual orientation, religious opponents again invoked an argument that there must be parity and 'equality' in the harassment provisions relating to sexual orientation and religion and belief.[137]

During the passage of the EA 2010 there were various attempts to extend the harassment provisions to cover sexual orientation. For instance, in Commons Committee an amendment was unsuccessfully proposed to extend harassment provisions to sexual orientation, albeit with a 'narrower definition' of harassment than that applied to other protected characteristics so as to meet 'the need to have respect for freedom of speech'.[138] In the Lords, various amendments were proposed that would have extended protection from harassment on the basis of sexual orientation in schools, as well as in services and public functions.[139] There

---

131 HM Government, op. cit.
132 S.29(3) Equality Act 2010.
133 S.29(6) Equality Act 2010.
134 S.29(8) Equality Act 2010.
135 S.33(3) Equality Act 2010.
136 S.33(6) Equality Act 2010.
137 HM Government, op. cit.
138 E. Harris, HC Committee, 18 June 2009, c.303.
139 HL Debate, 13 January 2010, c.575.

was considerable resistance to this and the argument made against extending harassment provisions to cover sexual orientation was that it would limit freedom of religious speech (an argument similar to that made against 'hate speech' legislation, which we discuss in Chapter 5). In response to the argument that 'some people use their religion as a vehicle for cultural bigotry' and that harassment provisions were necessary to protect sexual minorities,[140] it was argued that 'one person's bigotry is another person's belief' and that extending harassment provisions would 'create a risk to free speech'.[141] As a consequence, the EA 2010 provisions on harassment in respect of goods, services, facilities and premises continue to apply to other protected characteristics but not sexual orientation and religion or belief.

Conclusion

In this chapter we have examined the development of legislation specifically designed to address discrimination on the grounds of sexual orientation and discussed the ways in which this has been shaped by religion. The focus of our analysis has been the discourses deployed by religious groups and individuals to negotiate exceptions for organised religions and religious organisations from anti-discrimination law relating to sexual orientation. Supporters of religious exceptions repeatedly invoked the claim that sexual orientation and religion are in competition with each other and that the respective rights of each group necessitate careful balancing. Exceptions are needed, it is argued, to prevent a new 'orthodoxy' of sexual orientation equality infringing the essential need for religious believers to manifest their 'traditional' faith-based opposition to homosexuality. As we have demonstrated, this argument has been successful in shaping law that allows organised religions and religious organisations a unique and significant capacity to lawfully discriminate against individuals on the grounds of sexual orientation. Our analysis shows that discourses of religious freedom have been instrumental in producing a legislative landscape in which organised religions may apply a wider requirement related to sexual orientation in the sphere of employment than that available to other employers, and religious organisations can refuse to provide non-heterosexuals with goods, services, facilities and the use of premises. The consequence of this has been the creation of an equalities hierarchy in which sexual orientation is often afforded less protection than other protected characteristics. In the next chapter we show how a similar discourse was marshalled and extended in respect of law reform relating to same-sex partnership recognition.

140 D. Abbott, HC Committee, 18 June 2009, c.308.
141 J. Mason, HC Committee, 18 June 2009, cc.308–311.

Chapter 4

The secular and the sacred

Civil partnership and same-sex marriage

In this chapter we examine the evolution of legislation in the UK that has enabled same-sex couples to register civil partnerships and solemnise marriage. Our analysis of this sphere of lawmaking demonstrates the considerable impact of religious opposition to the legal recognition of same-sex partnerships upon successive legislation. During the passage of the Civil Partnership Bill 2004, and in response to MPs whom he characterised as '[t]hose who believe in God, and yet believe too in opposing the Bill', Alan Duncan MP described religious opposition in the following way:

> In my view, the Bill is a landmark in the clash between those who want to enforce their own moral code and choose to judge their fellow man and those who say that a couple's mutual love should be permitted and celebrated without the intrusion and interference of the state.[1]

Whilst Duncan rightly identifies a conflict between religious opponents of same-sex partnership recognition and those in favour of law reform, our analysis of ten years of parliamentary debate demonstrates that this has rarely become manifest as an explicit 'clash'. In comparison with the reform of the criminal law that we examined in Chapter 1, a key aspect of parliamentary debates in this area of law has been the relative absence of religious condemnations of homosexuality. Although religious opponents of legislative change have certainly sought to enforce 'their own moral code', they have consistently obfuscated and dissembled in order to avoid using discourse that would overtly 'judge their fellow man'. Duncan's description of a conflict between religion and homosexuality within the terms of the dispute between Devlin[2] and Hart[3] – as a battle between public (Christian) morality and private liberty – fails to adequately capture the complexity of the religious opposition to the legal recognition of same-sex partnerships.

---

1 HC Debate, 9 November 2004, cc.800–801.
2 P. Devlin, *The Enforcement of Morals*, Oxford: Oxford University Press, 1965.
3 H.L.A. Hart, *Law, Liberty and Morality*, Oxford: Oxford University Press, 1963.

Unlike the reform of criminal law relating to male homosexual acts, which represented an effective withdrawal of (Christian-inspired) law from the sphere of private life, the development of civil partnership and same-sex marriage legislation actively incorporates law into private intimate relationships. Those in favour of civil partnership and same-sex marriage legislation are not, as Duncan characterises it, against the 'intrusion and interference of the state' with 'a couple's mutual love' because such legislation fundamentally increases the state's involvement with couple relationships. Furthermore, a key aspect of the primary legal mechanism through which the state sanctions, legitimises and mandates particular couple relationships – the solemnisation of marriage – is that it is intimately bound up with religion. Although English law distinguishes 'civil marriage' from marriage solemnised according to religious rites and usages,[4] religion and law maintain a close relationship in respect of marriage.[5] Consequently, whereas debates about the regulation of male homosexual sex amongst Christians and other faith groups in the UK were, in the latter half of the twentieth century, premised on a question about the extent to which law should be 'rolled back', in respect of same-sex partnership rights the foundational question has been the extent to which law should be 'rolled out'.

This chapter examines the influence of religion on three significant pieces of legislation: first, the Civil Partnership Act 2004 which enabled same-sex couples to register a partnership in all jurisdictions of the UK; second, the Marriages and Civil Partnerships (Approved Premises) (Amendment) Regulations 2011 which allowed for civil partnerships to be registered on religious premises in England and Wales; and, third, the Marriage (Same Sex Couples) Act 2013 which made the marriage of same-sex couples lawful in England and Wales. In charting the development of this legislation, we consider a number of discursive strategies that have been adopted by religious opponents in their attempt to fashion law in particular ways. Whilst these strategies have been heterogeneous, their fundamental

---

4   S.35(2) Civil Partnership Act 2004 defines a 'civil marriage' as a 'marriage solemnised otherwise than according to the rites of the Church of England or any other religious usages'.
5   In this chapter our primary concern is with the statutory relationship between religion and marriage in England and Wales since 'An Act for the better preventing of clandestine Marriages' 1753 (26 Geo.2 c.33) required that all marriage (except 'amongst the People called Quakers, or amongst the Persons professing the Jewish Religion') be solemnised in a 'parish church or chapel' of the Church of England following the publication of banns or the issuing of a licence (except in the case of marriage by special licence, issued by the Archbishop of Canterbury). Although subsequent statutory changes have enabled the solemnisation of 'civil marriage', the extensive provisions relating to religion in the Marriage Act 1949 – which *inter alia* prescribes the methods of authorising marriages so that they may be solemnised according to the rites of the Church of England, the usages of the Jews and Society of Friends, or in other registered places of worship according to a form and ceremony that the persons to be married see fit to adopt – demonstrates the endurance of the close connection between religion and marriage in English law.

aim has been to maintain distinctions in law between same-sex and opposite-sex partnerships. As we demonstrate, religious opponents have been successful in shaping legislation to reflect and maintain the fundamental hostility of mainstream organised religions to sexual orientation equality.

Avoiding a clash: civil partnerships as secular relationships

The Civil Partnership Act (CPA) 2004 enabled a same-sex couple in the UK to register a partnership that afforded legal rights and responsibilities equivalent to heterosexual marriage. On enactment, the CPA 2004 specified that '[n]o religious service is to be used while the civil partnership registrar is officiating at the signing of a civil partnership document'[6] and that registration must 'not be in religious premises'.[7] Furthermore, the CPA 2004 made the signing of a civil partnership document (or schedule in Northern Ireland and Scotland) the formal means by which a civil partnership is contracted, rather than the verbal declaration and contract made in the solemnisation of marriage. The inclusion of these provisions was neither inevitable nor uncontested. Baroness Rendell, for example, argued that '[m]any homosexual and lesbian people are deeply religious [. . .] and would like to feel their commitment to each other was made in the sight of God as well as man'.[8] In this section we discuss the reasons and justifications given for the inclusion of provisions in the CPA 2004 prohibiting the use of religious services and premises during the registration of a civil partnership.

As a background to the CPA 2004, it is important to note that the UK Parliament had twice before debated and failed to enact legislation that proposed to extend a legal status for same-sex partners equivalent to marriage. The Relationships (Civil Registration) Bill 2001[9] was introduced as a Ten Minute Rule Bill into the House of Commons and failed to progress beyond Second Reading, and the Civil Partnership Bill 2002[10] was introduced into the House of Lords as a Private Members' Bill that was discontinued after Second Reading.[11] Neither of these privately sponsored Bills was designed with an exclusive focus on same-sex couples but, rather, proposed that all cohabiting couples regardless of sex

---

6   S.2(5) Civil Partnership Act 2004 in respect of England and Wales. In Northern Ireland, religious content was prohibited by S.137(5) Civil Partnership Act 2004. In Scotland, religious content was prohibited because civil partnerships could only be registered by authorised registrars (S.85 Civil Partnership Act 2004) rather than approved celebrants.
7   S.6(1)(b) Civil Partnership Act 2004 in respect of England and Wales; S.93(3) Civil Partnership Act 2004 in respect of Scotland; Reg.12 Civil Partnership Regulations (Northern Ireland) 2005.
8   HL Debate, 22 April 2004, c.415.
9   HC Debate, 24 October 2001, cc.321–327.
10 HL Debate, 25 January 2002, cc.1691–1746.

should be able to register a partnership and gain access to legal rights associated with marriage. Neither Bill included any reference to religious premises or ceremony. Because of the emphasis placed by the sponsors of these Bills on the need to extend legal protections to cohabiting unmarried heterosexual couples, neither generated significant opposition towards same-sex couples during debates. Although Stuart Bell MP strongly opposed the Relationships (Civil Registration) Bill 2001 at its First Reading on the grounds that '[m]arriage [. . .] is a commitment between one man and one woman' and that 'every society has restricted marriages to heterosexual relationships',[12] there was a large majority in favour of it.[13] There was similar enthusiasm for the Civil Partnership Bill 2002 in the Lords, where only the Bishop of Guildford, John Gladwin, made a distinction between same-sex and opposite-sex couples in respect of the ceremonial aspects of contracting partnerships.[14]

It was not until the UK Government, via the Women and Equality Unit, issued the consultation *Civil Partnership: A Framework for the Legal Recognition of Same-Sex Couples*[15] in June 2003 that objections to same-sex civil partnerships began to be made. A significant aspect of these objections was that they originated from religious organisations or individuals with religious affiliations. The consultation document, which set out Government proposals to make specific legal provisions for the registration of same-sex partnerships,[16] contained no reference to religion – save for one mention in passing to 'marriage, whether religious or civil'[17] – but generated responses from churches and other religious organisations. The Government's own analysis of responses to the consultation showed that it had

---

11 On 11 February 2002, Lord Lester of Herne Hill stated that he would not be proceeding with the Bill in order to 'allow the completion of a cross-departmental Government review of the impact which the proposed reforms would have' and that he would 'call for a Select Committee of the House of Lords to examine the question of reform once the Government has concluded its review in autumn 2002'. House of Commons Research Paper 02/17, *The Relationships (Civil Registration) Bill and the Civil Partnerships Bill*, 19 March 2002.
12 HC Debate, 24 October 2001, c.324.
13 The House divided 179-59 in favour. HC Debate, 24 October 2001, Division No.41.
14 The Bishop of Guildford cited evidence of one same-sex couple who 'did not want a gay wedding in church, they wanted a party'. HL Debate, 25 January 2002, cc.1721–1722.
15 Women and Equality Unit, *Civil Partnership: A Framework for the Legal Recognition of Same-Sex Couples*, London: Department for Trade and Industry, June 2003.
16 The legislation was encouraged by the judgment in *Mendoza v Ghaidan* ([2002] EWCA Civ 1533), in which the Court of Appeal considered the entitlement of a survivor of a long-term same-sex partnership to a housing tenancy under the Rent Act 1977 which provided a right of succession to those 'living with the original tenant as his or her wife or husband'. The Court of Appeal, relying on the Human Rights Act 1998, held that the phrase 'as his or her wife or husband' had to be taken to mean 'as *if they were* his or her wife or husband' (§ 35) to include same-sex couples.
17 Women and Equality Unit, op. cit., § 2.7.

received responses from a number of nationally based religious groups and that 47 per cent (eight responses) were opposed to a same-sex civil partnership scheme.[18] The analysis further showed that the Government received responses from a number of individual religious groups and congregations and of these 85 per cent (17 responses) were opposed. The majority of religiously based objections at the consultation stage therefore came from religious groups and congregations such as 'Baptist, Evangelical, Free and Congregational churches'.[19] In addition to these, the Christian Institute had encouraged individuals to submit a bespoke postcard to the consultation and this had resulted in 202 objections.[20] Qualitative analysis of the religious views expressed during the consultation show that faith underpinned both support for civil partnerships – with one Church of England vicar, for example, arguing, 'I warmly and wholeheartedly endorse the proposals for Civil Partnership registration for lesbian and gay couples'[21] – and opposition – with, for example, one Baptist minister responding that 'I cannot see how gay relationships can possibly be equated to marriage'.[22]

A key aspect of the Government's response to religious arguments was to state that it would not 'interfere in matters that are clearly for religious groups to decide for themselves' and that the 'registration of a civil partnership would be a purely civil process and involves (sic) no religious element'.[23] To achieve this, the Government relied upon the existing legal framework regulating the solemnisation of heterosexual 'civil marriage'.[24] In England, for example, since 1837, heterosexual couples have been able to solemnise a marriage on the authority of superintendent registrar's certificate in register offices (and subsequently approved premises[25]) in a manner that must not involve any religious service.[26] Currently,

---

18 Women and Equality Unit, *Responses to Civil Partnership: A Framework for the Legal Recognition of Same-Sex Couples*, London: Department for Trade and Industry, November 2003.
19 Ibid., § 2.14.
20 Ibid., § 2.6.
21 Ibid., § 3.11.
22 Ibid., § 3.10.
23 Ibid., § 3.12.
24 The Church of England has disputed the distinction between 'civil' and 'religious' marriage, arguing that in English law 'there is one social institution called marriage, which can be entered into through either a religious or a civil ceremony. To suggest that this involves two kinds of marriage is to make the category error of mistaking the ceremony for the institution itself.' Church of England, 'A response to the Government Equalities Office consultation "Equal Civil Marriage" from the Church of England', June 2012.
25 S.46A and S.46B Marriage Act 1949.
26 S.21 Marriage Act 1836 (commenced 1837) enabled couples to 'contract and solemnize Marriage at the Office and in the Presence of the Superintendent Registrar'. S.12 Marriage and Registration Act 1856 explicitly prohibited the use of any religious service during the

when marriage is solemnised in this way the only similarity it has with a marriage solemnised in registered buildings (places of religious worship) is in the verbal declaration and contract made by a couple to legally formalise their partnership.[27] By using civil marriage as a model and omitting the element of the declaratory and contracting words, the Government constructed civil partnership registration in such a way to ensure it was completely disinvested of any sacred quality.

Appeasing religious opposition through secularism

The Government's argument that the registration of a civil partnership should be entirely isolated from any aspect of religion in order to protect religious freedoms can be seen as a strategy to both avoid confrontation with and appease religious groups. A key aspect of this strategy has been the assertion that civil partnership is a 'measured and proportionate response' to the 'disadvantages which same-sex couples face in the way they are treated by our laws' because it offers a 'secular solution'.[28] As the Bishop of Peterborough, Ian Cundy, argued, the Government's commitment to 'a secular solution' was 'honoured in a number of ways: [. . .] a distinctive procedure with no specific wording; a document signed before a civil partnership registrar; without religious, or indeed any, defined ceremony'.[29] Yet, although Government ministers argued that it was important to ensure that a civil partnership was a 'purely secular legal relationship', because 'there are [. . .] people who take a secular view and would want to be reassured that there was a purely secular route for entering a civil partnership or civil marriage',[30] the target audience for its 'reassurance' was not secularists. Rather, the emphasis placed on the secular quality of civil partnership was a response to those religious organisations and individuals who expressed hostility towards civil partnership because of a perceived similarity with marriage.

For example, during the CPA 2004 debates the Bishop of Oxford, Richard Harries, argued that there was 'a concern to some in the Churches that the

---

soleminisation of marriage in this way; a prohibition continued by S.45(2) Marriage Act 1949 which states: 'No religious service shall be used at any marriage solemnized in the office of a superintendent registrar.' S.46B(4) Marriage Act 1949 extends this prohibition to marriages soleminised on approved premises.

27 The declaratory and contracting words that are common to marriages solemnized in register offices and registered buildings in England and Wales are specified in S.44(3)–(3A) Marriage Act 1949. Marriage solemnised according to the rites of the Church of England and the usages of the Jewish religion and Society of Friends are not subject to this requirement.
28 Baroness Scotland of Asthal, HL Debate, 22 April 2004, c.388.
29 HL Debate, 22 April 2004, c.422.
30 J. Smith, HC Committee, 21 October 2004, cc.80–81.

legislation [...] parallels that for marriage at almost every point'.[31] It was commonly asserted by parliamentarians that civil partnership was 'absolutely parallel with marriage',[32] 'driven too much by an attempt to shadow the provisions for marriage',[33] 'a parody on marriage'[34] and 'introduces homosexual marriage by any other name'.[35] Some religious opponents compared similarities in the solemnisation of civil marriage and civil partnership registration as evidence of this. Baroness O'Cathain, for example, argued that the prohibition on religious premises and services was inadequate to distinguish civil partnership from marriage because a civil partnership 'must be solemnised in front of a registrar in the presence of two witnesses, exactly like marriage'.[36] Although O'Cathain and other opponents successfully resisted an amendment to the CPA 2004 that would have added a verbal contracting statement, similar to that used in the solemnisation of marriage, to the civil partnership registration process – on the grounds that 'married people will be deeply offended that the civil marriage ceremony is to be adopted in the formation of civil partnerships'[37] – it was still claimed that civil partnership too closely resembled marriage.

Religious opponents of the CPA 2004 used arguments about 'similarity' and 'resemblance' to argue that 'opposition to [civil partnership] comes from those who feel that it is an attack on Christian marriage or, indeed, on civil marriage, which has its roots in a Christian tradition'.[38] All marriage, it was argued, regardless of how it is solemnised is 'sanctified by the sacramental tradition of Christianity'[39] and is the outcome of a 'doctrine [...] grounded in the Christian tradition'.[40] Because marriage is 'a solemn and holy thing'[41] and a 'unique and holy'[42] institution, religious opponents claimed that the CPA 2004 'will further undermine the institution of marriage – the holiest state of matrimony. At the same time, it will be an affront to Christians and other faith communities.'[43] This view reflected the Church of England's argument that marriage occupies a 'special position' and has a 'unique status' in society.[44] Such arguments were given forceful re-expression in various responses to subsequent consultations on same-sex

31 HL Debate, 22 April 2004, c.389.
32 Lord Elton, HL Debate, 22 April 2004, c.420.
33 Bishop of Chester, HL Committee, 13 May 2004, c.208.
34 Lord Tebbit, HL Debate, 24 June 2004, c.1367.
35 E. Leigh, HC Debate, 9 November 2004, c.731.
36 HL Debate, 22 April 2004, c.404.
37 HL Committee, 10 May 2004, c.54.
38 Lord St John of Fawsley, HL Debate, 24 June 2004, c.1357.
39 Lord St John of Fawsley, HL Debate, 17 November 2004, c.1462.
40 Bishop of Rochester, HL Debate, 24 June 2004, c.1367.
41 I. Paisley, HC Debate, 12 October 2004, c.223.
42 E. Leigh, HC Debate, 9 November 2004, c.731.
43 C. Chope, HC Debate, 12 October 2004, c.213.
44 Church of England, 'Civil Partnership: Church of England response to DTI consultation document', Archbishops' Council, 30 September 2003.

marriage in England and Wales, as well as in Scotland. For example, Cardinal O'Brian of the Catholic Church in Scotland produced a letter to be read out in every Catholic church on its newly inaugurated 'National Marriage Sunday' in which he called on Catholics to defend the 'truth and beauty of the Sacrament of Matrimony'.[45]

The response to these arguments by supporters of the CPA 2004 was not to contest the claims being made in respect of the religious nature of heterosexual marriage. Rather, supporters sought to appease religious objectors by confirming the claim that marriage retained a special religious significance distinct from the 'purely secular legal relationship' of civil partnership. For example, Alan Duncan MP asserted that '[w]hile marriage is an ancient institution with special religious significance, civil partnership is a secular legal arrangement', and because a 'religious service is specifically banned during the signing of the register', the 'clear distinction between a civil secular partnership and the institution of marriage [is] preserved'.[46] Similarly, Chris Bryant MP stated that 'marriage is an institution that is ordained of God and should be celebrated between a man and a woman' and that 'we should have in law separate institutions that reflect that reality'.[47] These arguments attributed a religious substance to all heterosexual marriage to distinguish it from secular civil partnerships. As Jacqui Smith MP argued:

> [W]e have used civil marriage as the template for creating a completely new legal relationship, that of the civil partnership [...] The whole point, however, is that civil partnership is not civil marriage, for a variety of reasons, such as the traditions and history – religious and otherwise – that accompany marriage. It is not marriage, but it is, in many ways – dare I say it? – akin to marriage. We make no apology for that.[48]

Edward Leigh MP described this as 'pure sophistry' designed to avoid affronting 'religious sentiment',[49] and many religious opponents argued that civil partnership was 'gay marriage in all but name'.[50] The reliance by supporters of the CPA 2004 on a distinction between 'sacred' marriage and 'secular' civil partnership was certainly problematic given that, although marriage in the UK has long been legally associated with religion, it was unsustainable to assert that religious tradition underpins marriage solemnised in civil contexts. Yet this distinction was central in the attempt to appease religious opponents and explains why the

---

45 Scottish Catholic Media Office, News Release, 22 August 2012. Available online at www.scmo.org/articles/cardinal-obrien-calls-on-politicians-to--sustain-rather-than-subvert-marriage.html (accessed on 3 December 2013).
46 HC Debate, 21 October 2004, c.185.
47 HC Committee, 21 October 2004, c.70.
48 HC Debate, 9 November 2004, c.776.
49 Ibid., c.780.
50 G. Howarth, HC Debate, 12 October 2004, c.239.

CPA 2004 was enacted with provisions that prohibited same-sex couples from registering a partnership on religious premises or including any reference to religion. The absence of religious content in the solemnisation of civil partnerships was therefore central to constructing a legal partnership that, whilst 'equal' to marriage in terms of rights and benefits, was distinctly 'separate'.

The geography of separation: places of worship and religious freedom

Although religious opponents of the CPA 2004 repeatedly claimed that the prohibition on religious premises and content in the registration of a civil partnership insufficiently distinguished it from heterosexual marriage, they vigorously argued that these provisions were essential in protecting religious rights and freedoms. For example, when an amendment was tabled to remove the restriction on registering civil partnerships on religious premises during the CPA 2004 debates, opponents argued that the prohibition was necessary to protect religious freedom:

> The amendment [. . .] would legalise civil partnership registration in a church, a mosque, a synagogue or temple. [A] great many clergy would regard it as totally unacceptable for a Government Bill to permit civil partnerships to be registered in a place of worship [. . .] This amendment directly concerns matters of religious belief. It is not about civil rights, since [. . .] a civil ceremony is freely available. It is, however, about theology and the views that religious people hold on homosexual practice. The amendment directly affects the internal affairs of religious bodies.[51]

It is striking that supporters of the CPA 2004 went to significant lengths to affirm that the protection of religious freedom required that churches be able to refuse to permit civil partnerships to be registered on their premises. Lord Alli argued that 'it is not for the state to dictate what the Church or any religious organisation should or should not do within their premises; it is up to them to decide on that',[52] and Alan Duncan MP argued that '[w]e have all been at pains to say that the Church should be allowed to determine what the Church wants to do and that we will not impose on it anything that might fetter its decision'.[53] Although Chris Bryant MP argued that the complete exclusion of all reference to religion during a civil partnership registration was 'anti-religious' rather than 'secular',[54] he

---

51 Baroness O'Cathain, HL Committee, 12 May 2004, c.135.
52 HL Committee, 12 May 2004, c.139.
53 HC Committee, 21 October 2004, c.67
54 Ibid., c.81.

agreed overall that it 'is not for the state to legislate' but 'for the Churches to decide whether they want to go down that route'.[55]

The argument, from both supporters and opponents of the CPA 2004, that churches must be free to determine their own practices was based on claims about the existing freedom of churches to decide the terms under which they will solemnise heterosexual marriage. Yet such claims are highly problematic because statute law has long placed requirements on ecclesiastical practice in respect of the solemnisation of marriage. For example, the Marriage Act 1540,[56] even if it did not affect the 'general marriage law',[57] specified prohibited degrees of relationship for the solemnisation of marriage. Since the Marriage Act 1753,[58] which introduced formal requirements for marriages solemnised by the Church of England that were previously governed solely by Canon law, marriage solemnised according to the rites of the Church of England has been subject to increasing statutory regulation. Similarly, although other organised religions retain significant autonomy and control in the solemnisation of marriage, statute law shapes their practice. The argument that a total prohibition on registering civil partnerships on religious premises was a fundamental requirement to preserve religious freedom from the encroachment of secular law therefore ignored the long-standing legal settlement between statute law and organised religions.

The more problematic aspect of the total prohibition on registering a civil partnership on religious premises was that it prevented organised religions from allowing it even if they wished to. This issue was present in the CPA 2004 debates – the Bishop of Oxford, Richard Harries, for example, argued that the prohibition 'infringes the proper freedom of religious authorities to control [. . .] premises' and that it was for 'those authorities and not for the state to decide whether or not their premises should be available to be used for registration purposes'[59] – but it remained muted. However, during the passage of the Equality Act (EA) 2010, this argument was reconfigured to make the claim that removing the prohibition would be within the 'tradition of standing up for religious freedoms'.[60] This view found wide support amongst Peers with records of voting on religious grounds against law reform aimed at extending gay and lesbian legal equality. For example, Baroness Butler-Sloss, who had opposed the introduction of the Equality Act (Sexual Orientation) Regulations 2007 (which we discussed in Chapter 3),[61] argued:

---

55   HC Debate, 9 November 2004, c.742.
56   'Concerning precontractes and degrees of consanguinite' 1540 (32 Hen.8 c.38).
57   *R v Chadwick* [1847] 11 QB 205 at 216.
58   'An Act for the better preventing of clandestine Marriages' 1753 (26 Geo.2 c.33).
59   HL Debate, 22 April 2004, c.399.
60   Lord Alli, HL Debate, 15 December 2009, c.1444.
61   HL Debate, 21 March 2007, Division No.1.

> I am utterly persuaded by [the removal of the prohibition on religious premises]. I would be totally opposed to it being a requirement, because many churches would find this utterly abhorrent; but in so far as there are churches and synagogues and other faith places that would like this to happen, it is entirely appropriate and I support [it].[62]

There was hostility to this argument from some religious opponents. For example, Baroness Royall argued that allowing registration of civil partnerships on religious premises 'blurs the line between what is a civil partnership and something that has elements of a religious partnership'.[63] The Bishop of Bradford, David James, argued that 'when Parliament introduced civil partnerships just a few years ago, it drew a clear distinction between the new legal status and marriage' and that changing this would create a 'muddle' between 'civil rights and religious freedoms'.[64] Or, as Lord Tebbit argued, it would 'equate civil partnership with marriage', which was problematic because a 'civil partnership is not a marriage, cannot be a marriage, never will be a marriage and should be treated entirely separately from marriage. Marriage is celebrated within a church.'[65] These opponents argued that the restriction on registering a civil partnership on religious premises was pivotal in maintaining the distinction between same- and opposite-sex partnerships. 'Christians and others', the Bishop of Chester, Peter Forster, argued, 'will continue to resist any blurring of the distinction between marriage and civil partnership'.[66]

Yet a central reason why a number of parliamentarians previously hostile to the CPA 2004 supported the removal of the prohibition was that they were persuaded that it enhanced religious freedom rather than furthered sexual orientation equality. As Baroness Royall described it: 'The amendment raises issues of fundamental religious conscience. This is not a question about civil rights for lesbians and gay men.'[67] The majority of religious supporters of the removal of the prohibition on religious premises ostensibly regarded it as a mechanism to strengthen the capacity of religious organisations to exercise autonomy in refusing to register civil partnerships. As a result of this support, the prohibition on religious premises (but not religious services) in England and Wales was repealed by the EA 2010,[68] and, following a consultation process, the Marriages and Civil Partnerships (Approved

---

62 HL Committee, 25 January 2010, c.1200.
63 HL Debate, 2 March 2010, c.1437.
64 Ibid., c.1430.
65 Ibid., c.1436.
66 HL Debate, 23 March 2010, c.866.
67 HL Debate, 2 March 2010, c.1439.
68 S.202(2) Equality Act 2010 repealed sections S.6(1)(b) and S.6(2) Civil Partnership Act 2004 which prohibited the use of religious premises for the registration of a civil partnership.

Premises) (Amendment) Regulations 2011 enabled religious premises to be approved for the purpose of registering civil partnerships.[69]

The Marriages and Civil Partnerships (Approved Premises) (Amendment) Regulations 2011 places no obligation on a religious organisation to 'opt in' to allowing the registration of civil partnerships on their premises. As a consequence, despite claims that removing the restriction would result in churches losing their religious freedom,[70] the majority of organised religions do not permit the registration of civil partnerships on their premises. The Church of England, for example, stated that 'the position under the new arrangements is that no Church of England religious premises may become "approved premises" for the registration of civil partnerships without there having been a formal decision by the General Synod to that effect'.[71] The General Synod has made no such decision and maintains a prohibition on the registration of civil partnerships on their religious premises.[72] In this sense, the removal of the prohibition has effectively enabled the Church of England and other mainstream religions to enforce and affirm a geography of separation[73] through which a hierarchical distinction between the value of same-sex and opposite-sex partnerships is maintained. As we examine below, arguments about this form of religious 'freedom' were essential in shaping the legislation enabling same-sex marriage in England and Wales.

Reaffirming separatism: same-sex marriage and religious rites

When, in 2012, the UK Government announced its intention to legislate to make marriage of same-sex couples lawful in England and Wales, it adopted the same discursive framework used in the CPA 2004 debates to make a fundamental distinction between profane 'civil marriage' and sacred 'religious marriage'. The Government proposed that it would not make any changes to 'religious marriage'

---

69 Marriages and Civil Partnerships (Approved Premises) (Amendment) Regulations 2011, amending Marriages and Civil Partnerships (Approved Premises) Regulations 2005. It is worth noting that the Explanatory Memorandum to the 2011 Regulations states: 'This change is being introduced as part of the Government's commitment to advancing equality for Lesbian, Gay, Bisexual and Transgender people and ensuring freedom of religion for people of all faiths.'
70 Baroness O'Cathain, HL Debate, 15 December 2011, c.1409.
71 Church of England, 'Civil partnerships in religious premises: note from the Secretary General', 1 December 2011, GS Misc 1005.
72 There has been an attempt to enable civil partnership registration in Church of England premises through a Private Members' Motion (John Ward, February 2012) in the General Synod but at the time of writing this has not yet been selected for debate.
73 A. Lemon and O. Williams, *Apartheid: A Geography of Separation*, Farnborough: Saxon House, 1976.

and that 'marriages solemnized through a religious ceremony and on religious premises would still only be legally possible between a man and a woman'.[74] However, following an initial consultation the Government subsequently announced that 'there is strength in the argument that, once marriage is made available to same-sex couples, religious organisations should be permitted to conduct such ceremonies if they wish to'.[75] The reason for this change in policy was that a number of religious organisations had argued that prohibiting same-sex marriage on religious premises curtailed religious freedom. The Religious Society of Friends, for example, argued for 'a permissive law which allows religious freedom'.[76] Such 'freedom' is qualitatively different to the removal of the spatial prohibition on the use of religious premises for the registration of a civil partnership because it opens the possibility of including same-sex couples in the social and cultural practice of solemnising marriage according to religious rites. In light of strong opposition by the Church of England, Catholic Church, Muslim Council of Britain and other mainstream faith groups to the solemnisation of same-sex marriage, the Government stated that 'it will remain unlawful for a religious organisation to marry same-sex couples unless it expressly consents and opts in according to a formal process put in place by legislation'.[77] As a consequence of this, when the Marriage (Same Sex Couples) Bill 2013 was introduced it was already shaped by religious opposition and drafted in such a way to ensure that the solemnisation of same-sex marriage by religious organisations was by default unlawful. Although some high-profile figures in the Church of England and Church in Wales expressed 'complete shock' at the position adopted by the Government and stated that it was not based on any consultation,[78] the approach taken by legislators was consistent with that taken in the CPA 2004 and unsurprising in light of mainstream religious opposition.

The 'quadruple lock' and the Church of England

The Government described the provisions relating to religion in the Marriage (Same Sex Couples) Act (MSSCA) 2013 as a 'quadruple lock' designed to 'promote' religious freedom.[79] The four 'locks' included in the MSSCA 2013 are: that solemnising same-sex marriage in places of worship or in another place

---

74 Government Equalities Office, *Equal Civil Marriage: A Consultation*, London: Home Office, 2012.
75 HM Government, *Equal Marriage: The Government's Response*, London: Home Office, 2012.
76 Religious Society of Friends (Quakers), 'Equal civil marriage: a consultation, Britain Yearly Meeting response', 17 May 2012.
77 HM Government, op. cit.
78 S. Jones, 'Church of England and Church in Wales protest at gay marriage ban', *Guardian*, 13 December 2012.
79 M. Miller, HC Debate, 5 February 2013, c.129.

according to religious rites or usages requires a religious organisation to 'opt in';[80] that no person or religious organisation can be compelled to undertake an 'opt-in activity' or refrain from undertaking an 'opt-out activity' in respect of same-sex marriage;[81] that any person or religious organisation that does not conduct, participate in or consent to a marriage in a place of worship or in another place according to religious rites or usages, for the reason that it is the marriage of a same-sex couple, does not contravene anti-discrimination law relating to the provision of services and the exercise of public functions;[82] and that the Church of England and Church in Wales are unable to opt-in to solemnising same-sex marriage in the same way as other religious organisations. In respect of the Church of England, the provisions in the MSSCA 2013 to prevent the solemnisation of same-sex marriage are extensive: no duty of a member of the Church of England clergy to marry is extended to same-sex couples;[83] the provisions for religious organisations to opt-in do not relate or have any reference to marriage solemnised according to the rites of the Church of England;[84] and the extension of marriage to same-sex couples has no effect in respect of the Measures and Canons of the Church of England or any subordinate legislation.[85]

It is striking that the provisions in the MSSCA 2013 relating to Church of England Canon law remained almost wholly unaddressed in parliamentary debate. This is significant given the wide-ranging implications of the MSSCA 2013 provision that:

> No Canon of the Church of England is contrary to section 3 of the Submission of the Clergy Act 1533 (which provides that no Canons shall be contrary to the Royal Prerogative or the customs, laws or statutes of this realm) by virtue of its making provision about marriage being the union of one man with one woman.[86]

---

80 The Marriage (Same Sex Couples) Act 2013 contains provisions that permit a marriage of a same-sex couple to be solemnised according to religious rites and usages when a religious organisation has followed the relevant 'opt-in' procedures. These provisions are found in: S.4–5, amending Pt.3 Marriage Act 1949, in respect of marriage solemnised on the authority of superintendent registrar's certificates in places of worship or in another place according to religious rites or usages; S.6, amending Pt.5 Marriage Act 1949, in respect of marriage solemnised in naval, military and air force chapels; S.7, amending Marriage (Registrar General's Licence) Act 1970, in respect of marriage solemnised on the authority of a Registrar General's Licence ('deathbed marriage'); and Sch.6 in respect of marriage solemnised by Order in Council.
81 S.2(1) Marriage (Same Sex Couples) Act 2013.
82 S.2(6) Marriage (Same Sex Couples) Act 2013, creating Sch.3 Pt.6A Equality Act 2010.
83 S.1(4) Marriage (Same Sex Couples) Act 2013.
84 Pt.3 S.26A(5) Marriage Act 1949 created by S.4 Marriage (Same Sex Couples) Act 2013.
85 S.11(6) Marriage (Same Sex Couples) Act 2013.
86 S.1(3) Marriage (Same Sex Couples) Act 2013.

This provision allows the definition of marriage as 'one man with one woman' contained in Church of England Canon law[87] to exist in parallel with the MSSCA 2013 definition of marriage. As a result, English law now contains two conflicting definitions of marriage: in existing England and Wales legislation 'a reference to marriage is to be read as including a reference to marriage of a same sex couple',[88] whereas in Canon law marriage refers exclusively to opposite-sex couples. Allowing this diametric opposition between Canon and statute law is without direct equivalence in the time since the Submission of the Clergy Act (SCA) 1533 was enacted, and the provision to allow Canon law to be contrary to statute law therefore represents an important legislative (and constitutional) event.[89] Although there have been previous exemptions of Canon law from the SCA 1533 – for example, in the Church of England (Worship and Doctrine) Measure 1974 (No.3) which provided the General Synod with autonomy in respect of determining doctrine and worship[90] – the MSSCA 2013 represents arguably the most significant de-coupling of statute and Canon law. The Bishop of Chester, Peter Forster, called this provision in the MSSCA 2013 'unprecedented in statute law'.[91] Its consequence is that, until such time as it chooses to solemnise same-sex marriage and amend its Canon law, the Church of England can continue to assert a heteronormative framework of marriage in English law.[92]

---

87 Canon B 30 'Of Holy Matrimony' in: Church of England, *The Canons of the Church of England (7th Edition)*, London: Church House Publishing, 2011.
88 Sch.3 Pt.1 Para.1(1)(a) Marriage (Same Sex Couples) Act 2013.
89 S.3 'An Acte for the submission of the Clergie to the Kynges Majestie' 1533 (25 Hen.8 c.19) '[p]rovided alway that no canons [. . .] shalbe contraryaunt or repugnant to the [. . .] customes lawes or statutes of this Realme'. This was re-expressed and applied by S.1(3)(b) Synodical Government Measure 1969. The content of the current Canon law of the Church of England, the result of the Code promulged by the Convocations of Canterbury and York in 1964 and 1969 which replaced the previous Code of 1603, was guided by the fundamental principle that Canons cannot be 'contrary to the laws and customes of the state'. P. Boulton, 'Twentieth-century revision of Canon law in the Church of England', *Ecclesiastical Law Journal* 26, 2000, 362. Subsequent revisions of Canon law by the General Synod (for a list of these, see 'Table of Promulgation of Canons' in: Church of England, op. cit.) have followed that principle.
90 S.6(1) Church of England (Worship and Doctrine) Measure 1974 (No.3). A further example can be found in S.1(3) Church of England (Miscellaneous Provisions) Measure 1976 relating to ordination and admission to an office.
91 The Bishop of Chester argued: 'In the government documents there is an attempt to draw a parallel with divorce, although that hardly applies at all because the canons of the Church of England have never forbidden divorce. There has always been a legal permission to divorce under the canons of the Church of England, and so the changes that have happened in divorce law have never come into conflict with the canons – for the very good reason that it was always permitted in statute law. It is also there in the Old and the New Testament. Therefore, this clause is unprecedented in our legislative history.' HL Debate, 3 June 2013, c.995.
92 For the purposes of the Human Rights Act 1998, Church of England Canon law has the status of subordinate (secondary) legislation. For a discussion, see: M. Hill, R. Sandberg

A further significant aspect of the MSSCA 2013 in respect of the Church of England (and Church in Wales) is the exclusion from the 'opt-in' provisions that enable other religious organisations to solemnise same-sex marriage. The MSSCA 2013 amends Part 3 of the Marriage Act (MA) 1949 to allow religious organisations to opt-in to solemnising same-sex marriage on the authority of two certificates of a superintendent registrar but, importantly, states this does not 'relate or have any reference to marriages solemnized according to the rites of the Church of England'.[93] The MA 1949 already provided that marriage could be solemnised on the authority of superintendent registrar certificates according to the rites of the Church of England in lieu of the publication of banns.[94] This was amended by the MSSCA 2013 so that, now forming one of the ways in which marriage may be solemnised for which no opt-in is necessary, marriage solemnised on the authority of superintendent registrar certificates according to the rites of the Church of England relates only to 'a marriage of a man and a woman'.[95] In light of this amendment, it is arguable that the blanket exclusion of the Church of England from the opt-in provisions is therefore unnecessary. The MSSCA 2013 could have been written to include the Church of England in the opt-in provisions relating to marriage by registrar certificate in Part 3 of the MA 1949, and an opt-in provision could have been included in respect of Part 2 of the MA 1949 relating to marriage according to the rites of the Church of England, in order to provide the Church of England with the same permissive legal framework available to all other religious organisations. In the absence of the Church of England deciding to opt-in, the same strong protection available to all other religious organisations provided by the no 'compulsion to solemnize' provisions would apply.[96] The justification given by the Government for the blanket exclusion of the Church

---

and N. Doe, *Religion and Law in the United Kingdom*, Alphen aan den Rijn: Kluwer Law International, 2011, p.35.

93 Pt.3 S.26A(5) Marriage Act 1949 created by S.4 Marriage (Same Sex Couples) Act 2013.

94 Pt.2 S.5(d) Marriage Act 1949 provides that a marriage according to the rites of the Church of England may be solemnised on the authority of certificates issued by a superintendent registrar. Pt.2 S.17 Marriage Act 1949 specifies that a marriage solemnised in this way may take place 'in any church or chapel in which banns of matrimony may be published or in the case of a marriage in pursuance of section 26(1)(dd) of this Act [marriage of a person who is house-bound or is a detained person at the place where he or she usually resides] the place specified in the notices of marriage and certificates as the place where the marriage is to be solemnized: Provided that a marriage shall not be solemnized as aforesaid in any such church or chapel without the consent of the minister thereof or (wherever the marriage is solemnized) by any person other than a clergyman'. Pt.3 S.26(1)(e) again specifies that solemnisation of marriage under these circumstances may take place in 'any church or chapel in which banns of matrimony may be published'.

95 Pt.3 S.26(1)(e) Marriage Act 1949 as amended by S.3 Marriage (Same Sex Couples) Act 2013.

96 S.2 Marriage (Same Sex Couples) Act 2013.

of England from the opt-in provisions was the need to recognise its 'special circumstances in relation to marriage law', specifically the common law duty of Church of England clergy to solemnise the marriage of a parishioner in their parish church or one to which they have a qualifying connection.[97] Yet the MSSCA 2013 includes a separate provision that explicitly states that no existing duty of clergy to solemnise marriage is extended to same-sex couples.[98] The most likely reason for excluding the Church of England from the opt-in provisions is the Church's own explicit request that the legislation not enable it to opt-in to solemnising same-sex marriage.[99] The exclusion from the opt-in provisions provides the Church of England with more 'protection' insofar as any future solemnisation of same-sex marriage is dependent on the General Synod passing a Measure to amend the MA 1949. In addition to the other legal changes that the Church of England would have to make in order to solemnise same-sex marriage – for example, the revision of its Canon law on marriage – its exclusion from the opt-in provisions can be seen as a further 'hurdle' (both symbolic and practical) preventing it from doing so. Therefore, although the Church of England argues that the 'locks' in the MSSCA 2013 'simply make clear that the legislation leaves marriage according to the rites of the Church of England unchanged',[100] it may be more accurate to say that the legislation represents, in the Government's own words, a 'deference' to those who wish to ensure that it remains unchanged.[101]

Marriage 'locks' and the litigious homosexual

The inclusion of the religious protections in the MSSCA 2013 was significantly encouraged by the assertion of organised religions that same-sex marriage posed a 'threat' to religious freedoms. Such claims by religious organisations have been ubiquitous in parliamentary debates since the time of the CPA 2004. During the CPA 2004 debates, for example, there was considerable discussion of the 'problems that the Church of England may face', such as 'challenges in the occasional offices of baptism, marriage and funerals'.[102] During subsequent debates about the removal of the prohibition on registering civil partnerships

---

97 *Argar v Holdsworth* (1758) 2 Lee 515.
98 'Any duty of a member of the clergy to solemnize marriages (and any corresponding right of persons to have their marriages solemnized by members of the clergy) is not extended by this Act to marriages of same sex couples.' S.1(4) Marriage (Same Sex Couples) Act 2013.
99 Department for Culture, Media & Sport and Government Equalities Office, 'Note for the Joint Committee on Human Rights: Marriage (Same Sex Couples) Bill', February 2013, § 44.
100 Church of England, 'Marriage (Same Sex Couples) Bill, Commons Second Reading briefing from the Church of England', Westminster: Church House, 2013.
101 Department for Culture, Media & Sport and Government Equalities Office, op. cit., § 44.
102 R. Key, HC Debate, 12 October 2004, c.208.

on religious premises, these claims intensified with, for example, the Bishop of Winchester, Michael Scott-Joynt, arguing that '[s]hortly down the line [...] is the likelihood of a steady and continuing pressure on, if not a forcing of, the churches, the Church of England among them, to compromise on our convictions that marriage has a character that is distinct from that of a civil partnership'.[103] The Bishop of Chichester, John Hind, similarly expressed the fear that removing the restriction on religious premises would put pressure 'on the incumbents of the parishes and lead to widespread disarray throughout the Church of England'.[104]

A key claim advanced by those who have opposed all reform in partnership law is that it affords homosexual 'litigious activists'[105] the ability to compel religious individuals and organisations to alter their practices and principles. As Baroness Paisley of St George's argued, 'pressure will be put on churches to [go] against their consciences, otherwise there will be a cry of discrimination'.[106] It is this discourse about the need to defend churches against the threat of litigation by homosexuals that underpinned the inclusion of the extensive religious protections in the MSSCA 2013. Many religious organisations, including the Church of England, expressed concern about the threat of a potential complaint in the European Court of Human Rights by same-sex couples challenging their default exclusion from solemnising marriage in Church of England churches or other registered premises. This argument was advanced without acknowledging that the European Court of Human Rights has held that no right is available to same-sex couples to marry under any article of the European Convention on Human Rights.[107] Yet the Church of England and other religious groups and organisations repeatedly claimed they would be 'forced' to solemnise same-sex marriage. The Muslim Research and Development Foundation, for instance, stated that:

> Gay rights organisations claim that they do not agree with forcing mosques, churches, synagogues or any other religious institution to conduct a 'gay marriage', the door is already ajar – it is only a matter of time before it is pushed wide open and they decide they be allowed to access all the rights permitted to heterosexual couples. It would only be a matter of time before an imam could be prosecuted for refusing to conduct a nikah for a gay couple.[108]

---

103 HL Committee, 25 January 2010, c.1202.
104 Ibid., c.1203.
105 Baroness O'Cathain, HL Debate, 15 December 2011, c.1409.
106 HL Debate, 23 March 2010, c.870.
107 For a discussion, see: P. Johnson, *Homosexuality and the European Court of Human Rights*, Abingdon: Routledge, 2013.
108 S. Haitham Al-Haddad, 'The responsibility of the Muslim community to oppose the gay marriage Bill', 21 August 2012. Available online at www.islam21c.com/fataawa/5159-the-responsibility-of-the-muslim-community-to-oppose-the-gay-marriage-bill (accessed 3 December 2013).

At the centre of claims about this threat to religious freedom is a social imaginary of litigious homosexuals intent on trammelling the rights of religious believers. For example, in his advice to the Catholic Bishops' Conference of England and Wales on the human rights implications of the MSSCA 2013, McCrudden described the ways in which homosexuals might use aspects of the European Convention on Human Rights 'as a sword to attack protections for freedom of religion' and overcome this 'shield'.[109] Such claims, as we outlined in the Introduction, reiterate the more general concern of religious individuals and groups that religious rights and freedoms are being diminished at the expense of the development of sexual orientation equality. Religious speakers mobilise a discourse about rights as a way to position themselves as vulnerable to gay men and lesbians who use anti-discrimination law as a device to oppress them. The deployment of this discourse, which relies on understandings of an 'aggressive homosexual community'[110] as a kind of 'folk devil',[111] underpinned the inclusion of the religious protections in the MSSCA 2013.

The Marriage (Same Sex Couples) Bill 2013 amendments

Before the Marriage (Same Sex Couples) Bill 2013 was introduced in Parliament, religious opponents were already advocating peremptory legislative reform on the basis that same-sex marriage would threaten religious freedoms. For example, Edward Leigh MP introduced the Equality (Marriage) (Amendment) Bill 2012-13 as a Ten Minute Rule Bill that proposed to 'amend the protected characteristics in the Equality Act 2010 to include a person's conscientious beliefs about the definition of marriage'.[112] Leigh's Bill received a successful First Reading[113] and, although it subsequently ran out of time, demonstrated support amongst some MPs for legislation further protecting 'conscientious' objections to same-sex marriage. A motivation for this was arguments made by churches, including the Church of England, that the MSSCA 2013 would have 'a "chilling effect" in public discourse'.[114] Such concerns continued throughout the parliamentary passage of the MSSCA 2013 and found expression in a large number of (mostly unsuccessful) amendments tabled with the objective of strengthening 'protections' for people of faith. The amendments cluster around four key issues, which we consider in turn below: the designation of same-sex marriage as different to opposite-sex

109 C. McCrudden, 'Human rights implications of the Marriage (Same Sex Couples) Bill: advice to the Catholic Bishops' Conference of England and Wales', London: Blackstone Chambers, 15 April 2013.
110 G. Howarth, HC Debate, 20 May 2013, c.943.
111 S. Cohen, *Folk Devils and Moral Panics: The Creation of the Mods and Rockers (Third Edition)*, London: Routledge, 2002.
112 HC Debate, 29 January 2013, c.799.
113 The House divided 86-31 in favour. HC Debate, 29 January 2013, Division No.145.
114 Church of England, 'Marriage (Same Sex Couples) Bill, Commons Second Reading briefing from the Church of England', op. cit.

marriage; conscientious objection of religious believers as grounds for refusing to provide public services to homosexuals; additional protections for religious organisations who do not wish to opt-in to solemnising same-sex marriage; and the protection of freedom of speech in order to criticise same-sex marriage.

Several unsuccessful attempts were made to amend the MSSCA 2013 during its parliamentary passage in order to maintain definitional distinctions in marriage based on sexual orientation. For example, in the Common's Public Bill Committee David Burrowes MP, Tim Loughton MP and Jim Shannon MP proposed that 'references to "marriage" in relation to same sex couples shall be changed to "union"' to distinguish them from opposite-sex marriage.[115] There were various similar attempts in the Lords to designate a same-sex partnership a 'union',[116] a 'marriage (same sex couples)',[117] or a 'same sex marriage',[118] whilst defining opposite-sex marriage as a 'traditional marriage'[119] or a 'matrimonial marriage'.[120] Greg Mulholland MP proposed a more opaque way of maintaining this distinction by tabling the amendment that '[t]wo people, whether they are of different or the same sex, may enter into a civil union' and that 'no religious service is to be used while the civil union registrar is officiating at the signing of a civil union document'.[121] The effect of Mulholland's amendment would have been that, through a repeal of the MA 1949, 'no religious minister [would be] able to convey the rights of legal marriage' but it would be 'perfectly possible, either through the presence of a registrar at a belief-based or religious marriage ceremony, or by another process, to have that conveyed at the same time'.[122] Although Mulholland argued that this would lead to greater equality, the legal system he proposed would have enabled organised religions to maintain complete authority in respect of permitting access to a 'religious marriage ceremony' and, through denying this to same-sex couples, uphold a symbolic distinction between 'civil unions' and 'marriage'. The parliamentarians who proposed these amendments were widely recognised as those from 'a strong religious tradition [. . .] which drives many of their views'.[123]

A wide range of amendments tabled during the MSSCA 2013 debates proposed to better protect those with faith-based objections to same-sex marriage.

---

115 HC Committee, 7 March 2013, c.425
116 Amendment 1 by Lord Hylton and Lord Cormack, HL Committee, 17 June 2013, c.11.
117 Amendment 2 by Lord Mackay of Clashfern, HL Committee, 17 June 2013, c.32.
118 Amendment 34 by Lord Edmiston and Lord Mawhinney, HL Committee, 17 June 2013, c.26.
119 Amendment 9 by Lord Carey of Clifton and Lord Dear, HL Committee, 17 June 2013, c.40.
120 Amendment 46 by Lord Armstrong of Ilminster, HL Committee, 17 June 2013, c.16.
121 HC Debate, 21 May 2013, c.1073.
122 Ibid., c.1092.
123 Lord Lester of Herne Hill, HL Committee, 17 June 2013, c.22.

Burrowes, Loughton and Shannon tabled a group of amendments in the Public Bill Committee[124] which later found expression at Report stage in the proposal that no person employed as a registrar of marriages could be placed under any duty to solemnise the marriage of a same-sex couple if a refusal to do so was 'based on the person's sincerely held religious or other beliefs'.[125] The Bishop of Leicester, Tim Stevens, with Baroness Cumberlege tabled a similar amendment.[126] Numerous amendments were also tabled that proposed changes to the EA 2010 in order to, for example, ensure that '[n]o person shall suffer any detriment in respect of his opposition to same sex marriage or the reasonable expression thereof' when 'motivated by his deeply and genuinely held religious or philosophical beliefs'.[127] Similarly, a new 'protection for beliefs about marriage' was advocated through the proposed inclusion of the provision that 'the protected characteristic of religion or belief may include the belief that marriage should only be between a man and a woman'.[128] The former Archbishop of Canterbury, George Carey, tabled an amendment to extend the 'protection' available to religious organisations and individuals so that *any* person would not contravene the EA 2010 if she 'does not conduct a service of blessing', 'is not present at, does not carry out, or does not otherwise participate in, a service of blessing', or 'does not consent to a service of blessing for a relevant marriage being conducted, for the reason that the marriage is the marriage of a same sex couple'.[129] All of these amendments were attempts to gain exemption for public authority (Christian) registrars who, as we discussed in Chapter 3, cannot refuse to provide goods and services to homosexuals on the grounds of religious belief.

Religious opponents also tabled a wide range of amendments that proposed to strengthen the provisions relating to religious organisations. For instance, Rob Wilson MP in the Public Bill Committee proposed that the Human Rights Act 1998 should be amended to include the clause '[n]o duty to solemnize the marriage of a same sex couple according to the rites of the Church of England shall be created by virtue of this Act or the schedules thereto'.[130] More specifically, Burrowes and others tabled the amendment that '[f]or the purposes of section 149 of the Equality Act 2010, no regard may be had by any public authority to

---

124 HC Committee, 26 February 2013, c.220.
125 HC Debate, 20 May 2013, c 965. On division, this amendment was defeated 150-340. HC Debate, 20 May 2013, Division No.6.
126 Amendment 11 by Baroness Cumberledge and Bishop of Leicester, HL Committee, 17 June 2013, c.103.
127 New Clause 11 by R. Wilson, Public Bill Committee Amendments as at 12 March 2013.
128 Amendment 19 by Lord Singh, marshalled list of Amendments to be moved in Committee, 14 June 2013.
129 Amendment 15 by Lord Carey of Clifton, HL Committee, 19 June 2013, c.284.
130 New Clause 13 by R. Wilson, Notice of Public Bill Committee Amendments given on 26 February 2013.

any decision by a relevant governing authority or relevant religious organisation to give any consent or to refuse to give any consent' in respect of the solemnisation of a same-sex marriage.[131] The objective of this amendment was to 'prevent public authorities from penalising religious organisations for deciding not to opt in to same-sex marriage'.[132] The reasons given for the necessity of this amendment was a newspaper report regarding a Christian-run care home that had its annual funding withdrawn after refusing an alleged request from a local authority to record the sexual orientation of its residents.[133] The facts of this story were highly disputed and the amendment rejected, but in response to similar and repeatedly voiced concerns about the potential for religious organisations to be penalised by local authorities, the Government amended the wording of the 'no compulsion to solemnize' clause, which originally read '[a] person may not be compelled', to include the words 'by any means (including by the enforcement of a contract or a statutory or other legal requirement)'.[134] This was to satisfy the Catholic Church which was 'intensely worried'[135] that the original wording allowed a public body to refuse to hire premises, enter into contracts or offer grants to a religious organisation that had not opted-in to same-sex marriage.[136] Although the Government consistently argued that the original wording was sufficient, it amended the wording to 'simply make clear' its scope.[137] Yet the inclusion of the phrase 'by any means' is unusually wide in statute law and prompted one religious opponent to commend the Government for 'a courageous use of language' that provides 'an all-embracing' protection for religious organisations.[138]

Numerous amendments were tabled during the MSSCA 2013 debates that proposed additional protections to ensure freedom of speech. For example, the Bishop of Leicester, Tim Stevens, proposed that the EA 2010 include in its general interpretations that 'the expression by a person of the opinion or belief that marriage is the union of one man with one woman does not of itself amount to discrimination against or harassment of another'.[139] Stevens argued that the amendment was 'largely about establishing cultural norms and expectations about what will continue to be acceptable in terms of public discourse about marriage' because 'we cannot expect those cultural assumptions and norms to change overnight or at the speed at which legislation may emerge'.[140] Stevens' specific

---

131 HC Committee, 5 March 2013, c.332.
132 Ibid., c.334.
133 T. Loughton, HC Committee, 5 March 2013, c.340.
134 S.2(1)–2(2) Marriage (Same Sex Couples) Act 2013.
135 C. McCrudden, op. cit.
136 J. Rivers, 'Memorandum submitted to Joint Committee on Human Rights', February 2013.
137 Lord Wallace of Tankerness, HL Debate, 8 July 2013, c.100.
138 Lord Brennan, HL Debate, 8 July 2013, c.105.
139 Amendment 46C by Bishop of Leicester, HL Committee, 24 June 2013, c.599.
140 HL Committee, 24 June 2013, cc.600–601.

motivation was to ensure that employees could express in their workplace an antipathy to same-sex marriage without infringing the discrimination or harassment provisions of the EA 2010.[141] In the context of the significant exceptions for organised religions and religious organisations from equality law in respect of sexual orientation that were previously negotiated by religious opponents, which we discussed in Chapter 3, this can be seen as a further attempt to introduce exceptions for individual religious believers. The amendment was criticised on the grounds that Article 9 of the Human Rights Act 1998 protects the expression of a 'traditional' view of marriage, and was consequently withdrawn.

The MSSCA 2013 does contain one significant 'free speech' provision that was inserted as an amendment during its parliamentary passage. Burrowes, Loughton and Shannon first proposed in the Public Bill Committee that the saving provision in the Public Order Act (POA) 1986 (see Chapter 5) which excludes the 'discussion or criticism of sexual conduct or practices or the urging of persons to refrain from or modify such conduct or practices' from the scope of the offence of hatred on the grounds of sexual orientation[142] be amended to include reference to 'discussion or criticism of same-sex marriage'.[143] Shannon argued that although the motivation for the amendment was to protect the freedom of speech of those who hold to 'Christian standards and marriage as a divine institution', he was 'not solely concerned with people of religious conviction' but with 'protecting those who have a core belief [. . .] that marriage is between one man and one woman'.[144] The amendment was withdrawn and also failed when it was tabled at Report stage in the Commons.[145] A similar amendment was subsequently introduced in the Lords that proposed to protect 'the expression by a person of the opinion or belief that marriage is the union of one man with one woman'.[146] Simultaneously, the Government introduced a sexual orientation neutral provision that amends the POA 1986 to provide that 'any discussion or criticism of marriage which concerns the sex of the parties to marriage shall not be taken of itself to be threatening or intended to stir up hatred'.[147] The Government sponsor stated that the amendment 'makes it clear' that if a 'church wanted to demonstrate against same-sex marriage, it would be perfectly lawful'.[148] We discuss the full implications of the saving provision in Chapter 5.

141 Ibid., c.600.
142 Pt.3A S.29JA(1) Public Order Act 1986.
143 HC Committee, 28 February 2013, c.286.
144 Ibid., cc.291–292.
145 HC Debate, 20 May 2013, c.927.
146 Amendment 54 by Baroness Berridge and Baroness O'Loan, HL Committee, 17 June 2013, c.57.
147 Sch.7 Pt.2 Para.28 Marriage (Same Sex Couples) Act 2013, creating Pt.3A S.29JA(2) Public Order Act 1986.
148 Baroness Stowell of Beeston, HL Committee, 17 June 2013, c.77.

Distancing homophobia: a transformation in rhetoric

A key aspect of the ten years of UK parliamentary debate that we have examined in this chapter is the ubiquity of strong assertions by religious opponents that their opposition to law reform is not equivalent to homophobia. Rather, reflecting the general change in parliamentary discourse that we have detailed in previous chapters, religious opponents have carefully attempted to distance any religiously based opposition to same-sex civil partnership and marriage from an association with being 'anti-gay'. Because of this, despite occasional pleas from some parliamentarians for those who think 'homosexuality is wrong and a sin' to be 'honest',[149] there have been very few explicitly moral statements about homosexuality in these debates. Although occasionally some opponents have made explicit religious arguments about the morality of homosexuality – such as Christopher Chope MP who argued that 'as a matter of Christian doctrine' he could not accept that 'a [homosexual] relationship is a valid one under the laws of God'[150] – this has been highly unusual. Whilst in the MSSCA 2013 debates there were continuous references to religious doctrine on marriage to argue against legislative change, the use of theology to condemn homosexuality was conspicuously absent. One reason for this has been the argument made by those in favour of law reform that by legislating for same-sex partnerships parliamentarians are 'merely acknowledging the reality' of same-sex relationships which does 'not mean that any [. . .] individual has to approve or disapprove of their existence'.[151] This rhetorical approach has attempted to avoid moral and religious discussion of homosexuality and discourage religious objections to homosexual sexual relationships.

Nevertheless, religious opponents have gone to significant lengths to fend off any association with homophobia. Throughout the CPA 2004 and MSSCA 2013 debates there was a consistent concern amongst opponents to avoid 'certain innuendos' attached to objections to same-sex partnership legislation.[152] For example, Gerald Howarth MP argued that those who opposed civil partnership were 'decent people' who:

> are not homophobes, bigots or any of the other epithets so readily thrown about. They are tolerant and generally neither inquire nor want to be told what other people do in the privacy of their own home. However, they recognise that our laws ought to have a moral basis. They also recognise that the law sends a moral signal, for good or ill.[153]

---

149   C. Bryant, HC Debate, 12 October 2004, c.227.
150   HC Committee, 19 October 2004, c.32.
151   Baroness Scotland of Asthal, HL Committee, 12 May 2004, c.140.
152   M. Smyth, HC Debate, 12 October 2004, c.235.
153   HC Debate, 12 October 2004, c.238.

In many ways this represents a reiteration of an older and established discourse through which, as we discussed in Chapter 1, law is regarded as the primary vehicle for enforcing a religious (Christian) intolerance of homosexuality. However, during these debates this discourse further evolved when religious opponents sought to distinguish the desire to enforce religious morality in public law from sexual orientation discrimination. As Baroness Paisley of St George's argued, although she did 'not believe in discrimination because of a person's orientation [. . .] it is wrong and dangerous to overthrow certain limits'.[154] Or, as the Bishop of Oxford, John Pritchard, argued, individuals should not be 'accused of being homophobes' because of their commitment to the 'traditional ethical teaching on sexual morality of the Christian churches and many other faiths'.[155] By invoking religious 'tradition', opponents sought to combat 'accusations of being homophobic, toxic, [or] odious'.[156] This strategy is often successful because, as Bourdieu argues, those who appeal to 'religious tradition' can make claims that appear to be impartial statements about how the world *is* rather than how it *should be* and, as a result, make persuasive declarations about why it would be 'wrong and dangerous' to change it. As Archbishop Peter Smith argued:

> [Christians] are not trying to do down homosexuals; I know many homosexuals and I get on very well with them. However, at the end of the day we as bishops and as a Church have a duty to teach what Christ taught, rooted in his background of the Old Testament, and it is not for us as bishops to change that teaching.[157]

Such claims continue to shape the law in important ways (for example, by encouraging the inclusion of the extensive religious 'protections' in the MSSCA 2013 that we discussed above) because, even in a contemporary context so frequently described as secular, they are accorded both authority and respect.

'Equality' not 'sameness'

During the MSSCA 2013 debates, religious opponents sought to distinguish their opposition to same-sex marriage from 'homophobia' by making a distinction between 'sameness' and 'equality'. The widespread use of this distinction – although clearly drawing on debates in education, gender studies and elsewhere – was a novel element of the discourse of religious opponents of marriage

---

154 HL Debate, 23 March 2010, c.870.
155 HL Debate, 15 December 2011, c.1420.
156 Baroness O'Cathain, HL Debate, 15 December 2011, c.1446.
157 Witness evidence of Archbishop Peter Smith, HC Committee, 12 February 2013, c.30.

reform.[158] An early use of this was by the Catholic Church which, in its opposition to same-sex marriage, stated that:

> 'Equality' should not be confused with 'sameness'. Various professions require strength or fitness tests for their members. The tests are not the same for men and for women, but they do provide a fair and equal test for both sexes, recognising their differences. That is equality in its true sense; a just provision for different groups which takes appropriate account of their differences. For same-sex couples, equality in that proper sense has already been fully provided by the Civil Partnerships Act.[159]

The central premise of this argument is that equality depends upon recognition of essential differences between homosexual and heterosexual couples, and, consequently, 'equality in the true sense' is achieved through separate but equal institutions rather than the attempt to approximate 'sameness'.[160] Whilst the analogy used in this particular case is misleading – because it relies on the example of a mechanism that exists to *eliminate* inequalities in access to institutions created by recognised difference to argue for the *maintenance* of institutional distinctions based on recognised difference – it is a form of argument that is widely used by religious opponents of same-sex marriage. It draws upon and subverts a wider political discourse about the relationship between equality and diversity – in which, in respect of sexual orientation, there is a long-standing debate about the role of

---

158   This rhetoric about the relationship between 'sameness' and 'equality' can be seen to draw upon long-standing and wider debates about equality in relation to, for example, education (C.J.B. Macmillan, 'Equality and sameness', *Studies in Philosophy and Education* 3, 1964–65, 320–332), gender (S. Liff and J. Wajcman, '"Sameness" and "difference" revisited: which way forward for equal opportunity initiatives?', *Journal of Management Studies* 33, 1996, 79–94) and race and ethnicity (A.P. Harris, 'Equality trouble: sameness and difference in twentieth-century race law', *California Law Review* 88, 2000, 1925–2016). Many of these debates focus on the relationship between essentialism and social (in)equality. Debates about sameness and difference in respect of gay and lesbian equality have been present in popular discourse since at least the 1990s (see: D.J. Saunders, 'Homosexual marriages: does equality mean sameness?', *Sarasota Herald-Tribune*, 16 December 1996) and reflect broader political debates in lesbian and gay politics about the extent to which equality requires sameness and, vice versa, the extent to which equality produces similarity, assimilation and normalisation (see: M. Bernstein, 'Celebration and suppression: the strategic uses of identity by the lesbian and gay movement', *American Journal of Sociology* 103, 1997, 531–565).
159   Catholic Bishops' Conference of England and Wales, 'Response from the Catholic Bishops' Conference of England and Wales to the Government consultation on "Equal Civil Marriage"', June 2012.
160   This argument is long established in opposition to same-sex marriage. See: B.J. Cox, 'But why not marriage: an essay on Vermont's civil unions law, same-sex marriage, and separate but (un)equal', *Vermont Law Review* 25, 2000/01, 113–147.

sameness in achieving equality[161] – to make the claim that legally recognised difference in respect of marriage is necessary to ensure equality.

This was the argument advanced by the Archbishop of Canterbury, Justin Welby, to justify his opposition to the MSSCA 2013:

> It [the Marriage (Same Sex Couples) Bill 2013] assumes that the rightful desire for equality [...] must mean uniformity, failing to understand that two things may be equal but different. As a result, it does not do what it sets out to do. Schedule 4 distinguishes clearly between same-gender and opposite-gender marriage, thus not achieving true equality. The result is confusion. Marriage is abolished, redefined and recreated, being different and unequal for different categories [...] [W]e think that traditional marriage is a cornerstone of society, and rather than adding a new and valued institution alongside it for same-gender relationships [...] the Bill weakens what exists and replaces it with a less good option that is neither equal nor effective.[162]

Welby argues that attempts to produce legal 'uniformity' between couples that are different will inevitably fail to produce 'true equality'. His evidence for this is the distinction between opposite- and same-sex couples retained in law in respect of adultery[163] and consummation[164] (neither of which applies to same-sex couples). Yet these distinctions in divorce or nullity are not the product of differences based on sexual orientation but are the result of the unwillingness of legislators to address previously established heteronormative concepts in law about sexual acts and fidelity. This does not therefore support the claim that essential differences between same-sex and opposite-sex couples necessitate legal distinctions but, on the contrary, demonstrates how law produces and sustains such differences. Yet, like Welby, the Archbishop of York, John Sentamu, appealed to legislators to enact law that, 'precise in its use of language' like the CPA 2004, 'recognised the intrinsic difference between the loving, life-long commitment of same-sex couples and the loving, life-long commitment of male and female couples in marriage'.[165] Although Welby later argued that this rhetoric was 'utterly overwhelmed' by support for marriage equality, and that the 'majority of the population' that 'rejects homophobic behaviour' sometimes 'look at us [the Church of England] and they see what they don't like',[166] there was no

---

161 D. Richardson, 'Desiring sameness? The rise of a neoliberal politics of normalisation', *Antipode* 37, 2005, 515–535. See also: N. Levit. 'A different kind of sameness: beyond formal equality and antisubordination principles in gay legal theory and constitutional doctrine', *Ohio State Law Journal* 61, 2000, 867–934.
162 HL Debate, 3 June 2013, cc.953–954.
163 S.1(2)(a) Matrimonial Causes Act 1973.
164 S.12(1)(a)–12(1)(b) Matrimonial Causes Act 1973.
165 HL Debate, 17 June 2013, c.36.
166 G. Drake, 'Church must accept there is sexual revolution, Welby tells Synod', *Church Times*, 5 July 2013.

suggestion in parliamentary debates that faith-based opposition to the MSSCA 2013 constituted homophobia. On the contrary, many parliamentarians in support of same-sex marriage stated that it has 'never ever been our case [...] that opposition is homophobic'.[167]

Conclusion

The influence of religion in a decade of UK parliamentary debates about same-sex civil partnership and marriage legislation could be regarded as both marginal and declining. Parliamentarians have rarely engaged in faith-based moral condemnations of homosexuality and there has been a general absence of explicit religious hostility to the development of some partnership rights for same-sex couples. However, when examined within the context of the legislative settlement that has emerged, it is clear that religion has played a fundamental role in shaping the legal landscape. Successive governments have routinely deferred to religious opposition and produced legislation that has maintained distinctions between same-sex and opposite-sex couples. Whilst, as we have shown, some of these distinctions have subsequently been removed – such as the prohibition on registering civil partnerships on religious premises in England and Wales – others remain. As we have argued, the MSSCA 2013 maintains a fundamental difference in English law between opposite-sex couples who have an effective right to solemnise a marriage in a Church of England parish church (because of the common law duty placed upon Church of England clergy) and same-sex couples who do not.

The religious 'protections' in the MSSCA 2013, we would argue, can be viewed as a monument to religious hostility and intolerance of homosexuality. During its enactment, the Government described the legislation as 'not just about allowing same-sex couples to marry [but] about protecting and promoting religious freedom'.[168] What the MSSCA 2013 'protects' is the ability of organised religions to exercise legal authority to solemnise the marriage of opposite-sex couples in their places of worship whilst refusing to extend this to same-sex couples. Whilst the MSSCA 2013 is permissive legislation that allows some organised religions to opt-in to solemnising same-sex marriage, its various 'locks' are essentially designed to protect organised religions that wish to exclude same-sex couples. The amendment that the MSSCA 2013 makes to the EA 2010 explicitly states that a refusal to conduct, be present at, carry out, participate in, or consent to a 'relevant marriage' (marriage in a place of worship or in another place according to religious rites or usages, or a religious ceremony following registrar's marriage) for the reason that it is the marriage of a same-sex couple does not constitute unlawful discrimination.[169] Describing this as a legal provision to promote 'religious freedom' obscures the discrimination that it protects. Yet

---

167 Lord Fowler, HL Debate, 15 July 2013, c.544.
168 Baroness Stowell of Beeston, HL Debate, 3 June 2013, c.938.
169 S.2(6) Marriage (Same Sex Couples) Act 2013, amending Sch.3 Equality Act 2010.

the approach of legislators in the UK to affording organised religions the capacity to discriminate on the grounds of sexual orientation has been central to attempts to appease their hostility to law reform. In the next chapter we explore how such appeasement had a significant influence in shaping law designed to protect sexual minorities from 'hate speech'.

Chapter 5

Homophobic hate speech and freedom of religious expression

In this chapter we consider the role of religion in the creation of the offence of 'Hatred on the grounds of sexual orientation' in England and Wales by the Criminal Justice and Immigration Act 2008.[1] This offence is one element of a wider set of legislative changes designed to combat 'hate crime' based on sexual orientation. Although hate crime is a concept of comparatively recent lineage,[2] it has gained widespread acceptance amongst legislators and criminal justice practitioners in the UK (as well as in many other jurisdictions), where attempts have been made to deal with 'bias-motivated' crimes directed at individuals or groups because of their actual or perceived sexual orientation.[3] The offence that we focus on in this chapter – which is popularly understood to criminalise forms of anti-gay 'hate speech' – is distinguishable from the type of hate crime legislation now found in many jurisdictions which provides for enhanced sentences in cases where crimes against the person are motivated by bias based on sexual orientation.[4] Our emphasis in this chapter is not on the philosophical or political

---

1 S.74 and Sch.16 Criminal Justice and Immigration Act 2008, amending Pt.3A Public Order Act 1986. A similar, although more broadly drawn, offence of incitement to hatred on the grounds of sexual orientation has been in force in Northern Ireland since it was introduced by S.3 Criminal Justice (No. 2) (Northern Ireland) Order 2004. For a discussion, see: K. Goodall, 'Challenging hate speech: incitement to hatred on grounds of sexual orientation in England, Wales and Northern Ireland', *International Journal of Human Rights* 13, 2009, 211–232; F. Ashe, 'Iris Robinson's excitable speech: sexuality and conflict transformation in Northern Ireland', *Politics* 29, 2009, 20–27. There is currently no general offence of this type in Scottish law, although 'expressing hatred of, or stirring up hatred against, an individual based on [. . .] sexual orientation' is a criminal offence in relation to a regulated football match (Offensive Behaviour at Football and Threatening Communications (Scotland) Act 2012).
2 T. Newburn and M. Matassa, 'Policing hate crime', *Criminal Justice Matters* 48, 2002, 42–43.
3 For discussion, see: P. Johnson, 'Hate crime', in J. Brown (ed.), *The Future of Policing*, Abingdon: Routledge, 2013, pp. 317–332.
4 For a comparative study of European law on homophobic hate crime, see: L. Trappolin, A. Gasparini and R. Wintemute (eds), *Confronting Homophobia in Europe: Social and Legal Perspectives*, Oxford: Hart Publishing, 2012.

legitimacy of hate speech regulation or its efficacy in protecting vulnerable groups (issues that have been considered extensively elsewhere).[5] Rather, we provide a critical analysis of the discourses deployed in Parliament by those who sought to limit the scope of the offence.[6] We pay particular attention to how opponents and sceptics of the offence mobilised representations of religious persecution by the police and the 'aggressive' homosexual community to successfully argue for the inclusion of a saving provision that arguably narrows the scope of the law. We also emphasise how debates over the offence were characterised by frequent depictions of an equalities hierarchy in which religion and sexual orientation were understood to be in competition as categories of difference deserving legal protection. As we demonstrate, although parliamentarians differed in where they sought to position religion and sexual orientation in this equalities hierarchy, there existed a rarely challenged consensus amongst parliamentarians that religious objections to homosexuality provided a legitimate rationale for limiting the scope of the hate speech protections offered to sexual minorities.

'Hatred on the grounds of sexual orientation' and the 'freedom of expression' saving provision

In October 2007, the UK (Labour) Government announced its intention to introduce new legislation in England and Wales to criminalise incitement to hatred on the grounds of sexual orientation. The proposed offence was modelled on the Racial and Religious Hatred Act 2006, and its creation was explicitly informed by the Government's view that inciting hatred on the grounds of sexual orientation 'is harmful and divisive in the same way as is inciting hatred on the grounds of race or religion'.[7] While the Government emphasised that 'there are offences on the statute book aimed at tackling crime against individuals that is motivated by antipathy or hatred of the sexuality of that person', it identified a 'lacuna' in relation to certain forms of anti-gay speech and expression that did not target specific individuals.[8] The Government and other supporters of the legislation argued that existing law failed to capture forms of speech and expression – such as some far-right political propaganda and certain forms of reggae and rap

---

5   For contrasting views on the legitimacy and likely effectiveness of hate speech bans in relation to sexual orientation, see: E. Heinze, 'Cumulative jurisprudence and human rights: the example of sexual minorities and hate speech', *International Journal of Human Rights* 13, 2009, 193–209; Goodall, op. cit.
6   Pt.3A S.29AB Public Order Act 1986 provides the meaning of 'hatred on the grounds of sexual orientation' as 'hatred against a group of persons defined by reference to sexual orientation (whether towards persons of the same sex, the opposite sex, or both)'. Whilst this definition includes bisexuality, no parliamentary consideration was given to this, and as such we focus solely on the deployment of discourses about gay men and lesbians to provide a realistic account of the terms of the debate in Parliament.
7   M. Eagle, HC Committee, 29 November 2007, c.661.
8   Ibid., c.663.

lyrics – that, although not directed at identifiable individuals, were nonetheless viewed as inciting 'homophobic hatred'.[9] After extensive parliamentary debate, the Criminal Justice and Immigration Act (CJIA) 2008 introduced the offence of 'Hatred on the grounds of sexual orientation' which, amending the Public Order Act (POA) 1986, provides that:

> A person who uses threatening words or behaviour, or displays any written material which is threatening, is guilty of an offence if he intends thereby to stir up religious hatred or hatred on the grounds of sexual orientation.[10]

The most contentious issue in parliamentary debates about this legislation involved the types of speech that the law would capture and the types of speakers who would be most affected. Specifically, opponents and sceptics argued that the legislation as originally drafted would be used in attempts to criminalise those who expressed religiously motivated objections to homosexuality. Although the Government provided assurances that religious speech that did not intend to incite hatred would fall outside the ambit of the law, legislators (predominantly Conservative, but with some cross-party support) successfully argued for the inclusion of a saving provision in the legislation to ensure (it was claimed) the 'protection of freedom of expression'.[11] The utility of the saving provision was strongly rejected by the Government and characterised by some as a wrecking amendment intended to render the legislation largely unenforceable.[12] However, its supporters insisted that it simply added 'clarification' to the offence.[13] Whilst the House of Commons rejected inclusion of the saving provision,[14] it was included in the CJIA 2008 at the insistence of the Lords.[15] Consequently, Part 3A of the POA 1986 states that:

---

9   The term 'homophobic hatred' was widely used in parliamentary debates to characterise the offence (for example, D. Burrowes, HC Committee, 16 October 2007, c.69), although it does not appear anywhere in the Criminal Justice and Immigration Act 2008.
10 S.74 and Sch.16 Criminal Justice and Immigration Act 2008, amending Pt.3A S.29B Public Order Act 1986. Prior to being amended, Pt.3A Public Order Act 1986 dealt exclusively with incitement to religious hatred.
11 However, many of the most vocal champions of the saving provision also attempted to block the repeal of the offences of blasphemy and blasphemous libel (S.79 Criminal Justice and Immigration Act 2008), undermining assertions that their advocacy of the saving provision represented a deep ideological commitment to freedom of expression. For example, see: Baroness O'Cathain's argument for the preservation of blasphemy in the *Church Times*, 7 March 2008.
12 J. Bercow, HC Debate, 26 January 2009, c.53.
13 Lord Dear, HL Debate, 3 March 2008, c.932.
14 At ping pong the Commons voted 338-136 to disagree with the inclusion of the saving provision. HC Debate, 6 May 2008, Division 168.
15 At ping pong, the Lords voted 178-164 to insist on the inclusion of the saving provision. The Bishops' Bench voted 2-0 in favour, with the Bishops of Chichester and Norwich in support. HL Debate, 7 May 2008, Division No.2.

for the avoidance of doubt, the discussion or criticism of sexual conduct or practices or the urging of persons to refrain from or modify such conduct or practices shall not be taken of itself to be threatening or intended to stir up hatred.[16]

The extent of the Government's hostility to the inclusion of the saving provision was such that it took the unusual decision of delaying the commencement of the offence and attempted (unsuccessfully) to repeal the saving provision in the next parliamentary session (in the Coroners and Justice Bill 2009).[17] This generated a further round of extensive parliamentary debate about the offence which, as a result, was not commenced until March 2010.

With a greater intensity than any of the other legislative changes that we have examined in this book, debates over the hate speech offence in the CJIA 2008 were characterised by repeated and forceful assertions about the growing marginalisation and persecution of Christians and other religious believers. However, as we demonstrate below, contrary to claims about marginalisation, religious speech and speakers were in fact often represented by parliamentarians from across the political spectrum in privileged ways. Parliamentarians repeatedly weighed religion and sexual orientation in relation to one another as categories worthy of protection and, in so doing, often portrayed religiously motivated hostility to homosexuality as a legitimate rationale for limiting the scope of the protection to be extended to sexual minorities. This perspective on the legitimacy

16   Pt.3A S.29JA Public Order Act 1986 on enactment of Criminal Justice and Immigration Act 2008, now Pt.3A S.29JA(1) as amended by Marriage (Same Sex Couples) Act 2013. There is considerable debate about the actual implications of the saving provision, with opponents describing it as 'objectionable', a 'menace' and an example of legislative 'mischief'. Wintemute argues that the saving provision, 'if interpreted broadly, could deprive the [offence] of most of its symbolic and practical value'. See: R. Wintemute, 'Homophobia and United Kingdom law: only a few gaps left to close', in L. Trappolin, A. Gasparini and R. Wintemute (eds), op. cit., p.238. Guidance from the Government, however, indicates that the saving provision does not 'affect the threshold required for the offence to be made out' and thus offers no additional protection (Coroners and Justice Bill 2008, Explanatory Note to Bill, 15 January 2009). At the time of writing, there has been only one successful prosecution under the offence – of three Muslim men who distributed leaflets advocating capital punishment for those committing homosexual acts (Derby Crown Court, 20 January 2012) – and it is therefore difficult to assess the actual impact of the saving provision on the decisions of the courts. The interpretation of the provision also has potentially significant implications for policing, given that police have to exercise discretion in making arrests, and their understanding of the saving provision will impact upon decisions about when to investigate complaints or make arrests.
17   The Lords voted 179-135 in favour of an amendment that defeated the Labour Government's attempt to remove the saving provision. The Bishops' Bench voted 3-0 in favour of the saving provision with the Bishops of Chester, Chichester and Winchester in support. HL Debate, 11 November 2009, Division No.3.

of religious hostility was never advanced in relation to the category of 'race', which was repeatedly invoked as a benchmark against which the claims for protection of both 'religion' and 'sexual orientation' were measured.[18] Crucially, this willingness to limit the scope of protections available to gay men and lesbians in light of religious opposition was apparent in both supporters and opponents of the saving provision, if often expressed in somewhat differing ways.

Reflecting broader transformations in the nature of parliamentary discourse (as documented in previous chapters), direct challenges were rarely articulated to the notion that sexual minorities needed and deserved a degree of legal protection from hate speech. Rather, parliamentarians hostile to the hate speech offence simultaneously proclaimed an abhorrence of 'homophobia' while constructing a case that the proposed offence went 'too far' or conflicted with the rights of other groups (particularly religious groups) and the interests of the (presumed heterosexual) 'wider public'.[19] In the remainder of the chapter we examine several key discourses which shaped debates over the scope of homophobic hate speech regulation. We first examine the particular logics of equality that pervaded the debates, in which religion and sexual orientation were represented as in competition for legal protection. We then demonstrate how opponents successfully ensured a special status for faith-based speech about homosexuality. We go on to show how opponents claimed that the legislation placed people of faith at serious risk of police investigation. Finally, we highlight how opponents depicted the legislation as an expression of a more general state-led persecution of Christians and other people of faith.

The logics of equalities

Conservative religious groups increasingly argue that their own rights to religious liberty are violated by legal measures that either require the equal treatment of sexual minorities (such as in equality law which we discussed in Chapter 3) or limit the form and content of anti-gay expression.[20] One of the key ways that advocates of including the 'freedom of expression' saving provision in the CJIA 2008 sought to advance their case was through the appropriation of the language

---

18 For a discussion of how legislation regarding hate crime and hate speech has developed through an analogical process whereby protections are extended to new categories of people based on the rationale that there are equivalencies with other categories to which protection has already been granted, see: E. Heinze, op. cit.
19 See the Introduction for a discussion of the evolution of this discursive strategy.
20 See, for example: S. Hunt, 'Saints and sinners: the role of conservative Christian pressure groups in the Christian gay debate in the UK', *Sociological Research Online*, 8, 2003; C.F. Stychin, 'Closet cases: "conscientious objection" to lesbian and gay legal equality', *Griffith Law Review* 18, 2009, 17–38.

of equalities that had been central to promoting homosexual law reform in previous debates. Although, in a rare challenge to the sincerity of this rhetoric, John Bercow MP commented that 'some – although not all – of [the saving provision's] supporters would not even know how to spell the word "equality", let alone sign up to it',[21] the discourse of equality proved instrumental in constructing a case that the saving provision was necessary to prevent gay rights from being privileged over those of religious traditionalists.

Supporters of the inclusion of the saving provision repeatedly drew attention to the existing Racial and Religious Hatred Act 2006 to highlight differences in the approach to regulating incitement to hatred in respect of race, religion and sexual orientation. The offence of racial hatred is the most widely drawn of the three offences.[22] It covers words or behaviour that are 'abusive' and 'insulting' (not just 'threatening') and it lacks the requirement of intent that was introduced in relation to the offence of incitement to religious hatred. The offence of hatred against persons on religious grounds,[23] in contrast, is limited to 'threatening' words and behaviour and it includes a 'free speech' saving provision (absent from the offence of racial hatred) that states:

> Nothing in this Part shall be read or given effect in a way which prohibits or restricts discussion, criticism or expressions of antipathy, dislike, ridicule, insult or abuse of particular religions or the beliefs or practices of their adherents, or of any other belief system or the beliefs or practices of its adherents, or proselytising or urging adherents of a different religion or belief system to cease practising their religion or belief system.[24]

The inclusion of this saving provision is commonly understood as a response to lobbying from civil libertarians who feared that, without such a provision, those making criticism of religious groups would be put at risk of criminal charges. However, it is important to note that the religious saving provision was also actively promoted by a number of Christian groups who argued that, without it, they could be prosecuted for criticising or proselytising believers from faiths other than their own.[25]

Given that the Government had previously accepted a saving provision in respect of religious hatred, those who advocated the sexual orientation saving provision argued that to omit it would represent an obvious privileging of one protected category over another. As Lord Waddington, a key proponent of the

---

21 HC Debate, 26 January 2009, c.36.
22 Pt.3 Public Order Act 1986.
23 Pt.3A Public Order Act 1986.
24 Pt.3A S.29J Public Order Act 1986.
25 See, for example, the Christian Institute, 'Incitement to Religious Hatred'. Available online at www.christian.org.uk/resources/theology/apologetics/christian-freedoms-and-heritage/incitement-to-religious-hatred (accessed on 5 December 2013).

saving provision, argued when replying to attempts to block it: 'It is clearly not right; how can it be, when there is a free speech clause in the religious hatred offence but no such clause here?'[26] Although this logic was not entirely uncontested, supporters of the legislation as originally drafted found it difficult to articulate convincing challenges to the argument that the existence of a saving provision in relation to offences of religious hatred necessitated the insertion of one in relation to homophobic hatred in order to achieve equality. Subsequent to the passage of the CJIA 2008, when the Government attempted to repeal the saving provision in the Coroners and Justice Bill 2009, the argument was again effectively deployed that to repeal the saving provision would send a powerful message that protecting religious traditionalists mattered less than protecting sexual minorities. This argument was instrumental to the defence of the saving provision mounted by the Lords and the then Conservative minority in the Commons (with future Prime Minister, David Cameron, and Minister for Women and Equalities, Theresa May, amongst those voting to preserve the saving provision).[27]

The saving provision in the CJIA 2008 uses a narrower wording than that found in the religious hatred provision. Its wording was originally drafted by Jim Dobbin MP in direct consultation with the Church of England and the Catholic Church.[28] The text proposed by Dobbin specified that the law should not be interpreted:

> in a way which prohibits or restricts discussion of, criticism of or expressions of antipathy towards, conduct relating to a particular sexual orientation, or urging persons of a particular sexual orientation to refrain from or modify conduct related to that orientation.[29]

Dobbin claimed that this wording demonstrated the moderate and compromising stance of the churches (in contrast to the aggressiveness of pro-gay activist groups) because 'the Churches have restricted the free speech protection to "discussion", "criticism", and "antipathy"', while not seeking protection of 'ridicule', 'insult' and 'abuse'.[30] However, this initial draft was widely criticised for its protection of expressions of 'antipathy', with even Lord Dearing (whose voting record reflects consistent opposition to gay equalities legislation) suggesting that this proposal went 'a little too far'.[31] Others, such as the Bishop of Chester, Peter Forster, expressed hesitancy about the draft's explicit focus on 'orientation' rather than the notion of sexual behaviour or conduct, given that this wording would have

---

26 HL Debate, 7 May 2008, c.611.
27 HC Debate, 24 March 2009, Division No.84.
28 HC Debate, 9 January 2008, c.449.
29 Ibid., c.441.
30 Ibid., c.450.
31 HL Debate, 3 March 2008, c.938.

inscribed protection for expressions of antipathy towards a category of people rather than a belief or practice.[32] Lord Waddington described his final draft of the saving provision as a 'more moderate' proposal than the Dobbins draft because of its focus on 'sexual conduct or practices' rather than orientation.[33] From Waddington's perspective, the revised version was a fair companion to the religious saving provision because both now focused on the criticism of 'choice': 'religion is – at least, to some extent – a matter of choice, whereas sexual orientation is not, but while sexual orientation does not involve choice, sexual behaviour obviously does.'[34]

In response to this comparison of sexual orientation and religious belief, a number of opponents of the saving provision invoked essentialist arguments about the innateness of sexual orientation to differentiate it from religion.[35] They argued that sexual orientation more closely resembled 'race' or 'ethnicity' (concepts that were themselves problematically conflated in the debates) than 'religion', and therefore the inclusion of a saving provision was inappropriate. As Baroness Turner of Camden explained: 'Religion is a belief whereas sexual orientation may be a state of being. Therefore different arrangements should apply.'[36] Many supporters of the saving provision rejected this comparison between race and sexual orientation. For example, the Bishop of Winchester, Michael Scott-Joynt, asserted that 'to pass law on the assumption that we can use the language of sexual orientation and believe that we are talking about something that is absolutely fixed and clear, as ethnicity might be thought to be, is a mistaken political orthodoxy'.[37]

In many respects it is unsurprising that debates about the fixed and innate quality of homosexuality and its implications for law would be debated in this way, given the long lineage of these discourses in Parliament (see Chapter 1). However, what is significant here is that even opponents of the saving provision who accepted an essentialist view of homosexuality still often (both implicitly and explicitly) 'ranked' it within a hierarchy of equalities as lower than race. They did so because of claims about the need to protect religious expression about homosexuality. Evan Harris MP, one of the most outspoken critics of the saving

---

32   Ibid., c.937. Similar to the distinction that was made in these debates about the difference between homosexual identity and practice, prior debates about the offence of incitement to religious hatred saw government supporters often maintaining a distinction between religious identity and belief to justify the protection of expressions of 'antipathy' and 'abuse' related to religious belief. For one perspective on the unsustainability of this distinction between identity and belief, see: E. Barendt, 'Religious hatred laws: protecting groups or belief', *Res Publica* 17, 2011, 41–53.
33   HL Debate, 7 May 2008, c.612.
34   HL Debate, 3 March 2008, c.924.
35   Lord Lester of Herne Hill, HL Debate, 9 July 2009, c.806.
36   HL Debate, 21 April 2008, c.1370.
37   HL Debate, 9 July 2009, c.806.

provision and a supporter of homosexual law reform, exemplified this tendency when he provided the following 'rational framework':

> Provisions on incitement to hatred need a rational framework, and we are slowly but surely getting there. Our laws on incitement to racial hatred have a very low threshold, in that there is no requirement to intend to stir up hatred and the language can be threatening, abusive or insulting [. . .] At the other end of the spectrum, we need a high threshold to capture cases involving the criticism of people's opinions, whether they be political or aesthetic; I include in that religious opinions, even though they are often felt more strongly. That is why the House got things absolutely right with the narrow offence for incitement to religious hatred, which required an intention to incite hatred and was restricted to threatening language. Given that opinion is not innate and given that the Government were not offering any concessions on the matter, it was appropriate to have a freedom of speech saver clause [. . .] Sexual orientation falls somewhere in between those two ends of the spectrum. It is towards the racial hatred end, in terms of requiring protection, because it is innate and part of a shared or common humanity; it is not something that one can alter or choose. However, it perhaps requires less protection because there is a great deal of sincerely held, often religious, opinion that extends to sexual orientation that does not – generally speaking, in this country, thank goodness – extend to race [. . .] The threshold for offences in relation to sexual orientation therefore needs to be middle-ranking.[38]

From this perspective, the persistence of fervent and 'sincerely held' religious beliefs about homosexuality necessitated that sexual orientation do not merit the same level of protection as race. While warranting stronger protection than religion, sexual orientation must in Harris' view remain 'middle ranking'.

The special status of religious speech

Although debates over incitement to hatred on the grounds of sexual orientation were characterised by frequent claims about the marginalisation of religious people in the process of lawmaking, the debates exemplify how parliamentarians often accord religious speakers a special status. The special status attributed to religion becomes most apparent through an examination of how particular categories of speaker and speech – whether real or hypothetical – were imagined to meet the key thresholds of the offence: that speech or behaviour be both 'threatening' and 'intended' to stir up hatred. Parliamentarians on both sides of the debate repeatedly invoked examples of speech that they thought reached this

---

38 HC Debate, 6 May 2008, cc.616–617.

threshold and, as such, should be criminalised. Forms of religious speech were very rarely invoked in this respect. Rather, speech believed to fall within the ambit of the offence was imagined to originate from two primary sources: far-right political propaganda and particular forms of popular music. In relation to the first, a number of parliamentarians invoked the British National Party (BNP) and other elements of the 'odious extreme political right'[39] as key sources of homophobic hate speech. For example, Lord Hunt of Kings Heath, when explaining the Government's stance, provided the following illustrations:

> I want to say why we have brought forward this proposal in the first place. The Government have seen evidence, and the committee in the other place took oral evidence, that gay people are a target for threatening words and behaviour which stir up hatred [...] As we have heard, it shows extreme political parties trying to whip up hatred against the gay community by associating homosexuality with child abuse or with the spread of disease. Recent BNP campaign literature distributed to voters in north Wales featured photographs of child murder victims and claimed that a majority vote by mainstream parties to equalise the age of consent indicated that MPs were trying to legalise child sex step by step.[40]

In these examples, associations of homosexuality with criminality or disease are represented as deliberate attempts to 'whip up' hatred on the grounds of sexual orientation.[41] Using this formulation, far-right speech that depicts homosexuals as a social or public threat – even if a specific violent act is not threatened by the speaker – is sufficient to meet the key thresholds of the offence. Parliamentarians also invoked certain forms of rap, reggae and dancehall music to illustrate the need for the sexual orientation hate speech offence. In Commons Committee, MPs heard testimony from Ben Summerskill, Chief Executive of Stonewall, who quoted excerpts from songs with lyrics such as 'Tek a Bazooka and kill batty-fucker' (interpreted by Summerskill to mean 'Take a rocket launcher and

---

39 Ibid., c.622.
40 HL Debate, 3 March 2008, c.940.
41 To clarify the definition of 'threatening', attempts were made (led by David Heath MP, Evan Harris MP and David Howarth MP) to make explicit in the legislation that discursively linking homosexuality with paedophilia could be understood as 'threatening' (even if violence was not explicitly threatened), but their efforts were repeatedly rejected by the Government as unnecessary. As explained by then Under Secretary of State for Justice, Bridget Prentice MP: 'I fully understand the motivation [...] but I believe that it is unnecessary. Allegations about offences, and specifically about child sex offences, are a very easy and damaging way of stirring up hatred on the grounds of sexual orientation. Such allegations are damaging and distasteful and should be challenged, but we believe that it is not necessary to mention them specifically in the offence. In many instances, allegations linking sexual orientation with child sex offences will be threatening as well as distasteful, and will be caught by the offence'. HC Debate, 24 March 2009, c.201.

shoot gay men').[42] A representative of Liberty argued that 'black dancehall artists'[43] seemed to be the key target of the legislation.

In contrast, religious speakers were depicted by parliamentarians in often starkly different language, even when it was recognised that the views that some anti-gay religious groups advanced helped foster a threatening social climate for sexual minorities. For example, Lord Alli argued that anti-gay religious speech about homosexuality should be protected because it was the expression of 'good men and women up and down this country discussing their views openly'.[44] It was argued that religious speech was the expression of beliefs that are 'sincerely held'[45] and that such beliefs could not be compared to those of the far right. Evan Harris MP stated that the claim that homosexuality is linked with paedophilia, for example, 'will not necessarily come from religious voices'.[46] Edward Garnier MP asserted that 'the Christian right, or those who do not think that the law is necessary, do not want to make members of minorities live in fear or suffer hatred'.[47] And Stonewall Chief Executive, Ben Summerskill, affirmed Garnier's claim by replying: 'I am sure that that is true.'[48]

Even when the content of religious speech about homosexuality showed little difference to the discourse of 'vile' gangsta rappers or the far right, anti-gay religious speakers were often represented as behaving in ways that failed to reach the key thresholds of the offence. For example, the practice of publicly reciting particular excerpts from Leviticus (which, in some contemporary translations, call for men engaging in same-sex behaviour to be killed) in a church was portrayed as differing in fundamental ways from a far-right activist calling for gay men to receive the same fate in the presence of a sympathetic crowd. Speaking to a 'vanload of skinheads' was argued to be 'a mile away from a preacher in a church or mosque' speaking to fellow believers.[49] Or, as one of the most outspoken opponents of the saving provision put it: 'If a charge was brought against a saintly religious leader whose intention was to save souls, I cannot see how anyone might think that an offence had been committed.'[50] Although performing a song in a dancehall calling for violence against homosexuals was said to demonstrate adequate 'intent' to incite hatred, reading scripture from a pulpit that advocated the same outcome was considered below that threshold. Furthermore, it was assumed that the audiences that a religious speaker might address (for example, church congregations) would not be incited to hatred by the speaker's words.

---

42 HC Committee, 16 October 2007, c.75.
43 G. Crossman, HC Committee, 18 October 2007, c.131.
44 HL Debate, 7 May 2008, c.601.
45 P. Cormack, HC Debate, 6 May 2008, c.612.
46 HC Debate, 6 May 2008, c.618.
47 HC Committee, 16 October 2007, c.85.
48 Ibid.
49 E. Garnier, HC Committee, 29 November 2007, c.671.
50 D. Howarth, HC Debate, 24 March 2009, c.189.

Policing and the 'climate of fear' for people of faith

Throughout the debates, attention was repeatedly focused on the potential law enforcement implications of the legislation for people of faith. Although hate speech legislation was introduced because of evidence of persistent and, in some places, rising rates of homophobic violence, parliamentary debate focused far less on the experiences of sexual minorities and more on the allegedly growing fear of religious people that their ability to object to homosexuality would be curtailed. Baroness O'Cathain, along with many others, argued that Parliament must:

> make sure that this legislation does not add to the climate of fear that already exists around the controversial subject of homosexuality [. . .] Noble Lords might not agree with the churchman who says that all sex outside marriage is a sin, but do we want an environment in which he feels afraid to express his point of view?[51]

Supporters of the saving provision repetitively discussed a series of cases (some of which had featured prominently in the press) involving police investigations of Christians and other religious speakers who had publicly criticised homosexuality. Andrew Selous MP described these in the following terms:

> [A]n elderly pensioner couple, a bishop of the Church of England, a Roman Catholic archbishop, a leading Muslim figure and a leading author have been investigated by the police, and when that happens people worry about the nature of our society. We must maintain that essential freedom of speech while avoiding the harm and upset that neither [the Government] nor I wants to see.[52]

In response to a repetitive series of similar assertions, the Government emphasised that these cases were irrelevant because they were each examples of one of two types of incident, neither of which related directly to the offence in question: first, incidents investigated under other public order provisions that have a lower threshold (such as S.5 of the POA 1986, which does not require 'intent' and allows for prosecutions for behaviour that is 'abusive' – and, previously, 'insulting'[53] – even if not 'threatening'[54]); or, second, incidents involving police

---

51 HL Debate, 3 March 2008, cc.932–933.
52 HC Debate, 6 May 2008, c.600.
53 The word 'insulting' was removed from S.5 Public Order Act 1986 by S.57(2) Crime and Courts Act 2013.
54 S.5 Public Order Act 1986. At the time of these parliamentary debates only one such case had been successfully prosecuted under S.5 Public Order Act 1986. The prosecution was of an evangelical Christian street preacher, Harry Hammond, who was arrested on

following hate crime guidance that requires them to investigate incidents perceived to be homophobic (guidance created largely to reassure sexual minorities that their complaints would be properly investigated, after years of problematic relations with the police).[55] Nevertheless, supporters of the saving provision used these forms of policing and policy to argue that the protection of sexual minorities had gone 'too far'.[56] Repeated criticism, and even ridicule, was directed at the definition of homophobia contained in the Crown Prosecution Service's guidance on the investigation of homophobic hate incidents and the prosecution of hate crimes,[57] which includes reference to perceptions of 'dislike', rather than simply 'hate', of a person's lifestyle or orientation.[58] This definition was said to exemplify the overextension of police authority to harass 'respectable' citizens over the expression of their opinions (however, such claims obscure the fact that expressions of 'dislike' are nowhere constituted in the criminal law and that these definitions have no direct bearing on the threshold of the hate speech offence).

Although very few of the examples recited in this 'succession of scandals'[59] involving the police resulted in any formal charges or prosecutions, supporters of the saving provision portrayed them as representative of large-scale cultural and political shifts. These shifts meant that, Gerald Howarth MP argued, 'those of us who now seek to defend [traditional Church of England] teaching are regarded almost as pariahs'.[60] Religious opponents invoked the 'scandals' in policing as evidence and 'truth'[61] of the need to protect religious speech with the saving provision. By focusing on the apparent vulnerability of religious speakers, religious opponents were able to appropriate the language of minority rights to argue that it was Christians and other citizens with 'strong views'[62] about homosexuality who were those at 'risk', in 'danger', and had cause to 'fear', rather than the sexual minorities the law was designed to protect. As Baroness Butler-Sloss argued:

13 October 2001 for breach of the peace after displaying a sign reading 'Stop Immorality', 'Stop Homosexuality' and 'Stop Lesbianism', and subsequently charged with an offence under S.5 Public Order Act 1986. A subsequent appeal was dismissed. *Hammond v Director of Public Prosecutions* [2004] EWHC 69 (Admin).

55 P. Johnson and R.M. Vanderbeck, '"Hit them on the nose": representations of policing in parliamentary debates about incitement to hatred on the grounds of sexual orientation', *Policing: A Journal of Policy and Practice* 5, 2011, 65–74.
56 Lord Stoddart of Swindon, HL Debate, 22 January 2008, c.168.
57 Crown Prosecution Service, *Policy for Prosecuting Cases with a Homophobic Element*, produced by the CPS Equality & Diversity Unit and the Policy Directorate, November 2002. This guidance has since been updated: Crown Prosecution Service, *Policy for Prosecuting Cases of Homophobic and Transphobic Hate Crime*, produced by the CPS Equality & Diversity Unit and the Policy Directorate, November 2007.
58 For example: Lord Waddington, HL Debate, 21 April 2008, c.1366; G. Howarth, HC Debate, 24 March 2009, c.191.
59 Lord Waddington, HL Debate, 3 March 2008, c.943.
60 HC Debate, 6 May 2008, c.620.
61 Lord Harrison, HL Debate, 7 May 2008, c.604.
62 E. Garnier, HC Committee, 29 November 2007, c.669.

> We are talking about homophobia, which I, like, I assume, everyone in this House, abhor, but there are religious groups, not only Christians, not only bishops, but many Jews and Muslims, which share strong views that they gain from the Bible, the Old Testament in particular, or the Koran. Those people are potentially at risk. It is very unlikely that they are at risk of prosecution, but in the speech that the noble Lord, Lord Waddington, made today and on a previous occasion, he set out that his area of concern is the people who say what is understood incorrectly to be within this proposed clause. It is those people who will potentially be intimidated; they will certainly be bothered and may go through an extremely unfortunate experience before calmer heads point out that under the new clause, as under older clauses, they have not committed any offence. It is those people whom the noble Lord, Lord Waddington, has spoken about who, despite everybody's objection to homophobia, none the less need some help.[63]

Baroness Butler-Sloss, like many other advocates for the saving provision, asserted that religious speakers would feel 'intimidated' by the provisions of the new law and, as such, she urged Parliament to offer them the 'help' they needed in the form of the saving provision. While the rhetoric of Butler-Sloss and others made no reference to the ways in which lesbians and gay men frequently restrict the public expression of their views and identities for fear of violence, it was repeatedly asserted that people of faith with conservative views on sexuality had to be able to speak in uninhibited ways: '[W]here people have religious convictions and feel that they have to express views based on their belief [...] they should have absolutely no inhibition whatever in expressing those views as a matter of their opinion'.[64] The saving provision was represented as a tool for offering clarification necessary for police forces that lacked good judgement and who allegedly sought to advance a pro-gay political agenda. It offered, as the Bishop of Newcastle, Martin Wharton, argued, 'some protection from petty harassment by overzealous police officers investigating vexatious complaints'.[65]

To illustrate the overzealous and 'heavy-handed approaches taken by the police'[66] in respect of religious speech, legislators consistently relied upon a small group of cases to argue that police were both overusing and enforcing the POA 1986 in a disproportionate manner. For example, two of these cases involved Mr and Mrs Roberts, and the Bishop of Chester:

> In 2005, a Christian couple – Joe and Helen Roberts – were interrogated by the police because they complained about their local council's gay rights policy. The police said that they were responding to a reported homophobic

---

63 HL Debate, 7 May 2008, c.600.
64 W. Cash, 6 May 2008, cc.621–622.
65 HL Debate, 21 April 2008, c.1372.
66 D. Burrowes, HC Committee, 29 November 2007, c.664.

incident under the guidelines. They later admitted that no crime had been committed and, following legal action by the Roberts, the police and the council issued a public apology. It all worked out in the end, but that is a rather alarming example of the chilling effect of legislation such as that proposed today. The Bishop of Chester was investigated by the Cheshire constabulary in November 2003, after he told his local newspaper of research showing that some homosexuals reoriented to heterosexuality. The police passed a file to the Crown Prosecution Service, which decided not to prosecute [...] Again, it all worked out in the end, but that is another alarming example of the chilling effect of such a law.[67]

While this account obfuscates the exact nature of both the offence that is being policed and the specific 'guidelines' that are supposedly being used to enable it, there is an implicit assertion that the police were using existing legislation to 'interrogate' people in an 'alarming' and 'chilling' manner. These 'high-profile incidents', it was argued, showed that police were investigating people who 'have done nothing more than express a religious view'.[68]

In responding to these 'frightening cases', Lord Stoddart of Swindon discussed the case of Lynette Burrows, a 'family values campaigner' who 'expressed the view on a radio programme that homosexual men may not be suitable for raising children'.[69] 'She was entitled to express that opinion', asserted Lord Stoddart, 'without the police coming down on her like a ton of bricks'.[70] Lord Clarke of Hampstead discussed a letter he had received from 'two people' who were described as 'pensioners and Christians':

> They heard that the council where they live wanted to display homosexual leaflets around the area. The couple asked a council officer whether they could distribute Christian leaflets. They were told that no, they could not. The reason given by the official was that homosexuals would find it very offensive. They said that they were not aggressive and did not raise their voices. They went home. Two or three days later they found out that the man they spoke to at the council had alerted the police.[71]

Lord Clarke further described how '[t]wo six-foot tall policemen turned up at their door' and 'interrogated' them 'in their own front room for 80 minutes' about their 'homophobic phone calls'. These 'two lovely old people'[72] were 'terrified by the police' and, Lord Clarke argued, this terror should be deplored

---

67 P. Hollobone, HC Committee, 29 November 2007, c.686.
68 A. Widdecombe, HC Debate, 9 January 2008, cc.454–455.
69 HL Debate, 22 January 2008, c.168
70 Ibid.
71 HL Debate, 21 April 2008, c.1368.
72 HL Debate, 7 May 2008, c. 605.

regardless of whether it takes place in Britain or 'in apartheid South Africa, in Iran or in many other parts of the world'.[73] In a subsequent account of the same incident by David Taylor MP, the 'two six foot police officers' were said to have arrived in 'body armour' to interrogate the couple.[74]

These and other examples depicting police interaction with 'vulnerable' members of the public were used to argue for provisions that provided 'protection' from the 'vexatious complaints' that the Bishop of Newcastle, Martin Wharton, asserted were routinely made by gay men and lesbians.[75] What Wharton did not consider was that, whilst he and other legislators repeatedly claimed that the police received a high volume of vexatious complaints, research shows that most incidents of homophobic hate crime go unreported.[76] Yet cases of disproportionate policing were repeatedly cited to encourage support for including the saving provision in the legislation: 'this quite modest amendment would be to deter such overzealous police officers from causing [. . .] anxiety'.[77] Without the saving provision, it was 'not impossible to envisage people being driven to the end of their tether by that sort of thing'.[78] Whilst Ann Widdecombe MP stated that policing in Britain had not yet reached the status of 'the KGB knocking on the door at dawn or people being shanghaied off to the Lubyanka', she argued that it was now 'an established fact' that 'people have been visited by the police for expressing an opinion'.[79] The police were repeatedly portrayed as having 'harassed, bullied, interrogated',[80] used the existing law to 'go for it tooth and nail',[81] created 'fear' through 'over-zealous pursuit',[82] 'threatened [Christians] with jail for what was described as homophobia',[83] and engaged in 'over-the-top and heavy-booted action'.[84] As a consequence of the 'special pleading'[85] by gay

---

73 HL Debate, 21 April 2008, c.1368.
74 HC Debate, 24 March 2009, c.196.
75 HL Debate, 21 April 2008, c.1372.
76 See: M.L. Williams and A.L. Robinson, 'Problems and prospects with policing the lesbian, gay and bisexual community in Wales', *Policing and Society* 14, 2004, 213–232; K. Wong and K. Christmann, 'The role of victim decision-making in the reporting of hate crime', *Community Safety Journal* 7, 2008, 19–35.
77 Lord Anderson of Swansea, HL Debate, 21 April 2008, c.1373.
78 P. Cormack, HC Debate, 6 May 2008, c.602.
79 HC Debate, 6 May 2008, c.615.
80 Lord Waddington, HL Debate, 7 May 2008, c.597.
81 Baroness Knight of Collingtree, HL Debate, 7 May 2008, c.604.
82 Lord Armstrong of Ilminster, HL Debate, 7 May 2008, c.606.
83 Lord Moran, HL Debate, 18 May 2009, c.1274.
84 D. Taylor, HC Debate, 9 November 2009, c.114.
85 Lord Stoddart of Swindon, HL Debate, 3 March 2008, c.935. This characterisation referred directly to Stonewall, which Lord Stoddart argued was an organisation that had 'undue influence on Government policy' and was exerting 'pressure' to shape the law to reflect its mistaken belief that 'gays are less able to stand up for themselves than everybody else' (HL Debate, 22 January 2008, c.169). Stonewall was often contrasted with other 'prominent homosexuals' (Lord Monson, HL Debate, 9 July 2009, c.808) such as Peter

men and lesbians, Christians and other people of faith were argued to suffer 'reverse discrimination'.[86]

The persecution of people of faith?

The representation of overzealous police officers was instrumental in encouraging the necessary support amongst legislators for the inclusion of the 'freedom of expression' saving provision in the CJIA 2008. It reframed a debate that originated with the question of how to balance the legal protection of freedom of speech with the protection of sexual minorities, to one that emphasised how best to address, as some parliamentarians asserted, an existing imbalance in the approach to freedom of religious speech. By sketching a 'past history' in which 'individuals who have sought to express perfectly reasonable criticism have received visits from the police', it was argued that '[w]e must ensure that such things do not happen' under the new law.[87] Even the Government minister responsible for taking the legislation through the final stages of the House of Commons agreed that, whilst it was important to protect gay and lesbian people, it was also vital to restrict 'overzealous investigations' by the police: '[t]hat is the balance that we need to strike'.[88]

Therefore, rather than considering the important role of the police service in arbitrating between the conflicting rights and interests of two different groups (however problematic this conceptualisation of distinct 'groups' may be, since it assumes that faith and homosexuality are mutually exclusive), the police were portrayed as exacerbators of this conflict. A consistent assertion, recalling nineteenth-century popular portrayals of the police as oppressive agents of a police state,[89] was that police forces adopted pro-gay, anti-Christian policies and used the law to 'silence' Christians. What is novel about this contemporary representation is that the police were depicted as seeking to oppress 'ordinary Britons' in order to advance the rights of homosexuals.[90] This marks a significant inversion of dominant cultural representations of policing in relation to sexual orientation: in contrast to long-standing images of police culture as inherently heterosexist and anti-gay, supporters of the saving provision depicted police forces as driving a pro-gay agenda that abused the rights of religious believers.

Lord Waddington, for example, stated that there 'is no doubt that there have been abuses in the sense of inappropriate action by the police'.[91] Such abuses were

---

Tatchell and Matthew Parris who were invoked as allies amongst those who believed that 'to attack this [hate speech] legislation is to be pro free speech' (Lord Waddington, HL Debate, 22 January 2008, c.171).
86 Earl Ferrers, HL Debate, 3 March 2008, c.931.
87 D. Grieve, HC Debate, 26 January 2009, cc.37–52.
88 M. Eagle, HC Debate, 6 May 2008, c.624.
89 R. Reiner, *The Politics of the Police (Third edition)*, Oxford: Oxford University Press, 2000.
90 A. Widdecombe, HC Debate, 9 November 2009, c.119.
91 HL Debate, 11 November 2009, c.863.

said to take the form of people having their speech 'gone over by the police' which not only 'creates an aura of fear' but amounts to 'reverse discrimination': '[w]e have seen it all over the place [...] That is what happens in a police state.'[92] The foundations for this 'reverse discrimination' were said to be the 'politically correct climate in which the police now operate' which makes officers feel 'obliged' to take 'silly' complaints seriously.[93] Officers were portrayed as being 'urged on by politically correct chief constables to step up their harassment'[94] of those with conservative views on homosexuality. One parliamentarian speculated on the motivations underpinning the 'politically correct' behaviour of officers: 'trying to shake off their old homophobic image perhaps, [the police] have been overzealous in investigating claims of homophobia'.[95] Legislators relied upon a range of anecdotal accounts of such 'overzealousness' to represent police officers routinely engaging in the suppression of criticism of homosexuality. David Taylor MP, for example, cited the case of 'an eminently calm and sensible' street preacher who, even though he 'had not even mentioned homosexuality', was subject to 'unfounded and unsubstantiated allegations of homophobia' by the police 'as a device for shutting him up'.[96] Taylor argued that there 'is a lot of public sympathy for these victims of police heavy-handedness in the area of gay rights' and new legislation should prevent the police from 'trampling on people's civil liberties'.[97] Ann Widdecombe MP argued that, whilst such 'misguided application' of the law by 'some PC Plod' produces an 'outcry' from the public,[98] the police continue to behave in ways suitable for 'totalitarian states'.[99] This alleged transformation in police culture and priorities was represented as the result of pressure from a Government that had become beholden to LGBT groups, particularly Stonewall. As Lord Dear argued: 'Is it, perhaps, that the Government have bowed to lobby groups that are more vociferous in the one category than in the other?'[100]

The Pauline Howe case

A close examination of the case of Pauline Howe – one of the 'horror stories' of 'over-policing' frequently cited during debates in both the Commons and the Lords – vividly illustrates how parliamentarians sought to depict religious individuals as both persecuted and in need of protection. The case of Howe, a pensioner and Christian who wrote a letter to Norwich Council to complain about

---

92 Earl Ferrers, HL Debate, 3 March 2008, c.931.
93 Baroness O'Cathain, HL Debate, 3 March 2008, c.933.
94 Lord Monson, HL Debate, 21 April 2008, c.1370.
95 Lord Lester of Herne Hill, HL Debate, 9 July 2009, c.797.
96 HC Debate, 9 November 2009, c.110.
97 Ibid., c.113.
98 HC Debate, 24 March 2009, c.202.
99 HC Debate, 9 November 2009, c.119.
100 HL Debate, 11 November 2009, c.853.

a Gay Pride March in the city, was reported widely in the British media in 2009. For example, the *Daily Telegraph* reported that in her letter Howe had stated that '[i]t is shameful that this small, but vociferous lobby should be allowed such a display unwarranted by the minimal number of homosexuals' and, referring to homosexuals as 'sodomites', she blamed 'their perverted sexual practice' for sexually transmitting diseases as well as the 'downfall of every Empire'.[101] The *Daily Telegraph* and other media focused on the response of the local authority, which was to pass the letter to the police on the basis that it potentially constituted an offence, and the subsequent 'investigation' by the police which consisted of a visit by officers to Howe's home. Media reports typically obfuscated the fact that Howe had also been distributing leaflets opposing homosexuality at the parade about which she had complained, and hence her rhetoric was not confined to a private letter to the council. Despite the police explaining that their response was simply to 'talk' to Howe, many commentators, including Ben Summerskill of Stonewall, described the actions of officers as 'disproportionate'.[102]

Howe's case was invoked frequently to argue for the need to protect religious believers from harassment. For example, David Taylor MP argued:

> Pauline Howe [. . .] is a 67-year-old grandmother who wrote to her council complaining about a gay pride march at which she says she was verbally abused. She used old-fashioned, politically incorrect words and several biblical references, and I doubt whether many of us in the House would have written a letter in those terms [. . .] Pauline Howe's letter certainly did not merit two officers interrogating her in her living room, and apparently frightening the living daylights out of her, but that is what happened.[103]

Lord Dear defended Howe in the following terms:

> Mrs Howe was not a shrill, loud-mouthed demonstrator, shrieking abuse in the streets. She did not carry a placard in public with abusive or insulting words written on it. Mrs Howe is an eminently respectable, highly principled, late-middle-aged, middle-class lady married to a clergyman [. . .] In July this year, she wrote a letter to Norfolk county council. She complained against the holding of a Gay Pride march in Norwich. The letter, which I have seen, was well constructed and forthright, but it was by no means inflammatory. However, the council officials in their wisdom saw fit to pass it to the police. In September, she was visited and interviewed in her own home by not one

---

101 The *Daily Telegraph*, 24 October 2009.
102 Summerskill's characterisation of the Howe case as an example of unreasonable police conduct was subsequently cited by parliamentarians to add weight to the argument for retaining the saving provision. See: HC Debate, 9 November 2009, c.111.
103 HC Debate, 9 November 2009, cc.110–111.

but two police officers from Norfolk Constabulary. She was interviewed for writing a letter, not for demonstrating in public.[104]

Speaking for the Government, Lord Bach challenged the benign representation of Howe by Lord Dear, highlighting her reference to 'sodomites' who, through their 'perverted sexual practice', were said to have brought about the 'downfall of every Empire'.[105] However, Lord Bach agreed with Lord Dear and others that Howe was 'absolutely entitled to make those remarks [and] whatever view you take of what she did, it was hardly threatening, nor was it intended to stir up hatred on the grounds of sexual orientation'.[106] Bach construed Howe's rhetoric as 'hardly threatening', despite drawing clear linkages between homosexuality and the spread of infectious disease, and constituting homosexuals as a group that threatens civilisation: both key features of the far-right discourse and musical lyrics that the Government sought to regulate with the criminal law. Howe's status as the Christian wife of a clergyman was effectively imagined to make it 'unreasonable' to construe her speech as inciting homophobic hatred, or even to warrant the investigation of a 'hate incident'; rather, she was represented as a persecuted victim.

Conclusion

In this chapter we have demonstrated that, within a changing social context where 'homophobia' is widely condemned, those seeking to limit the extension of legal protections to gay men and lesbians on religious grounds have developed new discursive strategies. As we argued in Chapter 3, these often take the form of appropriating the contemporary discourse of equalities to argue that 'gay rights' are creating inequalities in respect of religious belief. The parliamentary debates that we have analysed in this chapter show religious opponents advancing this discourse in novel ways to limit the scope of law designed to protect sexual minorities from hate speech. We have illustrated four key discursive strategies employed by religious opponents of the legislation: first, the deployment of particular logics of equality to represent religion and sexual orientation in a competitive and hierarchical relationship; second, the attribution of a special status to faith-based speech about homosexuality; third, the assertion that people of faith are at serious risk of police investigation; and, fourth, the representation of Christians and other people of faith as the victims of a more general state-led persecution. As we have demonstrated, a consensus existed in Parliament that the 'strongly' and 'sincerely' held objections of conservative religious believers necessitated that the offence of incitement to hatred on the grounds of sexual

---

104   HL Debate, 11 November 2009, c.854.
105   Ibid., c.861.
106   Ibid.

orientation have a higher threshold than the offence of incitement to racial hatred. Our analysis in this chapter shows how religion continues to hold a privileged ontological status within the process of lawmaking, even amongst some vocal supporters of rights and protections for gay men and lesbians. In the final chapter, we turn to consider the privileged role of religion in shaping the legal frameworks that govern the inclusion and exclusion of knowledge about homosexuality in British schools.

Chapter 6

Religion, homosexuality and state education

In this chapter we examine the relationship between religion and the legal frameworks that govern the inclusion and exclusion of knowledge about homosexuality within the curricula of British schools. The issue of how schools – and particularly, faith schools[1] – teach about homosexuality has been characterised by some commentators as 'the latest battleground in the culture wars'[2] between religion and sexual orientation. This 'war' has a long history, with its best-known 'battle' consisting of the 15-year struggle over the passage and repeal of so-called 'Section 28', which prohibited local authorities from promoting homosexuality in schools and other contexts.[3] Since the repeal of Section 28, debates have continued about how information about homosexuality is circulated, censored and shaped in schools by programmes of sex education, religious education and other aspects of the curriculum.

Schooling is arguably the arena of British public life in which religion remains most deeply institutionally embedded, and the public funding of religious schools 'represents one of the most controversial ways in which religion and the State interact'.[4] As of January 2013, 37 per cent of state-funded primary schools and

---

1 Until relatively recently, state-funded schools with a religious character were often referred to as 'church schools'. However, given the creation of a modest number of schools associated with other faiths, the broader term 'faith schools' has come into common usage. We use the term 'faith schools' here to refer to state-funded schools with an official religious designation or faith ethos. Although some commentators avoid the term 'faith schools' in favour of 'schools with a religious designation' (which is perceived as more legally precise, given that 'faith school' is not a category constituted in law), this terminology excludes an important category of school: academies and free schools with a religious ethos but not a formal religious designation (see below). Hence we use the term 'faith schools' to capture the full range of state-funded schools with either a religious designation or faith ethos.
2 A.J. Higginson, 'Faith schools: what really goes on behind closed doors', *Huffington Post*, 4 July 2013. Available online at www.huffingtonpost.co.uk/A.J.%20Higginson/faith-schools-what-really-goes-on_b_3545981.html (accessed on 5 December 2013).
3 S.28 Local Government Act 1988. Repealed by Ethical Standards in Public Life etc. (Scotland) Act 2000; Local Government Act 2003.
4 R. Sandberg, *Law and Religion*, Cambridge: Cambridge University Press, 2011, p.160.

19 per cent of secondary schools were designated as having a religious character.[5] Despite steep declines in levels of religious participation and identification in the population, successive governments have adopted and championed policies supporting faith schools.[6] Even those schools without a religious designation are legally required to organise acts of daily collective worship 'of a broadly Christian character'[7] and to provide pupils with religious education.[8] This deep penetration of the school system by religion is central to understanding if, how and when pupils are taught about issues concerning homosexuality during sex education and elsewhere in the curriculum.

We begin by examining the role of religion in relation to the passage and ultimate repeal of Section 28 and consider its ongoing legacy for the legal framework governing sex education in Britain. Following an overview of the complex nature of the English school system[9] and its entanglement with religion, we turn to consider three issues. First, we examine the role of religion in preserving the status of homosexuality in schools as what we term 'non-statutory knowledge' – that is, knowledge that is kept outside the requirements of the National Curriculum. Second, we explore recent debates about the implications of the Marriage (Same Sex Couples) Act 2013 in respect of the requirement that schools teach about 'marriage' in sex education. And, third, we demonstrate the role that religious considerations have played in protecting school curricula from challenges under equalities legislation. We argue that although religious arguments for severely circumscribing the discussion of homosexuality in schools have lost considerable persuasiveness, religious interests and considerations have contributed to shaping the law in ways that permit religiously inflected understandings of homosexuality to remain dominant in faith schools.

Religion and Section 28

Section 28 of the Local Government Act 1988 added a new section ('Prohibition on promoting homosexuality by teaching or by publishing material') to the Local Government Act 1986, specifying that local authorities shall not 'intentionally

---

5 Derived from Department for Education, 'Schools, pupils and their characteristics: January 2013'. Available online at www.gov.uk/government/publications/schools-pupils-and-their-characteristics-january-2013 (accessed on 5 December 2013). It is not possible with these data to determine whether or not free schools with a 'faith ethos' (a category of school we discuss later in this chapter) are included with schools designated as having a 'religious character'.
6 G. Walford, 'Faith-based schools in England after ten years of Tony Blair', *Oxford Review of Education* 34, 2008, 689–699.
7 S.70 and Sch.20 Para.3(2) School Standards and Framework Act 1998.
8 S.80(1) Education Act 2002.
9 We limit our analysis here to England given important differences between schooling in Wales, Scotland and Northern Ireland.

promote homosexuality or publish material with the intention of promoting homosexuality' or 'promote the teaching in any maintained school of the acceptability of homosexuality as a pretended family relationship'.[10] The battle over Section 28 has been one of the most written-about aspects of lesbian and gay law reform in Britain,[11] and we do seek to replicate existing discussions of the struggle over the legislation here. Rather, we are concerned specifically with the role of religious discourse in debates over Section 28 and the complex legacy left by Section 28 for sex education (including the status of teaching about homosexuality).

The role of religion in the enactment of Section 28

The enactment of Section 28 must be understood within the broader history of British sex education. Since the late Victorian period, sex education in Britain had developed in an *ad hoc* fashion with an overriding emphasis on a 'damage limitation' approach intended to protect young people from the moral dangers of premarital sex, pregnancy and the risk of infections.[12] The first direct statutory intervention on sex education did not occur until the 1980s. Rather than seeking to bolster sex education, the Education (No.2) Act 1986 sought to circumscribe provision in some local education authorities (LEAs) which had begun to move beyond emphases on the risks and biology of sex towards a model of 'social education'.[13] Described as a key element of a wider 'moral counter-revolution' in the 1980s related to sex education,[14] the Education (No.2) Act 1986 limited the power of LEAs by placing primary control of sex education in the hands of school governing bodies.[15] The Act also required LEAs and schools to take reasonable steps to ensure that any sex education provided had 'due regard to moral considerations and the value of family life'.[16] The transfer of power from LEAs reflected broader Conservative efforts in this period to restrict certain local authorities (particularly, although by no means exclusively, several inner London boroughs) that were perceived to have become left-wing bastions.[17] The 'loony

---

10 S.2A(1) Local Government Act 1986.
11 For example: D. Epstein, 'Sexualities and education: Catch 28', *Sexualities* 3, 2000, 387–394; J. Moran, 'Childhood sexuality and education: the case of Section 28', *Sexualities* 4, 2001, 73–89; M. McManus, *Tory Pride and Prejudice: The Conservative Party and Homosexual Law Reform*, London: Biteback Publishing, 2011.
12 L. Hall, 'In ignorance and knowledge: reflections on the history of sex education in Britain', in L.D.H. Sauerteig and R. Davidson (eds), *Shaping Sexual Knowledge: A Cultural History of Sex Education in Twentieth Century Europe*, London: Routledge, 2009, p.20.
13 J. Moran, op. cit., 79. For an example of the concerns about the 'promotion' of homosexuality by some London LEAs, see: Baroness Cox, HL Debate, 30 October 1986, cc.802–804.
14 A. Blair and D. Monk, 'Sex education and the law in England and Wales: the importance of legal narratives', in L.D.H. Sauerteig and R. Davidson (eds), op. cit., p.38.
15 S.18(2) Education (No.2) Act 1986.
16 S.46 Education (No.2) Act 1986, consolidated by S.403 Education Act 1996.

left' were accused of wasting the money of 'rates payers' on promoting homosexuality through the funding of youth groups, events and programmes of sex education in schools. These programmes of sex education included attempts to present positive images of homosexuals as part of efforts to combat discrimination – something viewed as urgent given the rising hostility towards homosexuality evident in the early years of the HIV/AIDS epidemic in the 1980s.

Despite the evident reservations that many parliamentarians harboured regarding the forms of sex education being provided by some LEAs, official sex education guidance to schools issued in 1986 presented a relatively moderate view on the teaching of homosexuality.[18] The guidance acknowledged that, although there was greater 'openness' about homosexuality in society, 'many individuals and groups within society hold sincerely to the view that [homosexuality] is morally objectionable' and that this creates 'difficult territory for teachers to traverse'.[19] Whilst the 1986 guidance noted that these difficulties may be particularly acute in schools where 'to accept that homosexuality may be a normal feature of relationships would be a breach of the religious faith upon which they are founded', it called for homosexuality to be dealt with 'objectively and seriously'.[20]

The tone of the 1986 guidance offers a sharp contrast to the rhetoric that would characterise debate later that year over a Private Members' Bill introduced in the Lords by the Earl of Halsbury.[21] The Bill sought to prohibit local authorities in England, Wales and Scotland 'from giving financial or other assistance to any person for the purpose of publishing or promoting homosexuality as an acceptable family relationship or for the purpose of teaching such acceptability in any maintained school'.[22] Although this Bill – popularly known as the 'Halsbury amendment' – is often noted as a precursor of Section 28, the extent to which debates over the Bill were characterised by religious discourse is rarely explicated. More than half of speakers at the Bill's Second Reading in the Lords invoked religion in some form, and almost all speakers expressed support for the intent of the Bill, if not its specific wording (only two Labour Peers expressed cautious reservations).[23] For example, the Earl of Longford stressed that he supported the

---

17   A. Blair, 'Negotiating conflicting values: the role of law in educating for values in England and Wales', *Education and the Law* 14, 2013, 39–56; M. Durham, *Sex and Politics: The Family and Morality in the Thatcher Years*, Basingstoke: Macmillan, 1991.
18   Department of Education and Science, 'Health education from 5 to 16', HMI Series: Curriculum Matters No.6, 1986.
19   Ibid., p.20.
20   Ibid.
21   Local Government Act 1986 (Amendment) Bill 1986–1987.
22   HL Debate, 18 December 1986, c.311.
23   Although he did not participate in this specific debate, one of the few identified opponents of the Bill was the Archbishop of York, John Habgood, who was cited multiple times to argue that the Bill encouraged undesirable centralisation of educational control (for example: Earl of Halsbury, HL Debate, 18 December 1986, c.311).

Bill from a 'conventional Christian point of view',[24] Baroness Cox emphasised that it provided necessary protections for Christian and Muslim parents who were subject to 'brutal intimidation' by left-wing LEAs,[25] and Baroness David worried that 'for some schools to accept [. . .] homosexuality [. . .] would be a breach of [their] religious faith'.[26] Perhaps most strikingly, Lord Denning invoked the Bible to convey his hope that the Lords would 'destroy' those 'gay' local councils that were promoting homosexuality:

> I wish to make a few remarks [. . .] on religion. I looked up the Book of Genesis again. 'But the men of Sodom were wicked and sinners before the Lord exceedingly. And the Lord destroyed Sodom and Gomorrah.' When I read the article in The Times this morning, I thought of altering those words and saying: 'But the councillors of the Borough of Haringey were gay, and corrupted the children of the borough exceedingly'. And, I should like to add, after this Bill, 'The Lords destroyed those councillors'. That is the religious aspect.[27]

Subsequent debates produced often exaggerated litanies of the range of pro-gay materials allegedly being promoted by some LEAs.[28] While the Halsbury amendment ultimately was unsuccessful,[29] then Prime Minister Margaret Thatcher expressed her hope that similar legislation would be introduced in the next Parliament.[30] When new sex education guidance was issued subsequently in 1987, it displayed a hostility to homosexuality similar to the Halsbury amendment by stating that 'there is no place in any school in any circumstances for teaching which advocates homosexual behaviour or presents it as the norm'.[31]

In the next parliamentary session, David Wilshire MP tabled an amendment to the Local Government Bill 1987–1988 to prohibit local authorities from

---

24 HL Debate, 18 December 1986, c.314.
25 Ibid., c.322.
26 Ibid., c.331.
27 Ibid., c.325.
28 For example, there was detailed discussion of sex education resources and stories for children and young people, most prominently the Danish children's book *Jenny Lives with Eric and Martin* (S. Bösche, London: Gay Men's Press, 1983) which assumed a kind of totemic status in the debates. See: J. Moran, op. cit.
29 The Bill passed through the Lords without any division. After a short Commons debate, the House divided 20-0 in favour but, with fewer than the 40 members required to proceed, the question was declared as not decided. HC Debate, 8 May 1987, Division No.159. For a detailed discussion of Parliamentary debate of the Bill, see: M. McManus, op. cit.
30 See: M. McManus, op. cit.
31 Department of Education and Science, 'Circular 11/87: Sex education in schools', 1987.

promoting homosexuality. Although the language of the clause was modified over the course of its passage through Parliament,[32] and several attempts were made to supplement it,[33] it was accepted and became Section 28 of the Local Government Act 1988. Although less pronounced than during the debates over the Halsbury amendment, religion remained an important axis of contention in the Section 28 debates. In addition to familiar, rhetorically self-sufficient claims about the need to protect children and young people from the risks of homosexuality (see Chapter 2),[34] Section 28 was represented by some proponents as a straightforward reflection of the 'Judaic-Christian principles which underlie our society'.[35] However, opponents questioned the interpretation of Christianity deployed by some parliamentarians and asked them to 'not seek by law to impose any religious or theological morality on anyone else'.[36] Lord Soper, for example, warned of the 'smell of fascism' that surrounded attempts to 'isolate problems like homosexuality as if they belonged to the category of evil just as heterosexuality may be regarded as the category of good'.[37] Those who claimed religious support for Section 28, however, did not receive unambiguous backing from the Bishops' Bench. Indeed, the Archbishop of York, John Habgood, spoke against Section 28, arguing that while he supported the goal of protecting children from actions by some LEAs that were 'excessive and stupid', the legislation represented 'a dangerous precedent in the control of ideas by central government'.[38] Nevertheless, although opposing Section 28, Habgood also referred to homosexuals as 'a group of people who we all recognise can behave and have in the past behaved

32 For a detailed history of the various amendments to the language of the clause, see: A. Thorp and G. Allen, 'The *Local Government Bill* [HL]: the "Section 28" debate', House of Commons Research Paper 00/47, House of Commons Library, 6 April 2000.
33 The key Commons vote took place on an amendment moved by Simon Hughes MP, who supported a ban on the promotion of homosexuality but sought to ensure that schools could teach about diverse sexual orientations in sex education. Hughes' amendment specified that a local authority 'may undertake Sex Education in the course of which an awareness of different sexual orientations may be taught' (HC Debate, 15 December 1987, c.987). This was defeated along party lines 309-205 (HC Debate, 15 December 1987, Division No.116). A further Commons vote occurred when an amendment was moved unsuccessfully by Jack Cunningham MP to weaken Clause 28 by exempting 'action undertaken for the purpose of discouraging discrimination against or protecting the civil rights of any person' (HC Debate, 9 March 1988, c.370). The amendment was defeated 201-254 (HC Debate, 9 March 1988, Division No.207). Amendments were also debated in the Lords that sought to protect artistic expression; for a detailed account, see: M. McManus, op. cit.
34 For example: J. Knight, HC Debate, 9 March 1988, c.386.
35 N. Bennett, HC Debate, 9 March 1988, c.393.
36 S. Hughes, HC Debate, 9 March 1988, c.390.
37 HL Debate, 1 February 1988, cc.876–877.
38 HL Committee, 2 February 1988, c.998. The Bishops' Bench ultimately divided 4-2 against the inclusion of Clause 28 in the Bill. Overall, the Lords divided 202-122 in favour of the inclusion of Clause 28. HL Committee, 2 February 1988, Division No.1.

with quite extraordinary foolishness'.³⁹ Reminiscent of Church of England discourse in debates over decriminalisation (see Chapter 1), Habgood's opposition to Section 28 did not constitute a rejection of homophobia but relied upon stigmatising rhetoric about homosexuality.

Debates over Section 28 also demonstrated an emerging tendency for parliamentarians to relativise 'religion' and 'sexual orientation' as competing categories of difference in need of equal recognition and protection (a rhetorical strategy which at this stage was uncommon but which would become increasingly prominent in debates at the start of the twenty-first century, as illustrated in previous chapters). Peter Pike MP, for example, contrasted guidance about the teaching of homosexuality with guidance on religious education:

> The hon. Member for Birmingham, Edgbaston (Dame J. Knight) referred to instructions to teachers about teaching homosexuality in a positive way. She objected to that [. . .] The hon. Lady really should examine the education guidelines in other fields such as religious education, which state that teachers should give a positive image of religions other than Christianity – such as the Hindu and Moslem religions. I am sure that those guidelines are not arguing that children should convert to those religions. It is right that they should be taught in a positive way about those religions so that they can understand them, just as we believe it is right that they should recognise that homosexuality exists, that people do not make a choice and that homosexuality should be recognised and fully understood.⁴⁰

Proponents of Section 28 similarly invoked a perceived conflict between religion and sexual orientation, in which the actions of local authorities were represented as privileging the rights of homosexuals over those of religious parents:

> By aggressive anti-heterosexist policies and by expenditure of large sums of public money on the active promotion of so-called positive images of homosexuality, [LEAs] have caused grave offence to many parents and have thus violated the trust invested in them to provide schools which should be serving their children in loco parentis. When some of these parents have tried to remonstrate with their local authorities, they have been intimated (sic) and harassed and have even been told that they have no rights over their children. When some of them, going to remonstrate at one local authority, said that this violated their fundamental religious beliefs, they were told by one councillor that people had been known to die for their religious faith and that perhaps they should be prepared to die too.⁴¹

---

39 HL Committee, 2 February 1988, c.999.
40 HC Debate, 9 March 1988, c.415.
41 Baroness Cox, HL Debate, 11 January 1988, c.1012.

Although it was recognised at the time that the direct influence of Section 28 was limited – given that school governors rather than LEAs had been given control of sex education by the Education (No.2) Act 1986 – its impact would nevertheless prove significant. Whilst no LEA was ever taken to court successfully for violating Section 28,[42] and guidance to schools further stressed that Section 28 had no direct bearing on them,[43] the legislation was perceived to have a substantial 'chilling effect' on the discussion of homosexuality within many schools. Research with teachers suggested that many were confused about the nature of their responsibilities under Section 28 and were therefore hesitant to raise or address issues concerning homosexuality in the classroom.[44] A number of commentators also argued forcefully that the stigmatising language of Section 28 contributed to already rampant homophobic bullying – something which many teachers reported feeling inhibited about challenging.[45] Despite being perceived as largely redundant in terms of its direct legal effects, opponents attributed Section 28 with major symbolic significance in the struggle for lesbian and gay equality, and campaigners worked vigorously for its repeal. While discourses of religious morality featured prominently in the passage of Section 28, its repeal would involve significant negotiations with religious organisations within and outside Parliament, with lasting implications for the legal framework governing sex education, as we discuss in the next section.

Religion, sex education and the repeal of Section 28

The Labour Party pledged to repeal Section 28 in its 1992 general election manifesto,[46] although this commitment was not directly repeated in its 1997 manifesto,[47] which contained weaker language about the need to promote change while maintaining 'social stability'.[48] However, the Labour Government subsequently attempted to repeal Section 28 in the Local Government Bill 1999–2000.[49] This move provoked well-funded campaigns of opposition in

---

42 The Christian Institute unsuccessfully attempted to take Glasgow City Council to court in relation to its support of an AIDS charity that allegedly promoted homosexuality.
43 A. Thorp and G. Allen, op. cit.
44 Ibid. Evidence of teacher confusion was often cited in parliamentary debates about repeal. For example: Lord Whitty, HL Debate, 7 February 2000, c.479.
45 D. Epstein, op. cit. In contrast, Chris Woodhead, the Chief Inspector of Schools, argued in 2000 that no evidence existed that teachers were impaired by Section 28 in dealing with bullying.
46 *It's Time to Get Britain Working Again*, London: Labour Party, 1992.
47 *New Labour Because Britain Deserves Better*, London: Labour Party, 1997. However, the Liberal Democrats' 1997 manifesto did pledge repeal. See: *Make the Difference*, London: Liberal Democrats, 1997.
48 A. Thorp and G. Allen, op. cit., p.19.
49 Clause 68 Local Government Bill 1999–2000.

which Christian, Muslim, Hindu and other religious leaders played prominent roles, although opinion polls suggested that a majority of the public also favoured the retention of Section 28.[50] The Muslim Council, for example, released a statement condemning the Government's plans:

> Any teaching in schools which presents homosexual practice as equivalent to marriage or in a morally neutral way is deeply offensive to Muslims [. . .] We believe that the repeal of Section 28 profoundly undermines the institution of the family and will damage the fabric of our society.[51]

Similarly, in Scotland the repeal efforts of the recently devolved Government were met with a concerted 'Keep the Clause' campaign funded by Brian Souter, a self-identified evangelical Christian. Resistance in Scotland proved far stronger than had been anticipated, as Scottish Government officials would acknowledge retrospectively.[52] The 'Keep the Clause' campaign received support from key religious leaders including Cardinal Thomas Winning (then President of the Catholic Bishops' Conference of Scotland) who called for the 'silent majority' to prevent repeal of Section 28.[53] Although repeal in Scotland (in contrast to England and Wales) succeeded in June 2000 by a strong majority, the Scottish Government, which had previously been resistant to a national framework for sex education, agreed as a concession to issue statutory guidance to schools in which marriage would play a prominent role.[54]

In England and Wales, the Government negotiated with the Church of England, the Catholic Education Service and other religious groups over the legal framework for sex education that would be put in place following the repeal of Section 28. Anticipating resistance to the repeal of Section 28 in the Lords, Government ministers sought to offer reassurances in the form of statutory guidance to schools on the nature of sex education which would emphasise the importance of 'marriage and traditional family life'.[55] Draft guidance was prepared

---

50 An Ipsos MORI poll in February 2000 found 54 per cent of British adults in favour of maintaining Section 28. Available online at www.ipsos-mori.com/researchpublications/researcharchive/poll.aspx?oItemId=1576 (accessed on 5 December 2013).
51 Muslim Council of Britain, as quoted by Lord Moran, HL Debate, 7 February 2000, c.412.
52 K. Scott, 'Scotland throws out Section 28', *Guardian*, 22 June 2000.
53 *BBC News Online*, 'Cardinal fires Section 28 broadside', 18 January 2000. Available online at http://news.bbc.co.uk/1/hi/scotland/607046.stm (accessed on 5 December 2013).
54 S.34 Ethical Standards in Public Life etc. (Scotland) Act 2000 repealed S.2A Local Government Act 1986. Education authorities are required to have regard to guidance on sex education issued by Scottish Ministers under S.56 Standards in Scotland's Schools etc. Act 2000. This guidance was issued in 2001: 'Scottish Executive, Standards in Scotland's Schools etc. Act 2000: Conduct of Sex Education in Scottish Schools', Circular 2/2001, Edinburgh: Scottish Executive, 2001.

in close consultation with the Church of England, with one church source noting publicly that 'the deal that is being done [...] is that we won't go to the wire over Section 28, in exchange for greater clarity over the guidelines'.[56]

As a result of these negotiations, the Bishop of Blackburn, Alan Chesters, then chair of the Church of England's Board of Education, introduced an amendment to the Local Government Bill 1999–2000 that sought to replace Section 28 with new provisions related to sex education (rather than simply repealing Section 28, as proposed by the original draft of the Bill). Chesters' amendment specified that local authorities must take steps to ensure that when pupils received sex education in maintained schools:

> (a) that marriage should be promoted as the fundamental building block of society and of family life and as the proper context for the nurture of children, and
> (b) that pupils are entitled to develop without being subjected to –
>   (i) any physical or verbal abuse about sexual orientation, or
>   (ii) the encouragement of sexual activity.[57]

Opposition to the amendment was led by Baroness Young (former Conservative leader of the House of Lords and patron of the Christian Institute) who argued that Chesters' proposed measures – while rightly seeking to make marriage the statutory core of sex education – were an inadequate substitute for Section 28 which, she and others insisted, placed a crucial check on local authorities even if it had limited direct applicability to schools. Opponents of repeal frequently cited the strength of religious objections across Britain in defence of their position:

> I am sure that the Government must have been surprised by the strength of public reaction to their proposal, first in Scotland and now in England and Wales, and in the stand taken by so many religious leaders. It must be a powerful cause that persuades the Chief Rabbi and the Muslim Council of Britain to take the same line.[58]

In contrast, supporters of repeal insisted that parliamentarians should 'not pretend that all the world's religions are on one side in this argument, and

---

55 R. Reeves, 'The gay law furore that ignited Middle England', *Guardian*, 30 January 2000. The nature of Government consultation with the Church of England and other faith groups over the nature of sex education guidance was referenced repeatedly during the course of debates, and was officially acknowledged via a written answer (HL Written Answer, 27 July 2000, c.76).
56 R. Reeves, op. cit.
57 HL Committee, 7 February 2000, c.396.
58 Lord Moran, HL Committee, 7 February 2000, c.412.

not only religious leaders deal with moral issues'.[59] However, the level of opposition to Chesters' proposed amendment was such that he withdrew it without a division.[60]

The Government's response was to attempt to placate opponents of repeal with measures concerning sex education contained in the Learning and Skills Bill 1999–2000. After much negotiation, the Government adopted an approach that would require the Secretary of State to issue guidance to schools.[61] Opponents of repeal argued that the language of the guidance was too mild and wanted any guidance issued to be made subject to parliamentary approval. Baroness Young unsuccessfully attempted to make provision that pupils must be 'taught that marriage provides a strong foundation for stable relationships and the most reliable framework for raising children'[62] (echoing a previous failed amendment from the Commons, moved by Gerald Howarth MP in explicitly Christian terms[63]). Her efforts failed by a narrow margin, with the opposition of nine bishops in this case decisive.[64] However, the Lords then supported without division an amendment by Chesters[65] which added language to the Government's proposal[66] requiring that guidance be issued to ensure that pupils 'learn the nature of marriage and its importance for family life and the bringing up of children'.[67] Chesters stressed

---

59 Lord Whitty, HL Committee, 7 February 2000, c.482.
60 It is interesting to note that, in the same debate, supporters of Section 28 – again led by Baroness Young – felt it necessary to counter charges that they showed insensitivity to the problem of homophobic bullying in schools. While not accepting that Section 28 had any culpability for encouraging bullying or obstructing efforts to ameliorate it, Young moved an amendment to specify that nothing in Section 28 should be taken to 'prevent the headteacher or governing body of a maintained school, or a teacher employed by a maintained school, from taking steps to prevent any form of bullying'. This amendment passed despite Government opposition to adding further provisions to a law they were attempting to repeal. Young's amendment was agreed 210-165 (HL Debate, 7 February 2000, Division No.1) with the Bishops' Bench dividing 3-1. However, the new language was removed at Committee stage in the Commons, and an attempt to reinstate it was defeated 133-305. HC Debate, 5 July 2000, Division No.253.
61 Such guidance to schools was in fact issued in July 2000, while debates over the Learning and Skills Bill 1999–2000 were ongoing. Department for Education and Employment, *Sex and Relationship Education Guidance*, July 2000.
62 Amendment 180E by Baroness Young and Lady Saltoun of Abernethy, Learning and Skills Bill [HL] – Amendments to be debated in the House of Lords, 18 July 2000.
63 HC Debate, 27 June 2000, cc.788–806. Howarth objected to language in the draft sex education guidance taking a neutral position on the 'promotion' of sexual orientation rather than giving 'proper, unambiguous, Christian, moral guidance to our young people to enable them to live more fulfilled lives' (ibid., c.799).
64 Young's efforts failed by a margin of 14 votes (220-234) with opposition from nine bishops. HL Debate, 18 July 2000, Division No.2. For a discussion of aspects of parliamentary manoeuvering in the debates over sex education guidance, see: M. McManus, op. cit.
65 HL Debate, 18 July 2000, c.876.
66 Ibid. cc.875–876.

that his amendment had been constructed in consultation with the Church of England Board of Education, the Catholic Education Service, and at an exceptional meeting of the Lords Spiritual.[68] He did so, arguably, because of an awareness of accusations from critics within the Church of England that, in the words of one member of General Synod, he was 'in the pocket of government'.[69]

While the Learning and Skills Act 2000 significantly altered the framework for sex education, the attempted repeal of Section 28 by the Local Government Bill 1999–2000 failed in that parliamentary session. In leading the defeat of the repeal, Baroness Young claimed 'support [...] from representatives of all the great religions: Christians, Jews, Muslims, Hindus and Sikhs',[70] although the Bishops' Bench divided 4-4.[71] The repeal of Section 28 in England and Wales was not achieved until the Local Government Act 2003.[72] Although there was again concerted opposition in both Houses, the final attempt to block repeal in the Lords – led by Baroness Blatch, a self-identified evangelical Christian and long-time ally of Baroness Young, by then deceased – failed following a debate that contained few direct references to religion and little participation from the Lords Spiritual (in many ways similar to debates over the Sexual Offences Act 2003 that we described in Chapter 1, where the use of religious rhetoric vanished after having featured prominently in previous debates).[73]

Although now defunct for more than a decade, the legacy of Section 28 persists in the form of the framework for sex education negotiated by the Labour Government with religious leaders in an attempt to assuage opponents of its repeal. While the repeal of Section 28 was seen by many to lift a powerful disincentive to schools regarding the discussion of homosexual relationships, there remains ongoing debate about how and when issues concerning homosexuality should be included in the curriculum. Writing against Section 28 in 2000, Sue Wise characterised opposition to repeal as part of 'the "last ditch" attempts of organised religions to have a say in the secular world of politics'.[74] In retrospect, however, this assessment significantly underestimated the extent to which religious interests would continue to influence the legal frameworks that govern the circulation of information about homosexuality in schools. In the sections

---

67 S.403(1A) Education Act 1996, as amended by S.148(4) Learning and Skills Act 2000.
68 HL Debate, 18 July 2000, c.857.
69 S. Bates, 'Church split over Section 28 repeal', the *Guardian*, 29 February 2000.
70 HL Debate, 24 July 2000, c.101.
71 The House divided 270-228, HL Debate, 24 July 2000, Division No.2.
72 S.122 Local Government Act 2003 repealed S.2A Local Government Act 1986.
73 Baroness Blatch proposed amendments (characterised by opponents as wrecking amendments) that would have required local authorities to organise parental ballots on the sex education policies of schools. Blatch's amendment was defeated 180-130, with the bishops dividing 1-1. HL Debate, 10 July 2003, Division No.3.
74 S. Wise, '"New right" or "backlash"? Section 28, moral panic and "promoting homosexuality"', *Sociological Research Online* 5, 2000, § 3.11.

that follow, we explore the status of teaching about homosexual relationships in English schools, including recent debates over how and to what extent schools with a religious character are obliged to offer information about same-sex relationships as part of their curricula.

Homosexuality and faith in the English school system

To place our analysis of the relationship between religion, education and homosexuality in context, it is necessary to explicate the distinctive ways in which religion is embedded in England's complex system of state-funded schools. Within the English school system there is no straightforward distinction between 'state schools' and 'faith schools' given that many faith schools are funded by the state. Rather, the key distinctions between types of school relate to their degree of independence from local authority control and whether they are required to follow the National Curriculum. Below, we briefly outline the nature of these distinctions as they relate to the main categories of state-funded schools in England.

Maintained schools

Maintained schools in England are funded by central government via their local authorities. The School Standards and Framework Act 1998 divides maintained schools into five categories:[75]

   a. community schools;
   b. foundation schools;
   c. voluntary schools, comprising –
       i. voluntary aided schools, and
       ii. voluntary controlled schools[76]
   d. community special schools; and
   e. foundation special schools.[77]

---

75 S.20(1) School Standards and Framework Act 1998.
76 Voluntary controlled schools have all of their capital costs met by the local authority; voluntary aided schools make a contribution to capital costs (this was originally 50 per cent, but is currently only 10 per cent – reduced from 15 per cent by the Labour Government – and this can be waived by the local authority) and the religious group or foundation of the school has a greater degree of autonomy from the local authority. For a discussion of these differences, see: Department for Education, 'Voluntary and faith schools', 19 June 2012. Available online at www.education.gov.uk/schools/leadership/typesofschools/maintained/b00198369/voluntary-and-faith-schools (accessed on 5 December 2013).
77 Community special schools and foundation special schools are specifically for students with special educational needs.

While community schools are not permitted to have a religious designation, foundation and voluntary schools can be designated by the Secretary of State as having a specific religious character.[78] While relatively few foundation schools have a designated religious character,[79] nearly all voluntary schools have such a designation. The overwhelming majority of voluntary schools with a religious designation are Church of England (71 per cent at primary level, 26 per cent at secondary level) or Roman Catholic (27 per cent at primary level, 68 per cent at secondary level) schools, while very small numbers are designated as Methodist, Jewish, Muslim, Hindu, Sikh, or 'other Christian faith'.[80] Schools with a religious character can lawfully discriminate on grounds of religion or belief in aspects of their admission of pupils, hiring of staff and appointment of governors, allowing them to favour those who belong to the designated faith of the school.[81] Of all state-funded (maintained or otherwise) schools in England, 35 per cent at primary level and 11 per cent at secondary level are voluntary schools with a religious character. All community, foundation and voluntary schools, regardless of religious designation, are required to teach the so-called statutory 'basic' curriculum which encompasses the National Curriculum,[82] religious education, and – for pupils of secondary age – sex education.[83] However, given its location outside the National Curriculum, no national programme of study exists for sex education.

Academies and free schools

In contrast to the maintained sector, academies and free schools are not required to follow the National Curriculum and have significantly greater overall curricular flexibility. The growth of academies and free schools has been one of the most significant recent transformations in the English education system. Academies and free schools function largely as independent (private) schools – although they are funded directly by government – with a much greater degree of autonomy in their

---

78 S.69(3)–(5) School Standards and Framework Act 1998, under which the Religious Character of Schools (Designation Procedure) Regulations that govern the process of designation are issued.
79 The figures are 6 per cent at primary level and 2 per cent at secondary level, all Church of England. Derived from: Department for Education, 'Schools, pupils and their characteristics: January 2013', op. cit.
80 Ibid.
81 On the law governing the different ways in which voluntary aided, voluntary controlled, and foundation schools with a religious designation can discriminate in pupil admissions and hiring based on religion or belief, see: R. Sandberg, *Law and Religion*, Cambridge: Cambridge University Press, 2011, pp.161–165.
82 Introduced by the Education Reform Act 1988.
83 S.80(1) Education Act 2002. Students with special educational needs, such as those in special schools, do not necessarily have to be taught the National Curriculum (S.92 Education Act 2002).

affairs than maintained schools. Academies were first introduced under a previous Labour Government[84] as a means of transforming underperforming schools, and the programme has been substantially and enthusiastically extended under the subsequent Conservative–Liberal Democrat coalition Government both to allow maintained schools to apply to become academies and to permit the creation of new academies referred to as free schools.[85] According to the Department for Education, free schools are set up by groups of parents, teachers, charities, religious groups and others 'in response to what local people say they want and need in order to improve education for children in their community'.[86] Independent schools can also apply to enter the state-funded sector as free schools. The scale of transformation in secondary education in England as a result of the academies programme has been dramatic: whereas in January 2011 these schools constituted only 11 per cent of state-funded secondary schools, the figure had risen to 50 per cent by January 2013.[87]

Some academies and free schools are associated with a sponsor (for example, a business, charity, university) and some of these sponsors are faith groups. Currently available data on academies suggest that a somewhat smaller proportion of academies/free schools have a religious character compared with the maintained sector (25 per cent versus 38 per cent at primary level, 16 per cent versus 23 per cent at secondary level). Confusingly, however, in addition to those academies and free schools with a formal religious designation, schools can also be registered as having a 'faith ethos', potentially allowing a faith group to influence admissions policy and the governance of the school.[88] Secularist organisations have raised a number of concerns about the growth of 'faith academies'.[89] There is a fear (dismissed by the Government[90]) amongst these groups that the free schools programmes will ultimately increase the influence of religion on state education.

---

84 Learning and Skills Act 2000. The schools were originally referred to as 'city academies' but this was changed simply to 'academies' by the Education Act 2002.
85 Academies Act 2010.
86 Department for Education, 'Free schools', 2013. Available online at www.education.gov.uk/schools/leadership/typesofschools/freeschools (accessed on 5 December 2013).
87 Derived from: Department for Education, 'Schools, pupils and their characteristics: January 2011', op. cit.; Department for Education, 'Schools, pupils and their characteristics: January 2013', op. cit.
88 Unfortunately, official data provided by the Department for Education do not currently allow one to disaggregate data for academies with a faith ethos, so data on the proportion of academies with a religious character likely underestimates the total that have some form of direct involvement of faith groups.
89 See, for example: British Humanist Association, '"Faith" Schools'. Available online at https://humanism.org.uk/campaigns/schools-and-education/faith-schools (accessed on 5 December 2013).
90 R. Butt, 'Gove defends faith schools', *Guardian*, 17 February 2011. Available online at www.theguardian.com/education/2011/feb/17/gove-faith-schools (accessed on 5 December 2013).

An analysis of Department for Education (DfE) data (released only after a freedom of information tribunal[91]) by the British Humanist Association suggests that at least 36 per cent of the successful free school applications approved by the DfE in the first three waves (2011–2013) of the programme either had a designated religious character or faith ethos (an estimated 46 per cent of total applications were for such schools).[92] Furthermore, a number of campaigners have expressed concerns about the Church of England's significant expansion plans via so called multi-academy trusts,[93] through which non-faith schools become affiliated with a single trust led by the Church. The academies programme, as described by then Archbishop of Canterbury, Rowan Williams, presents an opportunity in the 'middle-term future' for the Church of England to become 'quite conceivably the largest sponsor and provider of secondary education in this country'.[94]

Sexual orientation discrimination, victimisation and harassment in schools

Regardless of religious designation or faith ethos, all schools are now bound by aspects of equalities legislation that offer protections to pupils and prospective pupils from forms of sexual orientation discrimination. The Equality Act (Sexual Orientation) Regulations (EASOR) 2007 provided pupils with protection against discrimination based on sexual orientation by schools and educational establishments. These protections were extended by the Equality Act (EA) 2010 which – while providing certain exceptions that allow faith schools to discriminate in pupil admissions and staff hiring based on religion or belief – prohibits the responsible

---

91 British Humanist Association, 'Government releases list of proposed free schools to BHA', 19 February 2013. Available online at http://humanism.org.uk/2013/02/19/government-releases-list-of-proposed-free-schools-to-bha (accessed on 5 December 2013). A freedom of information request was initially rejected by the Department for Education, but the British Humanist Association won their request on appeal to the Information Tribunal.
92 British Humanist Association, 'Number of religious Free School proposals from 2011–13', 2013. Available online at http://humanism.org.uk/wp-content/uploads/Number-of-religious-Free-School-proposals-from-2011-13.pdf (accessed on 5 December 2013).
93 On arrangements for multi-academy trusts, see: Department for Education, 'Multi-academy trusts', 30 April 2012. Available online at www.education.gov.uk/schools/leadership/typesofschools/academies/primary/steps/b00205443/primarymodels/multi-academy-trusts (accessed on 5 December 2013).
94 D. Marley, 'C of E vows to be the biggest and the best', *TES Magazine*, 3 October 2011. Available online at www.tes.co.uk/article.aspx?storycode=6114406 (accessed on 5 December 2013). The Church of England's goal of extending its influence in education is discussed in its recent report: Church School of the Future Review Group, *The Church School of the Future Review*, London: Archbishops' Council Education Division, 2012.

bodies of schools from discriminating on the grounds of sexual orientation in relation to the admission and treatment of pupils.[95] The responsible bodies of schools are also prohibited from engaging in the victimisation of pupils or prospective pupils based on sexual orientation. Additionally, the governing bodies of both maintained schools and academies are subject to the public sector equality duty,[96] which requires that they have due regard to the need to 'eliminate discrimination, harassment, victimisation and any other conduct that is prohibited' by the EA 2010, 'advance equality of opportunity' and 'foster good relations'.[97] However, consistent with other provisions within the EA 2010, pupils or prospective pupils are not protected from harassment based on sexual orientation (see Chapter 3 for a discussion of harassment provisions relating to sexual orientation).[98]

Homosexuality as non-statutory knowledge

In the previous section we outlined the relationship between religion, schooling and equality legislation in respect of sexual orientation. In this section we explore the relationship between religion, homosexuality and the contemporary legal framework governing the provision of sex education in English schools. Specifically, we are concerned with how key aspects of sex education (and information about homosexuality in particular) have remained segregated from the National Curriculum – which is compulsory for maintained schools – and how this segregation has been sustained in part through appeals to the need to respect the 'ethos' (either explicitly or implicitly understood to mean the 'religious ethos') of schools and the necessity for 'flexibility' in relation to the religious and cultural backgrounds of particular groups of parents and pupils.

---

95 S.85(1)–(2) Equality Act 2010.
96 S.149 and Sch.19 Equality Act 2010. Academies were added by amendment to the list of 'public authorities' by the Equality Act 2010 (Public Authorities and Consequential and Supplementary Amendments) Order 2011.
97 S.149(1)(a)–(c) Equality Act 2010.
98 S.85(10) Equality Act 2010. In defending the harassment exception, the Government made two primary arguments: (1) that there was almost no evidence for sexual orientation harassment in schools and (2) that the exception was unimportant because victims could bring claims of direct discrimination if they experienced harassing behaviour. Indeed, an interpretation clause was added to make clear that the 'disapplication' of a prohibition on harassment did not prevent conduct from amounting to unlawful discrimination (S.212(5) Equality Act 2010). However, this logic was directly challenged by several parliamentarians (e.g. Lord Lester of Herne Hill, HL Debate, 13 January 2010, c.584) who considered that there could be cases of harassing behaviour not captured by discrimination provisions, and that the purpose of a harassment provision was to avoid the need for victims to establish a case of direct discrimination. See also R. Wintemute, 'Homophobia and United Kingdom law: only a few gaps left to close', in L. Trappolin, A. Gasparini, and R. Wintemute (eds), *Confronting Homophobia in Europe: Social and Legal Perspectives*, Oxford: Hart Publishing, 2012, pp.233–264.

As we noted above, the history of sex education in England is complex and multifaceted. As Meredith has argued, 'a large part of the theory and practice of school sex education [...] continues to hinge upon attitudes to homosexuality'.[99] Nothing in the National Curriculum in England currently requires that maintained schools provide any information about homosexuality and same-sex relationships. The National Curriculum programme of study for science includes aspects of human reproductive anatomy and physiology, and sexually transmitted infections (although explicit reference to teaching about 'sexual health' has been removed from the new science programme of study announced in September 2013).[100] Other aspects of sex education, while not part of the National Curriculum, are legally part of the 'basic curriculum' which is to be provided by all secondary maintained schools[101] (this is required to include information on HIV/AIDS[102]). Sex education is typically incorporated as part of a wider framework of so-called Personal, Social, Health and Economic education (PSHE). Parents have the legal right to withdraw children from those aspects of sex education that are not part of the statutory science curriculum.[103] However, an ongoing concern of children's rights advocates[104] is that there is no right for pupils to opt *into* sex education – even those of sufficient maturity to reject the values and/or religious beliefs of parents and who, according to the Fraser guidelines, would be considered eligible to be prescribed contraception.[105]

---

99 P. Meredith, *Sex Education: Political Issues in Britain and Europe*, London: Routledge, 1989, p.32.
100 Teaching about sexually transmitted infections is noted in: Qualifications and Curriculum Authority, *Science: Programme of Study for Key Stage 3 and Attainment Targets*, 2007, p.211. Prior to the announcement of the new National Curriculum in September 2013, schools were expected to provide opportunities at Key Stage 3 for students to 'consider how knowledge and understanding of science informs personal and collective decisions, including those on substance abuse and sexual health' (p.213). References to sexual health and sexually transmitted infections do not appear in the new science programme of study for Key Stage 3 released in 2013. Department for Education, *National Curriculum in England: Science Programmes of Study*, September 2013. At the time of writing, the programme for Key Stage 4 has not been released. On the first introduction of a requirement to study HIV/AIDS in National Curriculum science, and subsequent controversies, see: A. Blair and D. Monk, op. cit.
101 S.80(1)(c) Education Act 2002. A requirement for sex education was first legally introduced by S.241(1) Education Act 1993, and was later superseded by S.352(1)(c) Education Act 1996.
102 The requirement to teach about HIV/AIDS and other sexually transmitted infections as part of sex education is contained in S.579(1) Education Act 1996.
103 S.405 Education Act 1996.
104 For example: 'Memorandum Submitted by the British Humanist Association', House of Commons Public Bill Committee on the Children and Families Bill 2012–13, 6 March 2013, § 13.
105 The term 'Fraser guidelines' is used to refer to the guidelines set out by Lord Fraser in *Gillick v West Norfolk & Wisbech Area Health Authority* [1985] UKHL 7.

There is no set curriculum for sex education, now often referred to as sex and relationships education (SRE). Rather, as we discussed above in relation to the repeal of Section 28, the Secretary of State is legally required to issue guidance to schools on the provision of sex education for which schools must have regard.[106] Any guidance must be designed to ensure that when sex education is delivered to pupils:

a. they learn the nature of marriage and its importance for family life and the bringing up of children, and
b. they are protected from teaching and materials which are inappropriate having regard to the age and the religious and cultural background of the pupils concerned.[107]

Prior to the release of the new guidance in 2000,[108] the media reported fears, reinforced by comments to the press by some Department for Education and Employment sources, that it would 'be along the same lines' as Section 28.[109] However, rather than prohibiting the promotion of homosexuality, the guidance contains the more neutral statement that '[t]here should be no direct promotion of sexual orientation'.[110] While stressing the importance of marriage, the guidance indicates that the Government 'recognises that there are strong and mutually supportive relationships outside marriage' and, as such, 'children should learn the significance of marriage *and stable relationships* as key building blocks of community and society'.[111] Further, the guidance states that sex education must 'make sure that the needs of all pupils are met' and that 'teachers should be able to deal honestly and sensitively with sexual orientation, answer appropriate

---

106 The requirement for the Secretary of State to provide guidance is set out in the S.403(1A) Education Act 1996, as amended by S.148(4) Learning and Skills Act 2000. At the time of writing, the current guidance, which is more than 13 years old, is: Department for Education and Employment, *Sex and Relationship Education Guidance*, op. cit.
107 S.403(1A) Education Act 1996.
108 Department for Education and Employment, *Sex and Relationship Education Guidance*, op. cit.
109 L. Ward, 'Sex education plan "same as Section 28"', *Guardian*, 28 January 2000.
110 Department for Education and Employment, *Sex and Relationship Education Guidance*, op. cit., §1.30. Wintemute argues, however, that 'many people read "sexual orientation" as meaning same-sex sexual orientation, because they do not see heterosexual individuals as having a sexual orientation'. R. Wintemute, 'Homophobia and United Kingdom law: only a few gaps left to close', in L. Trappolin, A. Gasparini and R. Wintemute (eds), op. cit., p.242.
111 Department for Education and Employment, *Sex and Relationship Education Guidance*, op. cit., §1.21; our emphasis. The Government had proposed to include language in statute (rather than simply in guidance) concerning the importance of pupils learning about 'stable relationships' other than marriage, but this was unsuccessful. HL Debate, 23 March 2000, c.431.

questions and offer support'.¹¹² However, the guidance also makes clear that '[s]chools of a particular religious ethos may choose to reflect that in their sex and relationship education policy'.¹¹³ The Catholic Education Service, which provides guidance for voluntary aided Catholic schools, has interpreted this to mean that Catholic school governors 'must ensure that the sex education provided is in keeping with the teachings of the Church'.¹¹⁴

In recent years, evidence has accumulated that has raised concerns about the content and quality of sex education regarding same-sex relationships (as well as many other issues related to relationships and sexual health). It is well recognised that the non-statutory status of PSHE affects the priority that it is given in schools. Within the context of crowded timetables and exam pressures, schools often prioritise statutory subjects over non-statutory material that is not subject to the exams regime. A recent report by Ofsted on the quality of national PSHE provision found that SRE required improvement in nearly half of the 50 secondary schools inspected, and that homosexuality was classed as a 'controversial' issue that many teachers seemed to avoid, along with sexual abuse and pornography.¹¹⁵ This is reinforced by other research in which gay, lesbian and bisexual secondary pupils report that issues related to homosexuality are inadequately covered – if addressed at all – in PSHE and sex education.¹¹⁶ Homophobic bullying reportedly remains rife, and pupils surveyed by Ofsted have indicated that they are far more likely to have learned about racism or faith discrimination than homophobia.¹¹⁷ There is no systematic information about differences between maintained schools

112 Ibid., §1.30.
113 Ibid., §1.7.
114 *Catholic Voices*, 'New guidance on what constitutes a Catholic School's ethos', 12 October 2011. Available online at www.catholicvoices.org.uk/monitor-blog/2011/10/new-guidance-what-constitutes-schools-catholic-ethos (accessed on 5 December 2013).
115 Office for Standards in Education, Children's Services and Skills, *Not Yet Good Enough: Personal, Social, Health and Economic Education in Schools*, 2013, §12.
116 For example, research conducted by the University of Cambridge Centre for Family Research on behalf of Stonewall reports that only 33 per cent of gay young people discuss lesbian, gay and bisexual issues in PSHE education lessons, while only 22 per cent discuss gay people or their relationships during sex and relationship education. See: A. Guasp, *The School Report: The Experiences of Gay Young People in Britain's Schools in 2012*, Stonewall and Centre for Family Research, University of Cambridge, 2012.
117 Office for Standards in Education, Children's Services and Skills, op. cit., §39. In the northwest region, 88 per cent reported having been taught about racism but only 14 per cent about homophobia. Research by Stonewall with gay pupils suggests that students who attend faith schools report that these schools are less likely to make clear statements about the unacceptability of homophobic bullying, and that staff are less likely to intervene in bullying incidents. In July 2013, in the wake of substantial negative coverage of the Church of England's stance during debates over the Marriage (Same Sex Couples) Act 2013, Archbishop of Canterbury Justin Welby announced that although the Church would not change its teaching about marriage, it would launch a campaign against homophobic bullying in its schools. See: J. Bingham, 'Welby calls for Church to join the sexual "revolution"', *Daily Telegraph*, 5 July 2013.

with and without a religious character, nor is there a systematic body of evidence available regarding the practices of faith schools in relation to teaching about homosexuality. However, there is qualitative evidence that some faith schools still primarily teach about homosexuality as a form of sinful or immoral behaviour.[118] As many parliamentarians and others have noted, it is clear that PSHE, as a non-statutory subject, is often given a low priority compared with the teaching of subjects in the statutory National Curriculum. Furthermore, despite the official guidance of the Secretary of State, 'the needs of all pupils'[119] – including non-heterosexual ones – are not necessarily being met by sex education provision in many schools. This in turn has led many campaigning groups (including those also concerned with sexual health, sexual violence and consent, and other issues) to call for PSHE and SRE to be made part of the statutory National Curriculum, with a defined programme of study compulsory for all maintained schools regardless of religious designation.

Sequestering homosexuality from the National Curriculum

Plans were developed under the previous Labour Government to make PSHE part of the National Curriculum,[120] although, reportedly under pressure from Catholic groups, an amendment was introduced that would have allowed sex education to be taught 'in a way that reflects a school's religious character'.[121] However, as a result of Labour's 2010 electoral defeat, these plans were dropped. The subsequent coalition Government has stated that it will not make sex education part of the National Curriculum. Rather, the curriculum announced in 2013 specifies that SRE is part of the required general school curriculum for secondary schools but not the statutory National Curriculum.[122] This leaves the existing guidance, first issued in 2000, intact. However, the status of teaching on homosexuality was given direct consideration in the Government's Equality Impact Assessment[123] of its changes to the National Curriculum. Specifically, the

---

118 A. Guasp, op. cit. Qualitative evidence presented in this report from gay and lesbian young people suggests that many perceived discussions of homosexuality in faith schools to be stigmatising and moralistic.
119 Department for Education and Employment, *Sex and Relationship Education Guidance*, op. cit., §1.30.
120 A. Macdonald, *Independent Review of the Proposal to Make Personal, Social, Health and Economic (PSHE) Education Statutory*, Department for Children, Schools and Families, 2009.
121 HC Notices of Amendments Given on Wednesday, 10 February 2010: Amendment 70, Children, Schools, and Families Bill 2010. See also R. Williams, 'Bill "will allow schools to teach that homosexuality is wrong"', the *Guardian*, 18 February 2010.
122 Department for Education, *The National Curriculum in England: Framework for Key Stages 1 to 4*, §2.3.
123 Equality Impact Assessments are used to ensure that decisions made by public bodies meet their duties under the Equality Act 2010 (see Chapter 3 for a discussion of the Equality Act 2010).

Government's assessment considered and then rejected arguments made during consultations in favour of making some teaching about same-sex relationships part of the statutory National Curriculum. In rejecting these arguments, the Government asserted that homosexuality is best considered within the context of non-statutory PSHE (from which parents have the right to remove their children, unlike aspects of the National Curriculum).[124] For example, in relation to proposals to include discussion of diverse sexual identities and relationships within the context of statutory Citizenship Education, the Government stated that 'schools should continue to address different sexual identities and family structures as part of PSHE education, where it can more effectively be adapted to suit the needs of particular groups of pupils, rather than as part of the statutory citizenship curriculum'.[125]

Similarly, the idea that scientific education on reproduction could incorporate discussion of homosexuality was rejected:

> Representatives of some religious groups expressed concerns over aspects of the prescribed content which run counter to the core beliefs of their communities – chiefly the inclusion of evolution and sexual reproduction [. . .] It was argued that sex education should be included in PSHE only, to preserve the right of parents to withdraw their children from those lessons. Other stakeholders were critical of the focus on sexual activity being only on the context of reproduction (thereby excluding gay pupils) and was suggested that same-sex relationships should be specified as part of the theme of human reproduction in key stage 3 [. . .] On same-sex relationships, our view is that it is most appropriate for schools to cover this topic as part of PSHE education, where it can be adapted more effectively to suit the needs of particular groups of pupils.[126]

Although not explicitly designating pupils from conservative religious backgrounds as amongst those requiring adapted presentation of either scientific information about homosexuality or the diversity of identities/family forms, the language of 'particular groups of pupils' must be understood intertextually within the wider context of public and parliamentary debates about PSHE and sex education in schools. While objections to teaching about homosexuality are certainly not raised solely by religious parents, a coded language of 'particular groups', 'parental wishes' and the 'ethos' of schools continues to be used in Parliament to signify religious objections to homosexuality.[127]

---

124 Department for Education, *Reform of the National Curriculum in England: Equalities Impact Assessment*, 2013.
125 Ibid., pp.7–8.
126 Ibid., p.12.
127 For example: Bishop of Chester, HL Committee, 24 April 2013, c.415.

Sex education in academies and free schools

The situation of education relating to homosexuality is even less clear with regard to the rapidly growing number of academies and free schools with a religious designation or faith ethos, which are not obliged to follow the National Curriculum. While academies are required by their funding agreements to provide 'a broad and balanced' curriculum (in common with all schools), the requirements for the provisions of sex education are highly circumscribed. The Model Funding Agreements of free schools at the primary and secondary level state that academies:

> shall have regard to any guidance issued by the Secretary of State on sex and relationship education to ensure that children at the Academy are protected from inappropriate teaching materials and they learn the nature of marriage and its importance for family life and for bringing up children.[128]

Referred to by one parliamentarian as 'an incredibly partial interpretation of the importance of sex and relationship education',[129] the clause suggests that academies are obliged to have regard for the official guidance, but places no duty on academies to provide sex education as such. The specific terms of the funding agreement also make no direct mention of ensuring that pupils understand the importance of other forms of 'stable relationships' besides marriage.[130] No systematic evidence exists about how issues related to same-sex relationships are dealt with in academies with a religious designation or faith ethos, and proposals to make PSHE (including SRE) compulsory for academies have been rejected on several occasions by Parliament.[131]

Recent attempts by the Labour opposition to make PSHE a statutory subject in both maintained schools and academies have been defeated. Concurrent with debates about religious protections and exemptions within the Marriage (Same Sex Couples) Act 2013 (see Chapter 4), Labour MPs moved an amendment to

---

128 R. Long, 'Sex and relationship education in schools', House of Commons Library, 31 October 2011, p.6. Model funding agreements vary somewhat depending on the particular type of academy being created, but they contain the same language with regard to sex education. Funding agreements for academies were updated in July 2012 to harmonise them with those created in 2011 for free schools. Model funding agreements for academies and free schools also make them subject to S.405 Education Act 1996, regarding parents' right to have their children exempted from sex education.
129 Lord Knight, HL Debate, 7 July 2010, c.234.
130 This point has been raised in the popular press, where comparisons have been drawn between Model Funding Agreements and the provisions of Section 28. See, for example: J. Henry, 'Free schools and academies must promote marriage', *Daily Telegraph*, 3 December 2011.
131 Baroness Massey, for example, proposed an amendment to the Academies Bill 2010 which would have made PSHE a compulsory subject for academies, but this was opposed by the Government and defeated 156-245. HL Debate, 7 July 2010, Division No.1.

the Children and Families Bill 2012–13/2013–14 which proposed to add PSHE to the existing list of subjects in the statutory National Curriculum.[132] Additionally, the amendment sought to make SRE an explicit component of PSHE, and defined SRE to include 'information about same-sex relationships, sexual violence, domestic violence and sexual consent'. The amendment also sought to compel the Secretary of State to issue new guidance to develop a 'coherent approach' to SRE while also extending the requirement to teach a full programme of SRE not just to maintained schools but also to academies and free schools. Opposition to the ultimately unsuccessful amendment[133] emphasised the need to maintain 'flexibility' and to preserve the 'ethos' of particular schools. As Fiona Bruce MP argued:

> At present, all secondary schools must provide sex education by law,[134] and although there is no centrally determined curriculum, governors and teachers, in conversation and consultation with parents, should develop a curriculum on a school-by-school basis, according to the ethos of the school. When properly applied, that decentralised approach means that this sensitive subject can be framed in a manner that has regard for parental views and concerns. If the curriculum were set centrally, that could and probably would disappear.[135]

While efforts to incorporate information about homosexuality as part of the statutory National Curriculum have been blocked by the Government, the legalisation of same-sex marriage has triggered further debate and uncertainty about the place of homosexuality within the curriculum. We turn to these debates about faith schools, marriage and same-sex relationships below.

Religion and the teaching of same-sex marriage

Because children in English schools are required to 'learn the nature of marriage and its importance for family life and the bringing up of children',[136] the Marriage (Same Sex Couples) Act (MSSCA) 2013 has been interpreted by many to introduce a statutory requirement for schools to address same-sex relationships. Many religious groups opposed to same-sex marriage made the issue of schools and teachers prominent in their efforts to defeat or alter the MSSCA 2013. For example, Muslims Defending Marriage – a campaign organised by the Muslim

---

132 HC Debate, 11 June 2013, cc.272–273.
133 The proposed amendment was defeated 219-303. HC Debate, 11 June 2013, Division No.25.
134 This assertion is misleading given the status of academies and free schools, as we discussed above.
135 HC Debate, 11 June 2013, c.260.
136 S.403(1A)(a) Education Act 1996.

Council of Britain – expressed their fear that the MSSCA 2013 would 'force teachers to teach that same sex marriage is equivalent to a genuine marriage'.[137] The Coalition for Marriage (an umbrella group of individuals and organisations opposing same-sex marriage) asserted that, according to a ComRes opinion poll, more than 40,000 teachers (approximately 10 per cent of the total in England) 'face being disciplined or sacked' because they plan to refuse to teach the importance of same-sex marriage.[138] This figure was disseminated widely in the media and was quoted frequently in parliamentary debate by many opponents of the MSSCA 2013.[139] Similarly widely referenced was an open letter to the *Daily Telegraph* signed by 53 self-described 'leaders of Britain's major faiths' who claimed that the Bill provided inadequate legal safeguards to 'protect the teacher or the parent who, for religious, or philosophical reasons, supports the current definition of marriage'.[140]

The issue of schools and teachers featured prominently at Committee stage of the MSSCA 2013 when Secretary of State for Education Michael Gove MP sought to provide reassurance that, although teachers will have to teach the legal reality of same-sex marriage, nevertheless 'it is perfectly clear that there will be no requirement on any teacher to promote a view or doctrine with which they feel any discomfort'.[141] Gove stated:

> We would not expect teachers in any area to express strong or polemical opinions. In fact, there is legislation to ensure that overall when teachers are presenting anything that is political, they must ensure that children have access to a balanced view on the matter.[142] But any teacher, if asked direct or invited to share his view by a parent or a student, is perfectly at liberty to say, with equal marriage – as with adultery, divorce or abortion – what their own moral view might be.[143]

Gove further expressed that he saw no reason to amend the existing sex education guidance to address teaching regarding same-sex marriage.[144] Despite these

---

137 Muslims Defending Marriage, 28 May 2012, www.mdm-campaign.org.uk (archived at http://archive.is/Ydqy). See also: Coalition for Marriage, *Gay Marriage in Primary Schools: the Impact of Redefining Marriage on Education*, London: Coalition for Marriage, 2012.
138 Coalition for Marriage, 'Press Release: 40,000 teachers face being disciplined or sacked as they set out to defy Cameron over Marriage', 3 February 2013.
139 For example: J. Shannon, HC Committee, 14 February 2013, c.144.
140 'Same sex marriage', *Daily Telegraph*, 1 June 2013. For an example of reference to it in debate, see: Earl of Clancarty, HL Debate, 4 June 2013, c.1086.
141 HC Committee, 12 February 2013, c.6.
142 S.406–407 Education Act 1996. The Model Funding Agreements of academies and free schools specify that primary and secondary schools are also subject to these provisions.
143 HC Committee, 12 February 2013, c.9.
144 Ibid., c.8.

attempted reassurances, the claim that it was necessary to protect teachers who wished to express religious or moral 'conscientious objections'[145] to same-sex marriage provided impetus for numerous but unsuccessful 'freedom of conscience' amendments that were tabled during the passage of the MSSCA 2013 (for a broader discussion, see Chapter 4).

The 'Packer amendment'

In addition to disagreements over the need for individual-level conscientious objection protection, debate over the MSSCA 2013 also focused on the status of marriage education within different categories of state-funded schools. Those in support of the ability of faith schools to teach SRE from the perspective of a particular religious ethos were vocal about perceived conflicts between the religious character of these schools and the need to provide information about same-sex relationships. For example, the Parliamentary Unit of the Church of England submitted a briefing to the Commons urging Parliament to amend the Education Act 1996 to require official guidance on sex education to take account of the religious ethos of church schools:

> Whilst Church of England schools will fulfil the duty to teach about the factual nature of marriage in its new legally redefined form, there is residual unclarity over how that will interact with the continuing need for schools to reflect their religious ethos in their SRE policies. There is also at present nothing to prevent future Secretaries of State [. . .] amending the guidance as it currently stands. We believe therefore that in order to ensure that schools can continue to teach an understanding of marriage that is consistent with their religious foundations, the [MSSCA 2013] should amend the Education Act 1996 to ensure that any guidance issued by the Secretary of State under this clause must take account of the religious character of the school.[146]

Representing the Church's position, the Bishop of Ripon and Leeds, John Packer, tabled an amendment during the MSSCA 2013 debates that sought to amend the Education Act 1996[147] to require guidance on sex education to specify that education on marriage and family life 'must [. . .] be given to registered pupils at schools which have a religious character in accordance with the tenets of the relevant religion or religious denomination'.[148] Seeking to avoid accusations that the Church was again seeking 'exemption' from the law, Packer sought to frame the proposed amendment using the language of 'accommodation':

---

145 For example: D. Burrowes, HC Committee, 26 February 2013, cc.177–179.
146 The Church of England Parliamentary Unit, *Marriage (Same Sex Couples) Bill: Commons Report and Third Reading Briefing*, 16 May 2013, pp.2–3.
147 S.403 Education Act 1996.
148 HL Debate, 24 June 2013, c. 547. After debate in Committee, Packer withdrew the amendment.

The Church of England's established policy is that pupils should have the opportunity to examine the full range of views on same-sex relationships – including different Christian views – and develop their own considered position. Within that atmosphere of open discussion, church schools must nevertheless be in a position to teach the nature of marriage in a way that is in accordance with the tenets of the Church of England. The distinctive Christian ethos of church schools will be undermined unless that position is accommodated. Exactly the same goes for schools that belong to other religious traditions. The purpose of this amendment is simply to achieve that accommodation. It does not seek an exemption.[149]

Speaking for the Government, Baroness Stowell reassured Packer that the Government supported the intentions of the amendment but would oppose it on the grounds that it was unnecessary, because schools would remain able to teach their own denominational views of marriage:

In order for teachers to handle the very sensitive situations in which they often find themselves, [faith schools] already interpret the [. . .] guidance according to their religious tenets. This will be no different when marriage is extended to same-sex couples [. . .] If the tenets of a particular religion do not recognise same-sex marriage, they will be able to approach teaching about marriage in exactly the same professional way that they do now. Although teaching will of course need to cover the factual position that marriage under the law of England and Wales can be between both opposite-sex and same-sex couples, faith schools will also be able to explain the relevant tenets of their religion on this matter.[150]

Throughout the MSSCA 2013 debates, the notion that faith schools should be obliged to teach more than the 'factual position' of same-sex marriage was questioned only rarely. Rather, most parliamentarians accepted without critique the premise that, as Lord Alli articulated, 'it is right and proper that faith schools should be allowed to teach the importance of marriage as they see it in relation to family life'.[151] Baroness Richardson, addressing the Packer amendment, was unusual in directly questioning whether it was reasonable and appropriate for schools to teach that same-sex relationships are immoral given the potential effects on pupils and their families:

[T]his amendment sounds eminently reasonable until you try to imagine yourself a child within a classroom in a school of a religious foundation. If you are talking about marriage and you know that your parents, who are

149 Ibid., c.549.
150 Ibid., c.566.
151 Ibid., c.556.

legally married to each other, are both of the same sex, how would it make you feel if you were told that their union is legal but not moral and not in accordance with Christian teaching?[152]

The Packer amendment was unsuccessful. However, although schools will seemingly be obliged to acknowledge the 'fact' of same-sex marriage, controversy persists regarding the messages that will be conveyed in some faith schools about same-sex marriage, other forms of same-sex relationship and the moral and ethical status of homosexual sex. The controversies arise in part from specific instances where state-funded schools have been seen to disseminate anti-gay messages and materials to students. Recent examples involving faith schools include the promotion of an anti-same-sex marriage petition in Catholic schools by the Catholic Education Service,[153] the distribution of a booklet declaring that 'the homosexual act is disordered' in Catholic schools in the Lancashire region,[154] and the alleged promotion of a group supporting gay conversion therapy by a Jewish voluntary aided school in north London.[155] In the final section below, we examine how arguments regarding the need to preserve the ability of faith schools to teach about homosexuality from a 'religious ethos' have contributed to shaping equalities legislation in ways such that there is little legal recourse for parents or pupils who object to homosexuality being represented as immoral or sinful.

Religion, curriculum and equalities

The issue of how faith schools teach about homosexuality featured significantly in debates over both the EASOR 2007 and the EA 2010. These debates focused attention specifically on whether the curriculum of schools should be captured by the provisions of equalities legislation. The EASOR 2007 contained neither a blanket exception of school curricula from equalities legislation nor specific exceptions for faith schools from provisions related to sexual orientation equality, although these were lobbied for by some religious groups. For example, prior to the drafting of the EASOR 2007, the Christian Institute released a report in which it stated that the regulations 'could force highly controversial and explicit pro-gay resources into the classroom'.[156] In parliamentary debate of the EASOR 2007, these concerns were reiterated by Baroness O'Cathain:

---

152 Ibid.
153 J. Vasagar, 'Catholic church urges pupils to sign anti-gay marriage petition', the *Guardian*, 25 April 2012.
154 A. Wagner, 'Is it legal to teach gay hate in schools?', *UK Human Rights Blog*, 19 February 2012. Available online at http://ukhumanrightsblog.com/2012/02/19/is-it-legal-to-teach-gay-hate-in-schools (accessed on 5 December 2013).
155 R. Razaq, 'Jewish school in storm over US "gay conversion" group', *London Evening Standard*, 20 January 2012.
156 Christian Institute, *Curriculum in the Courtroom: How New Laws will Give Activists the Power to Sue Schools*, Newcastle upon Tyne, 2006, p.20.

If a priest is asked a direct question in an RE lesson, there could be litigation if he divulged what he really believes. The Government and the Minister [. . .] deny the curriculum is covered by these regulations. In that case, why do equivalent religious discrimination laws have exemptions in the curriculum? The Government may be the only ones who believe the curriculum is not covered. Others who believe to the contrary are the Joint Committee on Human Rights, the Church of England's lawyers, the counsel to the Joint Committee on Statutory Instruments, the seven denominations suing the Government in Northern Ireland[157] and a pro-gay group called No Outsiders. That group is already going around the country telling schools that the regulations mean they have to 'normalise' homosexuality to seven year-olds and read gay fairy tales in the classroom.[158]

The Government sought to reassure religious opponents of the EASOR 2007 that issues of curriculum would not be captured and that religious schools would not need to adjust the content of their teaching. As Baroness Andrews argued on behalf of the Government, the 'issues of religious liberty have been conflated also with issues of educational freedom' and claims of litigation against schools that did not positively promote homosexuality were 'the most extreme parody of the reality'.[159]

The Government's position in relation to curricular issues, however, ran directly contrary to the recommendations of the Joint Committee on Human Rights (JCHR). In scrutinising proposals for what became the EASOR 2007, the JCHR argued that:

> [T]here is an important difference between [. . .] factual information [about homosexuality] being imparted in a descriptive way as part of a wide-ranging syllabus about different religions, and a curriculum which teaches a particular religion's doctrinal beliefs as if they were objectively true [because the] latter is likely to lead to unjustifiable discrimination against homosexual pupils.[160]

The JCHR recommendation that the EASOR 2007 'make clear that the prohibition on discrimination applies to the curriculum' was ignored by the Government in the face of a number of vigorous objections from those who argued that it would create a litigious situation and damper freedom of expression (the JCHR recommendation was described as 'illiberal' by the Bishop of

---

157 Chapter 3 provides fuller discussion of this action taken by religious organisations in respect of the Equality Act (Sexual Orientation) Regulations (Northern Ireland) 2006.
158 HL Debate, 21 March 2007, c.1298.
159 Ibid., c.1293.
160 Joint Committee on Human Rights, *Legislative Scrutiny: Sexual Orientation Regulations*, Sixth Report of Session 2006–07, 2007, p.25.

Winchester, Michael Scott-Joynt).¹⁶¹ Additionally, many opponents of the JCHR recommendation drew on a logic of equivalences when arguing that to extend the EASOR 2007 to cover the curriculum would create an 'inequity' because the Equality Act 2006 provided an explicit exception for the content of the curriculum in respect of discrimination on the grounds of religion or belief.¹⁶²

The EA 2010 introduced a wider curriculum exception that states that nothing in the provisions relating to schools¹⁶³ 'applies to anything done in connection with the content of the curriculum'.¹⁶⁴ Government guidance to schools on the implications of the EA 2010 makes a distinction between curriculum content (which is explicitly exempted) and the manner in which that curriculum is delivered (which is covered by the EA 2010).¹⁶⁵ During the passage of the EA 2010, concerns were raised about this broad curriculum exception, with the JCHR focusing attention on the potential consequences for gay and lesbian pupils in faith schools.¹⁶⁶ Queried about its intention to introduce the broad curriculum exception, the Government responded that its primary motivation was not to protect faith schools, but rather 'to clarify the full educational freedoms of schools to decide what resources to use so that they will not have to justify or defend themselves from accusations of discrimination when they are following a reasonable and balanced approach to the curriculum'.¹⁶⁷ The JCHR, however, indicated that it was not 'reassured' by the Government's assertion that pupils would be protected if anti-gay materials were presented in a 'hectoring, harassing or bullying way'¹⁶⁸ and urged that the broad curriculum exception be reconsidered:

> [E]xempting the content of the curriculum from the duty not to discriminate means, for example, that gay pupils will be subjected to teaching that their sexual orientation is sinful or morally wrong [. . .] We remain of the view that this is likely to lead to unjustifiable discrimination against gay pupils, even if it is not presented in a hectoring, harassing or bullying way. It is the

---

161 Bishop of Winchester, HL Debate, 21 March 2007, c.1319.
162 S.50(2)(a) Equality Act 2006. The Bishop of Winchester was amongst those raising the issue of equivalences. HL Debate, 21 March 2007, cc.1318–1319. The Government argued that this provision was necessary in part as an added protection from challenges by other religious groups to teaching about religion in faith schools.
163 Pt.6 Ch.1 Equality Act 2010.
164 S.89(2) Equality Act 2010.
165 Department for Education, *Equality Act 2010: Advice for School Leaders, School Staff, Governing Bodies and Local Authorities*, February 2013.
166 Joint Committee on Human Rights, *Legislative Scrutiny: Equality Bill*, Twenty-sixth Report of Session 2008–09, London: HMSO, 2009.
167 Joint Committee on Human Rights, *Legislative Scrutiny: Equality Bill*, op. cit., section 219.
168 This interpretation is presumably in reference to S.85(2)(a) Equality Act 2010 which indicates that a school must not discriminate against a pupil 'in the way that it provides education for the pupil'.

content of the curriculum (the teaching that homosexuality is wrong), not its presentation, that is discriminatory.[169]

Teaching homosexuality as sin

Although the argument of the JCHR was rejected by the Government, the guidance for schools issued by the Equality and Human Rights Commission (EHRC) on the EA 2010 suggests that teaching the religious belief that homosexuality is immoral could provide grounds for claims of direct discrimination. The EHRC provided the following as illustration:

> A teacher at a Church of England school tells pupils that homosexuality is 'wrong' and that gay and lesbian people will 'burn in hell' unless they are 'cured of the disease'. A gay pupil in the class is deeply offended and intimidated by this hostile and degrading language. This may be direct discrimination on the grounds of sexual orientation.[170]

However, in this example the distinction between content and manner of delivery is ambiguous: only the content of what is being taught is clearly described by the EHRC, rather than anything about the manner of teaching.

The meaning and scope of provisions in the EA 2010 continue to both generate controversy and provoke uncertainty. This is well illustrated by recent objections raised by gay rights campaigners, secularist groups, the Trade Unions Congress (TUC) and others in relation to information being distributed in some Catholic schools about homosexuality. In 2012, the TUC General Secretary, Brendan Barber, wrote formally to the Secretary of State for Education, Michael Gove MP, expressing concerns about a booklet condemning homosexuality which was distributed to students in many Catholic schools in the Lancashire area.[171] The booklet, *Pure Manhood*, written by a self-described American 'chastity speaker', suggests that male homosexuality may stem from sexual abuse or an unhealthy relationship between a child and his father, and describes homosexuality as 'disordered' and 'directed against God's natural purpose for sex – babies and bonding'.[172] Barber argued that the use of the booklet in schools violated the EA 2010 and the duty of schools to combat prejudice. Gove's reply stressed that the content of the curriculum was exempt from the EA 2010 and that the schools in question were free to distribute materials with anti-gay content, but he went on to state:

---

169 Joint Committee on Human Rights, *Legislative Scrutiny: Equality Bill*, op. cit., section 220.
170 Equality and Human Rights Commission, *Technical Guidance for Schools in England*, 2013, p.32.
171 A. Wagner, op. cit.
172 J. Evert, *Pure Manhood*, San Diego, CA: Catholic Answers, 2011.

The way in which the curriculum (and thus SRE) is taught, however, is covered by the provisions of the [EA 2010]. If a school conveyed its beliefs in a way that involved haranguing, harassing[173] or berating a gay or lesbian pupil or group of pupils then this would be unacceptable in any circumstances and is likely to constitute unlawful discrimination [. . .] In the case of faith schools [. . .] the only requirement is for them to teach the statutory science curriculum, and to teach about AIDS/HIV as part of SRE.[174]

Some conservative religious commentators have represented the controversy as a prime example of growing 'secularist attacks' on faith schools.[175] Nevertheless, Gove's response regarding the scope of the curriculum exception in the EA 2010 has reassured those in the Catholic Church who forcefully assert a right to distribute material condemning homosexual practice to pupils.[176]

Conclusion

This chapter has examined the relationship between religion and the evolution of legal frameworks that govern the inclusion and exclusion of knowledge about homosexuality within the curricula of British schools. Whereas in the 1980s religious arguments and interests helped drive efforts to restrict the circulation of information about homosexuality in state-funded schools through Section 28 (even if its effects were indirect rather than direct), these arguments have lost much of their persuasiveness in the era of 'equalities'. However, as we have shown throughout this book, although the equalities discourse in relation to sexual orientation is strong, it has not been successful in supplanting the notion that a state-funded faith school should be permitted to teach about homosexuality from the perspective of its particular 'faith ethos'. The significant influence of religion in this sphere of lawmaking is demonstrated by the struggle over the repeal of

---

173 As discussed previously, relevant provisions on harassment in the Equality Act 2010 explicitly exclude sexual orientation and, contrary to Gove's claim, harassment is not captured.
174 M. Gove, Letter to Brendan Barber, 26 January 2012. Available online at http://adam1cor.files.wordpress.com/2012/02/michael-gove-letter-260112.pdf (accessed on 5 December 2013).
175 For example: W. Oddie, 'Secularist attacks on the Catholic faith get worse, on both sides of the Atlantic: here it's the TUC, in the US (where at least there's a fightback) it's Obama', *Catholic Herald*, 27 February 2012. Available online at www.catholicherald.co.uk/commentandblogs/2012/02/27/secularist-attacks-on-the-catholic-faith-get-worse-on-both-sides-of-the-atlantic-here-it's-the-tuc-in-the-us-where-at-least-there's-a-fightback-it's-obama/ (accessed on 5 December 2013).
176 For example: M. Teahan, 'Gove rejects call to ban Catholic booklet from schools', *Catholic Herald*, 23 February 2012. Available online at www.catholicherald.co.uk/news/2012/02/23/gove-rejects-call-to-ban-catholic-booklet-from-schools (accessed on 5 December 2013).

Section 28 which involved negotations between Government and religious leaders (particularly in the Church of England and the Catholic Church) and which has left a legacy in relation to the requirements for sex and relationships education. Although all schools, regardless of religious designation, are now prohibited by equality legislation from discriminating against pupils based on sexual orientation, religious interests and considerations have played an important role in maintaining education relating to homosexuality as 'non-statutory knowledge'. By sequestering knowledge about homosexuality outside of the requirements of the statutory National Curriculum for maintained schools, parents with either religious or other objections to teaching about homosexuality (or other aspects of sex education) maintain a right to withdraw children from sex education. Furthermore, children and young people who reject the beliefs of their parents have no right to access this knowledge in schools nor an ability to 'opt in'.

Changes to the definition of marriage by the MSSCA 2013 have provoked debates over what information schools will be obliged to convey to pupils regarding the nature of same-sex marriage. Government ministers assert that, although schools in England will be required to teach the fact that same-sex marriage exists, they will be able to continue to teach about marriage (and other dimensions of human sexuality) from the perspective of a school's particular religious ethos. The question of whether maintained faith schools should be obliged to teach more than the 'factual position' of same-sex marriage was very rarely addressed in parliamentary debates over the issue. The rapid growth in the number of faith academies and free schools – which currently have no obligation to provide sex education – has raised further worries about whether the needs of all pupils will genuinely be met in these schools. Equality legislation provides little recourse for those with concerns about whether state-funded schools should be able to present homosexual sex primarily through the lens of sin, given the broadly drawn curriculum exception contained within the EA 2010. Although the EHRC and Government ministers differentiate between the content of the curriculum (which is exempt) and the manner in which it is taught (which is captured by the EA 2010), this distinction can be ambiguous. In the interpretation of Government ministers, state-funded faith schools maintain a right to characterise homosexuality as immoral and sinful to pupils.

Conclusion

Throughout this book we have demonstrated that religion continues to exercise considerable influence in lawmaking in respect of homosexuality. Despite claims such as those made by the Archbishop of Canterbury, Justin Welby, that religious voices have been 'utterly overwhelmed'[1] by those who favour sexual orientation equality, we have shown that religion remains a powerful presence in the making of statute law. The consequences of the continued authority of religious discourse in the UK Parliament are wide and far-reaching. In some cases, religious discourse has supported the evolution of law that has been beneficial to lesbians and gay men. The recent deployment of faith-based arguments by many parliamentarians (some of whom self-identify as lesbian or gay) in support of the legalisation of same-sex marriage in England and Wales shows the positive and enabling role that religious discourse can play in respect of sexual orientation equality. However, as we have shown throughout the book, religious discourse has more often been deployed to shape law in ways that are detrimental to sexual orientation equality.

In relation to English law, anti-gay religious discourse has been instrumental in shaping a legal landscape in which:

- organised religions have a bespoke exception from law prohibiting sexual orientation discrimination in employment;
- religious organisations enjoy an exception from law prohibiting sexual orientation discrimination in the provision of goods and services and the control of facilities and premises;
- sexual orientation is not a protected characteristic in relation to harassment outside of employment;
- same-sex couples are excluded by default from solemnising marriage according to religious rites or in places of worship;
- incitement to hatred on the grounds of sexual orientation is a more narrowly drawn offence than incitement to racial hatred;

---

1 G. Drake, 'Church must accept there is sexual revolution, Welby tells Synod', *Church Times*, 18 July 2013.

- the provision of information about homosexuality remains sequestered from the requirements of the National Curriculum for maintained schools;
- and state-funded faith schools retain the ability to teach young people about homosexuality from the perspective of their own religious 'ethos'.

These aspects of law are not accidental remnants or unintended outcomes. They result directly from the influence of religious prejudice and intolerance of homosexuality upon lawmaking.

In analysing how religious discourse has influenced the making of law, we have shown that there has never been a singular or unified religious view amongst legislators. The nature and extent of religious discourse about homosexuality in the UK Parliament has evolved over time, influenced by a number of factors including: transformations in the religious landscape of the UK since the mid-twentieth century; significant changes in the social construction of sexuality; and the ascendency of equality and rights discourses. The forms of religious discourse deployed in parliamentary debates about the partial decriminalisation of male homosexual acts during the 1950s and 1960s, in which there was a near-universal Christian condemnation of homosexuality, have become rare. By the time that male homosexual offences were repealed during the first decade of the twenty-first century, explicitly religious condemnations of homosexual sex no longer had an accepted place in parliamentary debate. As we have shown, the emphasis of much religious discourse since that time has shifted from the moral regulation of private sexual behaviour towards shaping law in ways that maintain heteronormative social privilege. However, the displacement of religious discourse aimed at preserving hierarchical social distinctions on the grounds of sexual orientation – for example, during failed efforts to maintain the exclusion of same-sex couples from the adoption of children – has produced a further transformation. Operating in an embattled and defensive mode, religious opposition to homosexuality has now refocused on defending boundaries between 'sacred' and 'secular' social institutions and spaces to preserve heterosexist power and privilege.

The claim that religious believers should be given maximum protection to exercise 'conscientious objections' to homosexuality has become the dominant feature of anti-gay religious discourse in the twenty-first century. An objection to homosexuality rooted in 'conscience', it is asserted, is not akin to other forms of unsavoury bigotry, prejudice or intolerance. Rather, it is argued, it is the expression of 'deeply held', 'sincere' and 'traditional' beliefs. The importance of this discourse is that it is still often successful in distancing faith-based objections to sexual orientation equality from charges of 'homophobia'. The consequence of this, as we have shown, is that religious discourse has been able to continue to exercise important influences on lawmaking at a time when homophobia is widely derided. As a consequence, for example, it was possible for religious arguments to shape debates over the scope of the criminal offence of incitement to hatred on the grounds of sexual orientation. Yet the discursive construction of religious objections to law reform as matters of 'conscience' masks their real foundation, which is a long-standing moral intolerance of homosexual intimate relationships that historically underpinned draconian and violent forms of social control. Central to any opposition to law reform by the Church of England is its view that 'homosexual genital acts' are sinful[2] and that homosexuality is not 'congruous with the observed order of creation'.[3] Some would argue that the religious intolerance of homosexual sex (which has shaped English law since at least the thirteenth century, as we explored in Chapter 1) conforms to the definition of homophobia as extreme and irrational aversion to homosexuality. Yet, in the UK Parliament, religious discourse about homosexuality often circumvents such an association and, as a result, maintains a normative force.

Because we have tried to show religious discourse 'in action' during lawmaking, our primary focus has been an analysis of the content of UK parliamentary debates. However, any understanding of the religious discourse that circulates in Parliament must take account of the multiple and often competing sites from which it originates. The Lords Spiritual exercise a meaningful legislative role but they are just one (not necessarily unified) source of the religious discourse that circulates in Parliament. As we have shown, religious discourse in Parliament is shaped in relation to a range of external factors that include increasingly active conservative lobby groups. It is beyond the scope of our analysis to make causal links between lobby groups and parliamentary discourse, but it is clear that anti-gay religious organisations play an active role (just as pro-gay organisations do) in shaping debate on a wide range of issues. For example, the active engagement of a wide range of churches in various stages of the creation of equality legislation has had a significant impact on law in this area. Although we have shown that conservative religious groups are often unsuccessful or only partially successful in achieving their legislative ambitions, anti-gay religious discourse remains a fundamental aspect of UK parliamentary debate. Such discourse is unlikely to disappear from lawmaking in the near future. On the contrary, religious discourse orientated towards preserving distinctions in law that are rooted in religious hostility to homosexuality is likely to remain central to and influential upon lawmaking.

2 General Synod of the Church of England, 11 November 1987.
3 *Issues in Human Sexuality: A Statement by the House of Bishops of the General Synod of the Church of England*, London: Church House Publishing, 1991.

Index

Abbott, D. 123
Adebowale, Lord 83–4
Adoption and Children Act (ACA) 2002 59, 69–70, 92, 97–8; contested moralities 72–88; religion and child welfare 76–80; religion and 'evidence' of homosexual parenting 80–4; religion and symbolic politics of marriage 84–7
'age of consent' debates 5–6, 20–1, 52–64, 87; assertion of Christian morality: Sexual Offences (Amendment) Bill 1977 52–4; Christian rejection of legal equality 57–9; 'homophobia' and 'equality': Criminal Justice and Public Order Act 1994 54–60; triumph of equality over religion? Sexual Offences (Amendment) Act 2000 60–4
age discrimination 101
AIDS/HIV 58, 177, 191, 205
Alison, Michael 56
Allen, G. 179, 181
Alli, Lord 80, 86–7, 106–7 132, 133, 163, 200
Anderson of Swansea, Lord 168
Andersson, J. 9, 14
Andrews, Baroness 202
Aquinas, Thomas 15
armed forces 11, 60
Armstrong of Ilminster, Lord 143, 168
Arran, Lord 52, 100
Ash, F. 153
Ashbourne, Lord 71–2
Astor of Hever, Lord 82
Atkin, Lord 42

Bach, Lord 172
Bailey, D.S. 30–1, 42, 44
Baird, V. 121
Baldry, T. 24

Ball, C. 75, 76
Barber, Brendan 204
Barber, M. 45
Barendt, E. 160
Barker, Baroness 70
Barry, Russell (Bishop of Southwell) 43
Bates, S. 185
Beauchamp, Earl 38
Beckford, J.A. 11
Belgium 76
Bell, S. 60, 127
Bennett, N. 179
Bentham, J. 15
Bercow, John 155, 158
Berger, P. 11
Bernstein, M. 149
Berridge, Baroness 146
Bingham, J. 75, 193
Birkenhead, Viscount 39
birth certificates 90, 94
Black, C. 47
Blackstone, W. 36
Blair, A. 176–7, 191
Blair, Tony 56, 74
Bland, L. 39
Blatch, Baroness 66, 92, 185
Bodkin, A.H. 37, 38
Boothby, Robert 41, 43
Borris, K. 32, 33
Bösche, S. 178
Boswell, J. 30, 32
Boulton, P. 138
Bourdieu, P. 18, 22, 148
Boyson, Rhodes 57
Brady, S. 38
Bray, A. 33
Brazier, Julian 85–6
Brennan, Lord 82–3, 145

Brethren Christian Fellowship 92
Brickell, C. 21
British Humanist Association 189
British National Party (BNP) 162
Britton, P. 73
Brock, J. 23
Brooke, S. 49
Brown, C.G. 7, 9–12, 46
Brown, Laurence (Bishop of Birmingham) 52–4
Bruce, Fiona 197
Bruce, S. 9
Brundage, J.A. 33
Bryant, Chris 97, 131–3, 147
buggery: CJPOA 1994 59; heterosexual buggery 59, 63; SOA 2003 64; SOAA 2000 63
Buggery Act (BA)1533 32–4; repeals and re-enactments: 1533 to 1563 34–5; sixteenth century and onwards 16, 35–6, 39
bullying 181, 193, 203
Burg, B.R. 34
Burgwinkle, W. 31
Burridge, J. 6
Burrowes, David 143–6, 155, 166, 199
Burrows, Lynette 167
Burt, A. 97
Burt, L. 115
Butler-Sloss, Baroness 133–4, 165–6
Butt, R. 188

Cameron, David 5, 159
Canada 13
Canon law 30–2, 34–5, 133, 137–8, 140
Carey, George 13, 144; Archbishop of Canterbury 60–1
Carlisle, Bishop of 52
Casanova, J. 8, 11
Cash, W. 166
Cassidy, George (Bishop of Southwell and Nottingham) 115–16
Catholic Children's Society 69, 74
Catholic Church 33–4, 43, 119, 131, 136, 145, 149; Catholic Bishops' Conference of England and Wales 92, 109, 142; education 187, 193, 201, 204–6; homophobic hate speech 159
Catholic Education Service 182, 185, 195, 201
Catholic Parliamentary Office 118
Charles-Edwards, Lewis (Bishop of Worcester) 48–9

Chesters, Alan (Bishop of Blackburn) 105–6, 183–5
children *see* parenting
Children's Society 74–5
Chope, Christopher 130, 147
Christian Action Research and Education (CARE) 12, 69, 80, 92, 105
Christian Institute 12, 181, 183; civil partnerships 128; education 201; employment equality 101–2, 105, 106; homosexual sex 29, 64, 66; judicial review: EASORNI 2006 113; parenting 69, 81, 84, 92
Christmann, K. 168
Church of England 11–2, 14, 18, 22–5, 209; age of consent 60–2; Children's Society 74–5; civil partnership and same-sex marriage 128, 130, 133, 135–41, 142, 150–1; decriminalisation of male homosexual acts 42, 44–52; education 179–80, 182–3, 185, 187, 189, 199–201, 206; employment equality: sexual orientation exception 102–6, 119–20; EA 2010 118–20; goods, services, facilities and premises and religious exceptions 109; HFEA 2008 92, 95–6; homophobic hate speech 159; homosexual sex 16, 42, 44–52; Mission and Public Affairs Council 92, 95–6; Moral Welfare Society 42, 44; multi-academy trusts 189; parenting 74–5, 84, 92, 95–6; 'Section 28' 179–80, 182–3, 185, 206; voluntary schools 187; Wolfenden Report and 16, 44–7; *see also individual archbishops and bishops*
Church of Ireland 25
Church of Scotland 11, 25; Church and Society Council 92
Church in Wales 25, 136–7, 139
civil partnership 21–2, 24, 77, 84, 92, 106–7, 120, 124–6, 151; avoiding a clash: civil partnerships as secular relationships 126–32; distancing homophobia: transformation in rhetoric 5–6, 147–51; geography of separation: places of worship and religious freedom 132–5
Civil Partnership Act (CPA) 2004 22, 24, 92, 125–6, 129–36, 140, 147, 150
Clancarty, Earl of 198
Clark, A. 32
Clarke of Hampstead, Lord 66, 167–8
Clarke, V. 73
Clatworthy, J. 14
Coalition for Marriage 198

Cocks, H.G. 37, 39
Cohen, S. 142
Coke, E. 15, 32, 34–5
Conservative Party 87–8, 92, 155, 159, 176–7
Cook, M. 37
Cook, R. 55
Cooper, D. 12
Cooper, J. 44
Cormack, Patrick, 24, 143, 163, 168
'cottaging' 65–7
Cox, Baroness 20, 176, 178, 180
Cox, B.J. 149
Coxon, A.R.M. 82
Crime and Disorder Act (CDA) 1998 60–2
Criminal Justice and Immigration Act (CJIA) 2008 153, 155–7, 159, 169
Criminal Justice and Public Order Act (CJPOA)1994 54–60, 66; Ashbourne–Ryder amendment 71–2
Criminal Law Amendment Act (CLAA) 1885 37–9, 64
Crossman, G. 163
Crown Prosecution Service 165
Cumberlege, Baroness 71–2, 144
Cundy, Peter (Bishop of Peterborough) 129
Cunningham, Jack 179
Currie, Edwina 55–6, 60
Curtis-Thomas, Claire 96–7

Darzi of Denham, Lord 95
David, Baroness 178
Davidson, Randall (Archbishop of Canterbury) 39
Davie, G. 10
Davies, E. 18
Davies, P.M. 82
Dawson of Penn, Lord 41–2
Dear, Lord 6, 143, 155, 170, 171–2
Dearing, Lord 159
decriminalisation of male homosexual acts 64–7; partial 6, 15–16, 19–20, 40–52, 208; Sexual Offences Act 1967 6, 29, 39–40, 47–52, 54, 65; Wolfenden Report and Church of England 44–7
Deech, Baroness 92–3
Denmark 76
Denning, Lord 1–2, 18, 178
desecularisation 11
Devlin, P. 40, 44–5, 124
Dewey, G. 23
Doan, L.L. 38–9
Dobbin, Jim 159
Doe, N. 139

Donaldson, J. 111–12
Donnelly, Desmond 41, 42
Drake, G. 150, 207
Duncan, Alan 124–5, 131–2
Duncan, R.F. 111
Durham, M. 6, 177
Durrant, Anthony 56

Eagle, M. 154, 169
Ecclesiastical Committee 24
ecclesiastical courts 30–4
Edmiston, Lord 143
education 59, 174–5, 205–6; academies 187–90, 196–7, 206; basic curriculum 191; free schools 187–9, 196–7, 206; homosexuality as non-statutory knowledge 190–7; independent schools 188; maintained schools 186–8, 190, 191, 193–4, 206, 208; National Curriculum 187, 190–7, 206, 208; 'Packer amendment' 199–201; religion, curriculum and equalities 201–5; same-sex marriage 197–201, 206; 'Section 28' 20, 73, 77, 87, 175–86, 205–6; sexual health 191; sexual orientation discrimination 189–90; teaching homosexuality as sin 204–5, 206
Edward VI 34
Elizabeth I 34
Elton, Lord 94, 130
employment equality 59, 99–107, 207; Church of England and sexual orientation exception 102–5; EA 2010 119–20; parliamentary acceptance of exception 105–7
Employment Equality (Sexual Orientation) Regulations (EESOR) 2003 100–7, 118–20
Epstein, D. 5–6, 176, 181
Equality Act (EA) 2006 99, 107–10, 116, 203
Equality Act (EA) 2010 103, 118–23, 133–4, 142, 144–6, 151, 189–90, 201, 203–6
Equality Act (Sexual Orientation) Regulations (EASOR) 2007 17, 92, 110, 114–17, 133, 189, 201–3
Equality Act (Sexual Orientation) Regulations (Northern Ireland) (EASORNI) 2006 110–15, 118, 202
Equality and Human Rights Commission (EHRC) 204, 206
'equality' not 'sameness' 148–50

ethic of care 14
ethnicity 160
European Convention on the Adoption of Children 77
European Convention on Human Rights 63, 64, 142; Art 8: private and family life 60; Art 9: freedom of thought, conscience and religion 117; Art 14: discrimination 60, 100, 117
European Court of Human Rights 3, 16, 20, 55, 60, 117, 141
European Union; Directive 2007/78/EC 100–2, 105
Evert, J. 204
expression *see* freedom of religious expression

facilities, premises, goods and services 107–17, 144, 207; EA 2010 121–3; religious opposition to harassment protection for sexual minorities: EASORNI 2006 110–14; threat to religious liberty: EASOR 2007 114–17
faith schools 174–5, 186, 205–6, 208; academies 187–9, 190, 196–7, 206; free schools 187–9, 196–7, 206; maintained schools 186–8, 190–1, 193–4, 206, 208; 'Packer amendment' 199–201; religion, curriculum and equalities 201–5; sexual orientation discrimination 189–90
Ferrers, Earl 169, 170
fertility services: HFEA 2008 69–70, 88–97, 98
Fisher, Geoffrey (Archbishop of Canterbury) 45–6
Fitt, Lord 66
Fittall, W. 104–6, 119
Forster, Peter (Bishop of Chester) 92, 130, 134, 138, 156, 159–60, 166–7
Fortescue, Earl 38
Foucault, M. 4, 32, 35
Fowler, Lord 151
France 76
Fraser guidelines 191
freedom of religious expression 143, 145–6, 153–4, 172–3, 202; homophobic hate speech and the saving provision 154–7; persecution of people of faith 169–72; policing and 'climate of fear' for people of faith 164–9; special status of religious speech 161–3

Gamble, N. 89
Ganiel, G. 9

Garnier, Edward 163, 165
Gasparini, A. 153
Gay Liberation Front 55
Gladwin, John (Bishop of Guildford) 127
Goldhaber, M.D. 16
Golombok, S. 81, 83–4
Goodall, K. 153
Goodich, M. 31
goods, services, facilities and premises 107–17, 144, 207; EA 2010 121–3; religious opposition to harassment protection for sexual minorities: EASORNI 2006 110–14; threat to religious liberty: EASOR 2007 114–17
Goudie, Baroness 80
Gould of Potternewton, Baroness 74
Gove, Michael 198, 204–5
Greenwood, A. 47
Grey, A. 15–16, 40
Grieve, Dominic 67, 114, 169
Grimley, M. 43
gross indecency 16, 37–9, 51, 54, 59, 62–4; between women: Criminal Law Amendment Bill 1921 38–9
Guasp, A. 193–4
Guest, M. 6, 25

Habermas, J. 11
Habgood, John (Archbishop of York) 56–8, 177, 179–80
Al-Haddad, S. Haitham 141
Hall, G.D.G. 30
Hall, L. 176
Halsbury, Earl of 20, 52, 177–8
Hammond, Harry 164
harassment based on sexual orientation 207; employment 100; goods, services, facilities and premises 107–14, 122–3; schools 190
Harries, Richard (Bishop of Oxford) 1, 62, 75, 84, 129–30, 133
Harris, A.P. 149
Harris, Evan 83, 89, 105, 122, 160–3
Harrison, Lord 165
Hart, C. 101
Hart, H.L.A. 15, 40, 124
hate speech, homophobic 59, 146, 153–4, 172–3, 207–8; 'freedom of expression' saving provision and 154–7; logics of equalities 157–61; persecution of people of faith 169–72; policing and 'climate of fear' for people of faith 164–9; special status of religious speech 161–3
Heath, David 162

Heinze, E. 154, 157
Helmholz, R.H. 30
Henry, J. 196
Henry VIII 33
Herbert, Christopher (Bishop of St Albans) 92–3
Herman, D. 12
Hickson, F.C.I. 82
Higginson, A.J. 174
Hill, M. 138
Hinchliffe, David 74
Hind, John (Bishop of Chichester) 121, 141, 155, 156
Hindus 11, 61, 182; voluntary schools 187
HIV/AIDS 58, 177, 191, 205
Hollobone, P. 167
'homophobia' 6, 67, 172, 180, 193; Crown Prosecution Service 165; denial that faith-based opposition constitutes 20–2, 59, 82, 96–7, 109, 157, 208–9; hate speech, homophobic *see separate entry*; term introduced into parliamentary discourse 56–7; transformation in rhetoric 147–51
Homosexual Law Reform Society 15, 40, 46, 50, 55
homosexual sex: religion and legal regulation 12, 29–30, 67–8, 209; 'age of consent' debates 5–6, 20–1, 52–64; alignment between religion, statute law and (male) homosexual acts 36–40; decriminalisation of male homosexual acts 64–7; from Roman canon law to statute law 30–6; partial decriminalisation of male homosexual acts 6, 15–16, 19–20, 40–52, 208; prior to Wolfenden Report 40–4; Sexual Offences Act 1967 6, 29, 39–40, 47–52, 54, 65; Sexual Offences (Amendment) Act 2000 29, 60–4, 67; Wolfenden Report and Church of England 44–7
Howarth, David 162–3
Howarth, Gerald 114, 131, 142, 147, 165, 184
Howe, Earl 75, 80–1
Howe, Pauline 170–2
Hughes, Simon 56, 179
Human Fertilisation and Embryology Act (HFEA) 1990 88–9, 91–4
Human Fertilisation and Embryology Act (HFEA) 2008 26, 69, 70, 88–98; equalities and morality of conception by assisted means 95–7; licensing provisions 89–90, 92, 95; religious opposition to 90–2; status provisions 90, 92, 94–5; symbolism of fatherhood and 'truth' of genetic heritage 93–5
human rights 21, 26, 142; Equality and Human Rights Commission (EHRC) 204, 206; European Convention on Human Rights 60, 63–4, 100, 117, 142; European Court of Human Rights 3, 16, 20, 55, 60, 117, 141; Human Rights Act 1998 100, 144, 146; Joint Committee on Human Rights (JCHR) 202–4
Hume, D. 30
Hunt, A.J. 82
Hunt of Kings Heath, Lord 75, 84, 86, 162
Hunt, S. 12, 157
Hyde, H.M. 32–4
Hylton, Lord 66, 143

International Gay Association (now International Lesbian and Gay Association) 55
Islam 11, 14, 61, 86; Muslim Council of Britain 136, 182, 197–8; Muslim Research and Development Foundation 141; voluntary schools 187

Jakobovits, Lord 58, 61
James, David (Bishop of Bradford) 134
Jeffrey-Poulter, S. 55
Jenkins, R. 51
Johnson, Alan 89
Johnson, P. 20, 55, 60, 64–5, 67, 100, 141, 153, 165
Johnson, R. 5, 6
Jones, Edward (Bishop of St Albans) 47, 51
Jones, P. 9
Jones, S. 136
Jordan, M.D. 31
Judaism 11, 61, 125; Jewish schools 187, 201

Keen, A. 60
Kettle, S. 88
Key, Robert 87–8, 140
Knight, J. (Baroness Knight of Collingtree from 1997) 91, 168, 179–80
Knight, Lord 196
Knott, K. 11–12
Kornicki, R. 119
Krafft-Ebing, R. von 36
Kyle, C.R. 5

Labouchere, Henry 38
Labour Party 181, 196–7

Ladele v The London Borough of Islington 116–17
Lang, Cosmo Gordon (Archbishop of Canterbury) 41–2
Learning and Skills Act 2000 184–5
Lee, R. 89
left-wing politics 26
Leigh, Edward 19, 105, 130–1, 142
Leigh, I. 101
Lemons, A. 135
Lesbian and Gay Christian Movement 14, 106
Lester of Herne Hill, Lord 105, 107, 127, 143, 160, 170, 190
Levit, N. 150
Leviticus 31, 163
Lewis-Jones, J. 25
Liff, S. 149
Livingstone, K. 20
Lloyd of Berwick, Lord 92
local education authorities (LEAs) 176–81
Long, R. 196
Longford, Earl of 58, 177–8
Loudoun, Countess of 53, 54
Loughton, Tim 75, 143–6
Lucas-Tooth, H. 40
Lynch, G. 10, 12
McCandless, J. 89–90, 94, 95
McCormick, I. 35
McCrea, W. 17
McCrudden, C. 142, 145
Macdonald, A. 194
MacDonald, J.H.A. 30
Mackay of Clashfern, Lord 121, 143
Mackenzie, G. 33
Macleod of Fuinary, Lord 53
McLeod, H. 10

McManus, M. 87, 176, 178, 184
McManus, T.J. 82
Macmillan, C.J.B. 149
Macquisten, Frederick 39
Maitland, F.W. 30–1
Makeover, F. 34
Malmesbury, Earl of 38–9
marginalisation of religion 12–13; HFEA 2008 88–97
Marley, D. 189
marriage 8, 130–1; civil 8, 128–9; conflicting definitions of 137–8; parenting: religion and symbolic politics of 84–7; register offices or approved premises 128–9; same-sex *see separate entry*

Marriage Act 1540 133
Marriage Act 1753 133
Marriage Act (MA) 1949 125, 128–9, 137, 139–40, 143
Marriage (Same Sex Couples) Act (MSSCA) 2013 2, 5, 18, 24, 102, 125, 136–43, 145–8, 151, 156, 175, 196–200; Marriage (Same Sex Couples) Bill 2013 amendments 142–6; 'quadruple lock' and Church of England 136–40
Mary I 34
Mason, J. 121, 123
Massey, Baroness 196
Matassa, M. 153
Mawhinney, Lord 2, 143
May, Theresa 159
Mayfield, Christopher (Bishop of Manchester) 77–9, 83, 85
Mead, F. 37–8
medieval period 30–2
merchant ships 60
Meredith, P. 191
Methodists 43; voluntary schools 187
Mill, J.S. 44
Miller, M. 136
Mitchell, B. 41
Modell, D. 91
Monk, D. 176, 191
Monson, Lord 168, 170
Moon, D. 32
Moran, J. 6, 176, 178
Moran, L.J. 39
Moran, Lord 113, 168, 182–3
Morgan, D. 89
Morgan, P. 81–2
Morrow, Lord 111–2
Mortimer, Robert (Bishop of Exeter) 46–7
Mulholland, Greg 143
music 154–5, 162–3, 172

Naphy, W. 35
Navy Act 1661 35
Netherlands 76
'new right' politics 54
Newburn, T. 153
Nichols, F.M. 30, 33, 35
Noakes, Baroness 65–6
Norfolk, Duke of 58
Northern Ireland 3, 6, 16, 20, 55, 59, 63–4; Church of Ireland 25; civil partnerships 126; employment equality 100; EASORNI 2006 110–14; parenting 73
Norton, R. 35

Norway 76
Norwich, Bishop of 155

O'Brian, Cardinal 131
O'Cathain, Baroness 22, 77, 92, 108, 115–16, 120, 130, 132, 135, 141, 148, 155, 164, 170, 201–2
Oddie, W. 205
Oerton, S. 65
Offences Against the Person Act (OAPA) 1861 36–7, 59
Office for Standards in Education, Children's Services and Skills (Ofsted) 193
O'Loan, Baroness 146
Olson, E. 6, 25
O'Neill of Bengarve, Baroness 70
Orr-Ewing, Lord 59
Outhwaite, R. 33
Outrage! 55
Owen, M. 72

Packer, John (Bishop of Ripon and Leeds) 199–200
Paisley, Baroness 21–2, 141, 148
Paisley, Ian 16, 56, 130
Pakenham, Lord 45
parenting 5–6, 12, 16–17, 69–70, 97–8, 208; ACA 2002: contested moralities 72–88; Ashbourne–Ryder amendment 71–2; equalities and morality of conception by assisted means 95–7; marginalisation of religion: HFEA 2008 88–97; religion and child welfare 76–80; religion and 'evidence' of homosexual 80–4; religion and symbolic politics of marriage 84–7; religious opposition to HFEA 2008 90–2; symbolism of fatherhood and 'truth' of genetic heritage 93–5
Parliament Acts 1911 and 1949 52, 63
Parris, Matthew 168
Perry, John (Bishop of Chelmsford) 75, 78
personal, social, health and economic education (PSHE) 191, 193–7;
persecution of people of faith 169–72
Phoenix, J. 65
Pike, Peter 180
policing 3; 'climate of fear' for people of faith and 164–9; persecution of people of faith 169–72
Pollock, Bertram (Bishop of Norwich) 39
Pollock, F. 31
Portugal 76

postsecularity 11
premises, facilities, goods and services 107–17, 144, 207; EA 2010 121–3; religious opposition to harassment protection for sexual minorities: EASORNI 2006 110–14; threat to religious liberty: EASOR 2007 114–17
Prentice, Bridget 162
Prentis, Dave 106
Pritchard, John (Bishop of Oxford) 22, 148
proportionality 119–20
public authorities: EA 2010 118, 144–5, 190
public lavatory offence 65–7
Public Order Act (POA) 1986 146, 154–6, 158, 164–6
Purvis, M. 23

Quakers/Religious Society of Friends 43, 48, 92, 125, 136

race discrimination 101, 107
racial hatred 158, 160–1, 173, 207
Ramsey, Michael (Archbishop of Canterbury) 48, 50–1
Razaq, R. 201
Rees-Davies, W. 51
Reeves, J. 33
Reeves, R. 183
Reformation 23, 33
registrars 116–17, 144
Reiner, R. 169
religion or belief discrimination 101, 106–7, 110, 112, 116, 118, 122–3, 203; schools with religious character 187
religious hatred 158–9, 160, 161
religious rites: civil partnerships and geography of separation 21–2, 132–5; same-sex marriage: reaffirming separatism 18, 135–46, 151–2, 207
Religious Society of Friends/Quakers 43, 48, 92, 125, 136
Rendell, Baroness 126
reproductive technologies *see* Human Fertilisation and Embryology Act (HFEA) 2008
Richardson, Baroness 200–1
Richardson, D. 150
Richardson, Jo 100
Rivers, J. 145
Roberts, Joe and Helen 166–7
Robinson, A.L. 168
Robinson, I. 97
Robinson, Kenneth 47

Robinson, L. 26
Rochester, Bishop of 130
Roll, J. 73
Royall, Baroness 134
Rush, M. 5
Ryder, B. 13
Ryder of Warsaw, Baroness 59, 71–2

Sadgrove, J. 9, 14
Sainsbury of Turville, Lord 104
St John of Fawsley, Lord 130
Salih, S. 36
Saltoun of Abernethy, Lady 66, 87, 89, 91, 184
same-sex marriage 2, 5, 17, 124–6, 151–2, 207; distancing homophobia: transformation in rhetoric 5–6, 147–51; marriage 'locks' and litigious homosexual 140–2; Marriage (Same Sex Couples) Bill 2013 amendments 142–6; 'quadruple lock' and Church of England 136–40; reaffirming separatism: religious rites and 18, 135–46, 151–2, 207; religion and teaching of 197–201, 206; Second Church Estates Commissioner 24 'sameness' and 'equality' 148–50
Sandberg, R. 74, 119, 139, 175, 187
Santer, Mark (Bishop of Birmingham) 62
Sarmiento, S. 106
Saunders, D.J. 149
schools *see* education
Scotland 3, 19, 55, 59, 63–4; Church of Scotland 11, 25, 92; civil partnerships 126; employment equality 100; Free Church of Scotland 92; parenting 73; 'Section 28' 182; shameless indecency 60
Scotland, Baroness 107, 129, 147
Scott, K. 182
Scott-Joynt, Michael (Bishop of Winchester) 61, 75, 83–4, 92, 115, 141, 156, 160, 202–3
Second Church Estates Commissioner 24
'Section 28' 20, 73, 77, 87, 175–86, 205; religion, sex education and repeal of 181–6, 205–6; role of religion in enactment of 176–81
secularisation 17, 49–50, 205; changing religious landscape and 6–14; civil partnership: appeasing religious opposition 129–32
Selous, Andrew 82, 164
Sentamu, John (Archbishop of York) 16–17, 92, 94–7, 115–16, 119–20, 150

services, goods, facilities and premises 107–17, 144, 207; EA 2010 121–3; religious opposition to harassment protection for sexual minorities: EASORNI 2006 110–14; threat to religious liberty: EASOR 2007 114–17
Sewell, G. 45
sex *see* homosexual sex: religion and legal regulation
sex discrimination 102, 106–7, 120
sex education 20, 28, 174–9, 181–7, 190–9, 206
Sexual Law Reform Society 55
Sexual Offences Act (SOA)1956 16, 39, 54, 64, 148
Sexual Offences Act (SOA)1967 6, 29, 39–40, 47–52, 54–5, 59, 64–6
Sexual Offences Act (SOA) 2003 29, 64–7, 185
Sexual Offences (Amendment) Act (SOAA) 2000 29, 60–4, 67
Sexual Offences (Amendment) Bill 1977: assertion of Christian morality 52–4
sexual orientation equality: religious exceptions 99, 123, 145–6; employment 99–107, 119–20, 207; goods, services, facilities and premises 107–17, 121–3, 144, 207; religious opposition to EA 2010 118–23; schools 189–90
sexual orientation, hatred on grounds of *see* hate speech
Shannon, Jim 111, 143–4, 146, 198
Shaw, Jonathan 75, 85–6
Sheldon, S. 89–90, 94, 95
Shell, D. 23
Sikhs 11, 14, 61; voluntary schools 187
Simpson, D. 112
Singh, Lord 144
Slack, S. 24
Smith, A.M. 54
Smith, David 92
Smith, Iain Duncan 92, 93
Smith, Jacqui 74, 83, 129, 131
Smith, Peter (Archbishop of Southwark) 148
Smyth, M. 147
socialist politics 26
Soper, Lord 179
Souter, Brian 182
Spivak, G.C. 63
Stamp, Lord 53
Steinberg, D.L. 5, 6
Stephen, J.F. 15
Stevens, Tim (Bishop of Leicester) 144–6

Stockwood, Mervyn (Bishop of Southwark) 49–50
Stoddart of Swindon, Lord 57, 108, 165, 167–8
Stonewall 55, 121, 162–3, 170–1
Stopford, Robert (Bishop of London) 47
Stowell of Beeston, Baroness 146, 151, 200
Straw, Jack 63, 73–4
Streeter, Gary 93
Stychin, C.F. 12, 99, 111, 157
Submission of the Clergy Act (SA) 1533 33, 137–8
Summers, M. 69
Summerskill, Ben 121, 162–3, 171
Sutton, Keith 57
Sweden 76

Tamagne, F. 39
Tasker, F. 81
Tatchell, Peter 168
Taylor, David 168, 170–1
Taylor, S. 45
Teahan, M. 205
Tebbit, Lord 130, 134
Thatcher, Margaret 178
Thompson, Jim (Bishop of Bath and Wells) 62
Thorpe, A. 179, 181
Tomkins, Oliver (Bishop of Bristol) 47
Trade Unions Congress (TUC) 204
transsexuality 106–7, 120
Trappolin, L. 153
Turner of Camden, Baroness 100, 107, 160

Unitarian Church 43, 92

Valentine, G. 9, 12, 14
Vanderbeck, R.M. 9, 14, 165
Vasagar, J. 201

Waddington, Lord 159–60, 165, 168, 169
Wagner, A. 201, 204
Waite, L. 12
Wajcman, J. 149
Wakefield, Bishop of 100
Wales, Church in 25, 136–7, 139
Walford, G. 175

Walholf, D.R. 12
Wallace of Tankerness, Lord 145
Ward, J. 135
Ward, K. 9, 14
Ward, L. 192
Warnock, M. 89, 91
Weatherburn, P. 82
Weeks, J. 37
Welby, Justin (Archbishop of Canterbury) 48, 75, 150, 193, 207
Wharton, Martin (Bishop of Newcastle) 94, 107–8, 112, 166, 168
White, E. 90
Whitty, Lord 181, 184
Widdecombe, A. 167–70
Willett, G. 43, 49
Williams, Llywelyn 47
Williams, M.L. 168
Williams, O. 135
Williams, Rowan (Archbishop of Canterbury) 17, 26, 189
Wilshire, David 178–9
Wilson, Leonard (Bishop of Birmingham) 46–7
Wilson, R. 144
Wilson, Roger (Bishop of Chichester) 50–1
Winning, Cardinal Thomas 182
Wintemute, R. 14, 153, 190, 192
Winterton, Earl 43
Wise, S. 6, 185
Wolfenden Report 16; age of consent 52; Church of England and 44–7; religion and homosexuality prior to 40–4
Wolffe, J. 6, 25
women, gross indecency between: Criminal Law Amendment Bill 1921 38–9
Wong, K. 168
Wood, Maurice (Bishop of Norwich) 52–4
Woodhead, Chris 181
Woodhead, L. 7, 10–12
Worcester, Bishop of 106

Yamane, D. 8
Yeatman, L. 73, 75–6, 86
Yip, A.K.T. 14
Young, Baroness 58, 60–3, 74, 77, 102, 183–5